The Year of Living DANISHLY

The Year of Living DANISHLY

Uncovering the Secrets of the World's happiest country

Helen Russell

Published in the UK in 2015 by
Icon Books Ltd, Omnibus Business Centre,
39–41 North Road, London N7 9DP
email: info@iconbooks.com
www.iconbooks.com

Sold in the UK, Europe and Asia
by Faber & Faber Ltd, Bloomsbury House,
74–77 Great Russell Street,
London WC1B 3DA or their agents

Distributed in the UK, Europe and Asia
by TBS Ltd, TBS Distribution Centre, Colchester Road,
Frating Green, Colchester CO7 7DW

Distributed in Australia and New Zealand
by Allen & Unwin Pty Ltd,
PO Box 8500, 83 Alexander Street,
Crows Nest, NSW 2065

Distributed in South Africa by
Jonathan Ball, Office B4, The District,
41 Sir Lowry Road, Woodstock 7925

Distributed in India by Penguin Books India,
7th Floor, Infinity Tower – C, DLF Cyber City,
Gurgaon 122002, Haryana

ISBN: 978-184831-812-0

Typeset in Filosofia by Marie Doherty

Printed and bound in the UK
by Clays Ltd, St Ives plc

For Little Red, Lego Man and the woman
in the salopettes-'n'-beret combo.

Contents

Prologue

Making Changes – The Happiness Project

It all started simply enough. After a few days off work my husband and I were suffering from post-holiday blues and struggling to get back into the swing of things. A grey drizzle had descended on London and the city looked grubby and felt somehow worn out – as did I. 'There has to be more to life than this…' was the taunt that ran through my head as I took the tube to the office every day, then navigated my way home through chicken bone-strewn streets twelve hours later, before putting in a couple of hours of extra work or going to events for my job. As a journalist on a glossy magazine, I felt like a fraud. I spent my days writing about how readers could 'have it all': a healthy work-life balance, success, sanity, sobriety – all while sporting the latest styles and a radiant glow. In reality, I was still paying off student loans, relying on industrial quantities of caffeine to get through the day and self-medicating with Sauvignon Blanc to get myself to sleep.

Sunday evenings had become characterised by a familiar tightening in my chest at the prospect of the week ahead, and it was getting harder and harder to keep from hitting the snooze button several times each morning. I had a job I'd worked hard for in an industry I'd been toiling in for more than a decade. But once I got the role I'd been striving towards, I realised I wasn't actually any happier – just busier. What I aspired to had become a moving target. Even when I reached it, there'd be something else I thought was 'missing'. The list of things I thought I wanted, or needed, or *should* be doing, was inexhaustible. I, on the other hand, was permanently exhausted. Life felt scattered and fragmented. I was always trying to do too many things at once and always felt as though I was falling behind.

I was 33 – the same age Jesus got to, only by this point he'd supposedly walked on water, cured lepers and resurrected the dead. At the very least he'd inspired a few followers, cursed a fig tree, and done something pretty whizzy with wine at a wedding. But me? I had a job. And a flat. And a husband and nice friends. And a new dog – a mutt of indeterminate breeding that we'd hoped might bring a bucolic balance to our hectic urban lives. So life was OK. Well, apart from the headaches, the intermittent insomnia, the on/off tonsillitis that hadn't shifted despite months of antibiotics and the colds I seemed to come down with every other week. But that was normal, right?

I'd thrived on the adrenaline of city life in the past, and the bright, buzzy team I worked with meant that there was never a dull moment. I had a full social calendar and a support network of friends I loved dearly, and I lived in one of the most exciting places in the world. But after twelve years at full pelt in the country's capital and the second stabbing in my North London neighbourhood in as many months, I suddenly felt broken.

There was something else, too. For two years, I had been poked, prodded and injected with hormones daily only to have my heart broken each month. We'd been trying for a baby, but it just wasn't working. Now, my stomach churned every time a card and a collection went round the office for some colleague or other off on maternity leave. There are only so many Baby Gap romper suits you can coo over when it's all you've wanted for years – all your thrice-weekly hospital appointments have been aiming for. People had started to joke that I should 'hurry up', that I wasn't '*that* young any more' and didn't want to 'miss the boat'. I would smile so hard that my jaw would ache, while trying to resist the urge to punch them in the face and shout: 'Bugger off!' I'd resigned myself to a future of IVF appointments fitted in around work, then working even *more* in what spare time I had to keep up. I had to keep going, to stop myself from thinking too much and to maintain the lifestyle I thought I wanted. That I thought we needed. My other half was also feeling the strain and would come home furious with the world most nights. He'd rant about bad drivers or the rush-hour traffic he'd endured on his 90-minute commute to and from work, before collapsing on the sofa and falling into a *Top Gear*/trash TV coma until bed.

My husband is a serious-looking blond chap with a hint of the physics teacher about him who once auditioned to be the Milky Bar kid. He didn't have a TV growing up so wasn't entirely sure what a Milky Bar *was*, but his parents had seen an ad in the *Guardian* and thought it sounded wholesome.

Another albino-esque child got the part in the end, but he remembers the day fondly as the first time he got to play with a handheld Nintendo that another hopeful had brought along. He also got to eat as much chocolate as he liked – something else not normally allowed. His parents eschewed many such new-fangled gadgets and foodstuffs, bestowing on him instead a childhood of classical music, museum visits and long, bracing walks. I can only begin to imagine their disappointment when, aged eight, he announced that his favourite book was the Argos catalogue; a weighty tome that he would sit with happily for hours on end, circling various consumer electronics and Lego sets he wanted. This should have been an early indicator of what was in store.

He came along at a time in my life when I had just about given up hope. 2008, to be exact. My previous boyfriend had dumped me at a wedding (really), and the last date I'd been on was with a man who'd invited me round for dinner before getting caught up watching football on TV and so forgetting to buy any food. He said he'd order me a Dominos pizza instead. I told him not to bother. So when I met my husband-to-be and he offered to cook, I wasn't expecting much. But supper went surprisingly well. He was clever and funny and kind and there were *ramekins* involved. My mother, when I informed her of this last fact, was very impressed. 'That's the sign of a very well brought up young man,' she told me, 'to own a set of ramekins. Let alone to know what to do with them!'

I married him three years later. Mostly because he made me laugh, ate my experimental cooking and didn't complain when I mineswept the house for sweets. He could also be incredibly irritating – losing keys, wallet, phone or all of the above on a daily basis, and having an apparent inability to arrive anywhere on time and an infuriating habit of spending half an hour in the loo ('are you *redecorating* in there?'). But we were all right. We had a life together. And despite the hospital visits and low-level despair/exhaustion/viruses/financial worries at the end of each month (due to having spent too much at the *start* of each month), we loved each other.

I'd imagined a life for us where we'd probably move out of London in a few years' time, work, see friends, go on holidays, then retire. I envisaged seeing out my days as the British version of Jessica Fletcher from *Murder She Wrote*: writing and solving sanitised crime, followed by a nice cup of tea and a laugh-to-credits ending. My fantasy retirement was going to rock. But when I shared this vision with my husband, he didn't seem too keen. 'That's it?' was his response. 'Everyone does that!'

'Were you not *listening*,' I tried again, 'to the part about Jessica Fletcher?'

He began to imply that *Murder She Wrote* was a work of fiction, to which I scoffed and said that next he'd be telling me that unicorns weren't real. Then he stopped me in my tracks by announcing that he really wanted to live overseas someday.

'"Overseas"?' I checked I'd got this bit right: 'As in, "not in this country"? Not near *our* seas?'

'Yes.'

'Oh.'

I'm not someone who relishes adventure, having had

more than my fair share of it growing up and in my twenties. Nowadays, I crave stability. When the prospect of doing anything daring is dangled in front of me, I have a tendency to weld myself to my comfort zone. I'm even scared of going off piste on a menu. But my husband, it seemed, wanted more. This frightened me, making me worry that I wasn't 'enough' for him, and the seed of doubt was planted. Then one wet Wednesday evening, he told me he'd been approached about a new job. In a whole other country.

'What? When did this happen?' I demanded, suspicious that he'd been applying for things on the sly.

'Just this morning,' he said, showing me an email that had indeed come out of the blue earlier that day, getting in touch and asking whether he'd be interested in relocating ... to Denmark. The country of pastries, bacon, strong fictional females and my husband's favourite childhood toy. And it was the makers of the small plastic bricks who were in search of my husband's services.

'*Lego*?' I asked, incredulous as I read the correspondence. 'You want us to move to Denmark so you can work for Lego?' Was he kidding me? Were we in some screwed-up sequel to that Tom Hanks film where grown-ups get their childhood wishes granted? What next? Would Sylvanian Families appoint me their woodland queen? Were My Little Pony about to DM me inviting me to become their equine overlord? 'How on earth has this happened? And was there a genie or a malfunctioning fairground machine involved?'

My husband shook his head and told me that he didn't know anything about it until today – that a recruitment agent he'd been in touch with ages ago must have put him forward.

That it wasn't something he actively went looking for but now it was here, well, he hoped we could at least consider it.

'Please?' he begged. 'For me? I'd do it for you. And we could move for your job next time,' he promised.

I didn't think that this was an entirely fair exchange: he knew full well that I'd happily stay put forever in a nice little town just outside the M25 to execute Project Jessica Fletcher. Denmark had never been a part of my plan. But this was something that he really wanted. It became our sole topic of conversation outside work over the next week and the more we talked about it, the more I understood what this meant to him and how much it mattered. If I denied him this now, a year into our marriage, how would that play out in future? Did I really want it to be one of the things we regretted? Or worse, that he resented me for? I loved him. So I agreed to think about it.

We went to Denmark on a recce one weekend and visited Legoland. We laughed at how slowly everyone drove and spluttered at how much a simple sandwich cost. There were some clear attractions: the place was clean, the Danish pastries surpassed expectations, and the scenery, though not on the scale of the more dramatic Norwegian fjords, was soul-lifting.

While we were there, a sense of new possibilities started to unfurl. We caught a glimpse of a different way of life and noticed that the people we met out there weren't like folks back home. Aside from the fact that they were all strapping Vikings, towering over my 5′3″ frame and my husband's 5′11″-on-a-good-day stature, the Danes we met didn't *look* like us. They looked relaxed. They walked more slowly. They took their time, stopping to take in their surroundings. Or just to breathe.

Then we came home, back to the daily grind. And despite my best efforts, I couldn't get the idea out of my head, like a good crime plot unravelling clue by clue. The notion that we could make a change in the way we lived sparked unrest, where previously there'd been a stoic acceptance. Project Jessica Fletcher suddenly seemed a long way off, and I wasn't sure I could keep going at the same pace for another 30 years. It also occurred to me that wishing away half your life in anticipation of retirement (albeit an awesome one) was verging on the medieval. I wasn't a serf, tilling the land until I dropped from exhaustion. I was working in 21st century London. Life should have been good. Enjoyable. Easy, even. So the fact that I was dreaming of retirement at the age of 33 was probably an indicator that something had to change.

I couldn't remember the last time I'd been relaxed. Properly relaxed, without the aid of over-the-counter sleeping tablets or alcohol. *If we moved to Denmark,* I daydreamed, *we might be able to get better at this 'not being so stressed all the time' thing ... We could live by the sea. We could walk our dog on the beach every day. We wouldn't have to take the tube anymore. There wouldn't even be a tube where we'd be moving to.*

After our weekend of 'other life' possibilities, we were faced with a choice. We could stick with what we knew, or we could take action, before life became etched on our foreheads. If we were ever going to try to lead a more fulfilling existence, we had to start doing things differently. Now.

My husband, a huge Scandophile, was already sold on

Denmark. But being more cautious by nature, I still needed time to think. As journalist, I needed to do my research.

Other than Sarah Lund's Faroe Isle jumpers, Birgitte Nyborg's bun and *Borgen* creator Adam Price's knack of making coalition politics palatable for prime time TV, I knew very little about Denmark. The Nordic noir I'd watched had taught me two things: that the country was doused in perpetual rain and people got killed a lot. But apparently it was also a popular tourist destination, with official figures from Visit Denmark showing that numbers were up 26 per cent. I learned too that the tiny Scandi-land punched above its weight commercially, with exports including Carlsberg (probably the best lager in the world), Arla (the world's seventh biggest dairy company and the makers of Lurpak), Danish Crown (where most of the UK's bacon comes from) and of course Lego – the world's largest toymaker. Not bad for a country with a population of 5.5 million (about the size of South London).

'Five and a half million!' I guffawed when I read this part. I was alone in the flat with just the dog for company, but he was doing his best to join in the conversation by snorting with incredulity. Or it might have been a sneeze. 'Does five and a half million even *qualify* as a country?' I asked the dog. 'Isn't that just a big town? Do they really even *need* their own language?' The dog slunk off as though this question was beneath him, but I carried on unperturbed.

I discovered that Denmark had been ranked as the EU's most expensive country to live in by Ireland's Central Statistics Office, and that its inhabitants paid cripplingly high taxes. Which meant that we would, too. *Oh brilliant!*

We'll be even more skint by the end of the month than we are already... But for your Danish krone, I learned, you got a comprehensive welfare system, free healthcare, free education (including university tuition), subsidised childcare and unemployment insurance guaranteeing 80 per cent of your wages for two years. Denmark, I was informed, also had one of the smallest gaps between the very poor and the very rich. And although no country in the world had yet achieved true gender equality, Denmark seemed to be coming close, thanks to a female PM and a slew of strong women in leadership positions. Unlike in the US and the UK, where already stressed out and underpaid women were being told to 'lean in' and do more, it looked like you could pretty much lean any way you fancied in Denmark and still do OK. Oh, and women weren't handed sticks to beat themselves with if they weren't 'having it all'. This, I decided, was refreshing.

Whereas in the US and the UK we'd fought for more money at work, Scandinavians had fought for more *time* – for family leave, leisure and a decent work-life balance. Denmark was regularly cited as the country with the shortest working week for employees, and the latest figures showed that Danes only worked an average of 34 hours a week (according to Statistic Denmark). By comparison, the Office of National Statistics found that Brits put in an average of 42.7 hours a week. Instead of labouring around the clock and using the extra earnings to outsource other areas of life – from cooking to cleaning, gardening, even waxing – Danes seemed to adopt a DIY approach.

Denmark was also the holder of a number of world records – from having the world's best restaurant, in

Copenhagen's Noma, to being the most trusting nation and having the lowest tolerance for hierarchy. But it was the biggie that fascinated me: our potential new home was officially the *happiest country on earth*. The UN World Happiness Report put this down to a large gross domestic product (GDP) per capita, high life expectancy, a lack of corruption, a heightened sense of social support, freedom to make life choices and a culture of generosity. Scandinavian neighbours Norway and Sweden nuzzled alongside at the top of the happy-nation list, but it was Denmark that stood out. The country also topped the UK Office of National Statistics' list of the world's happiest nations and the European Commission's well-being and happiness index – a position it had held onto for 40 years in a row. Suddenly, things had taken a turn for the interesting.

'Happy' is the holy grail of the lifestyle journalist. Every feature I'd ever written was, in some way, connected to the pursuit of this elusive goal. And ever since defacing my army surplus bag with the lyrics to the REM song in the early 1990s, I'd longed to be one of those shiny, happy people (OK, so I missed the ironic comment on communist propaganda, but I was only twelve at the time).

Happy folk, I knew, were proven to earn more, be healthier, hang on to relationships for longer and even *smell* better. Everyone wanted to be happier, didn't they? We certainly spent enough time and money trying to be. At the time of researching, the self-help industry was worth $11 billion in the US and had earned UK publishers £60 million over the last five years. Rates of antidepressant use had increased by

400 per cent in the last fifteen years and were now the third most-prescribed type of medication worldwide (after cholesterol pills and painkillers). Even those lucky few who'd never so much as sniffed an SSRI or picked up a book promising to boost their mood had probably used food, booze, caffeine or a credit card to bring on a buzz.

But what if happiness isn't something you can shop for? I could almost feel the gods of lifestyle magazines preparing to strike me down as I contemplated this shocking thought. *What if happiness is something more like a process, to be worked on? Something you train the mind and body into? Something Danes just have licked?*

One of the benefits of being a journalist is that I get to be nosy for a living. I can call up all manner of interesting people under the pretext of 'research', with the perfect excuse to ask probing questions. So when I came across Denmark's 'happiness economist' Christian Bjørnskov, I got in touch.

He confirmed my suspicions that our Nordic neighbours don't go in for solace via spending (thus ruling out 90 per cent of my usual coping strategies).

'Danes don't believe that buying more stuff brings you happiness,' Christian told me. 'A bigger car just brings you a bigger tax bill in Denmark. And a bigger house just takes longer to clean.' In an approximation of the late, great Notorious B.I.G.'s profound precept, greater wealth means additional anxieties, or in Danish, according to my new favourite app, Google Translate, the somewhat less catchy '*mere penge, mere problemer*'.

So what *did* float the Danes' boats? And why were they

all so happy? I asked Christian, sceptically, whether perhaps Danes ranked so highly on the contented scale because they just expected less from life.

'Categorically not,' was his instant reply. 'There's a widely held belief that Danes are happy because they have low expectations, but when Danes were asked about their expectations in the last European study, it was revealed that they were very high *and* they were realistic.' So Danes weren't happy because their realistic expectations were being met; they were happy because their *high* expectations were also realistic? 'Exactly.'

'There's also a great sense of personal freedom in Denmark,' said Christian. The country is known for being progressive, being the first to legalise gay marriage and the first European country to allow legal changes of gender without sterilisation.

'This isn't just a Scandinavian thing,' Christian continued. 'In Sweden, for instance, many life choices are still considered taboo, like being gay or deciding not to have children if you're a woman. But deciding you don't want kids when you're in your thirties in Denmark is fine. No one's going to look at you strangely. There's not the level of social conformity that you find elsewhere.'

That's not to say that your average Dane wasn't conforming in other ways, Christian warned me. 'We all tend to look very much alike,' he told me. 'There's a uniform, depending on your age and sex.' Females under 40 apparently wore skinny jeans, loose-fitting T-shirts, leather jackets, an artfully wound scarf and a topknot or poker-straight blonde hair. Men under 30 sported skinny jeans, high tops, slogan or band T-shirts and 90s bomber jackets with some sort of flat-top haircut. Older men and women preferred polo shirts, sensible shoes, slacks and jackets. And everyone wore square Scandi-issue black-rimmed glasses. 'But ask a Dane how they're feeling and what they consider acceptable and you'll get more varied answers,' said Christian. 'People don't think much is odd in Denmark.'

He explained how social difference wasn't taken too seriously and used the example of the tennis club to which he belonged. This immediately conjured up images of WASP-ish, Hampton's-style whites, Long Island iced tea, and bad Woody Allen films but Christian soon set me straight. 'In Denmark, there's no social one-upmanship involved in joining a sports club – you just want to play sports. Lots of people join clubs here, and I play tennis regularly with a teacher, a supermarket worker, a carpenter and an accountant. We are all equal. Hierarchies aren't really important.'

What Danes really cared about, Christian told me, was trust: 'In Denmark, we trust not only family and friends, but also the man or woman on the street – and this makes a big difference to our lives and happiness levels. High levels of trust in Denmark have been shown time and time again in surveys when people are asked, "Do you think most people can be trusted?" More than 70 per cent of Danes say: "Yes, most people can be trusted." The average for the rest of Europe is just over a third.'

This seemed extraordinary to me – I didn't trust 70 per cent of my extended family. I was further gobsmacked when Christian told me that Danish parents felt their children were so safe that they left babies' prams unattended outside homes, cafés and restaurants. Bikes were apparently left unlocked and windows were left open, all because trust in other people, the government and the *system* was so high.

Denmark has a miniscule defence budget and, despite compulsory national service, the country would find it almost impossible to defend itself if under attack. But because Denmark has such good relations with its neighbours, there is no reason to fear them. As Christian put it: 'Life's so much easier when you can trust people.'

'And does Denmark's social welfare system help with this?' I asked.

'Yes, to an extent. There's less cause for mistrust when everyone's equal and being looked after by the state.'

So what would happen if a right-wing party came to power or the government ran out of money? What would become of the fabled Danish happiness if the state stopped looking after everyone?

'Happiness in Denmark isn't *just* dependent on the welfare state, having the Social Democrats in power or how we're doing in the world,' Christian explained. 'Danes want Denmark to be known as a tolerant, equal, happy society. Denmark was the first European country to abolish slavery and has history as a progressive nation for gender equality, first welcoming women to parliament in 1918. We've always been proud of our reputation and we work hard to keep it that way. Happiness is a subconscious process in Denmark, ingrained in every area of our culture.'

By the end of our call, the idea of a year in Denmark had started to sound (almost) appealing. It might be good to be able to hear myself think. To hear myself living. Just for a while. When my husband got home, I found myself saying in a very small voice, that didn't seem to be coming out of my mouth, something along the lines of: 'Um, OK, yes … I think … let's move.'

Lego Man, as he shall henceforth be known, did a rather fetching robotics-style dance around the kitchen at this news. Then he got on the phone to his recruitment consultant and I heard whooping. The next day, he came home with a bottle of champagne and a gold Lego mini-figure keyring that he presented to me ceremoniously. I thanked him with as much enthusiasm as I could muster and we drank champagne and toasted our future.

'To Denmark!'

From a vague idea that seemed unreal, or at least a long way off, plans started to be made. We filled in forms here, chatted to relocation agents there and started to tell people about our intention to up sticks. Their reactions were surprising. Some were supportive. A lot of people told me I was 'very brave' (I'm *really* not). A couple said that they wished they could do the same. Many looked baffled. One friend quoted Samuel Johnson at me, saying that if I was tired of London I must be tired of life. Another counselled us, in all seriousness, to 'tell people you're only going for nine months. If you say you're away for a year, no one will keep in touch – they'll think you're gone for good.' Great. Thanks.

When I resigned from my good, occasionally glamorous job, I faced a similarly mixed response. 'Are you mad?', 'Have you been fired?' and 'Are you going to be a lady of leisure?' were the three most common questions. 'Possibly',

'No' and 'Certainly not', were my replies. I explained to colleagues that I planned to work as a freelancer, writing about health, lifestyle and happiness as well as reporting on Scandinavia for UK newspapers. A few whispered that they'd been thinking of taking the freelance plunge themselves. Others couldn't get their heads around the idea. One actually used the term, 'career suicide'. If I hadn't been terrified before, I was now.

'What have I done?' I wailed, several times a day. 'What if it doesn't work out?'

'If it doesn't work out, it doesn't work out,' was Lego Man's pragmatic response. 'We give it a year and if we don't like it, we come home.'

He made it all sound simple. As though we'd be fools not to give it a go.

So, after welling up on my last day at work, I came home and carefully wrapped up the dresses, blazers and four-inch heels that had been my daily uniform for more than a decade and packed them away. I wouldn't need these where we were headed.

One Saturday, six removal men arrived at our tiny basement flat demanding coffee and chocolate digestives. Between us, we packed all our worldly possessions into 132 boxes before loading them into a shipping container to be transported to the remote Danish countryside. This was happening. We were moving. And not to some cosy expat enclave of Copenhagen. Just as London is not really England, Copenhagen is not, I am reliably informed, 'the real Denmark'. Where we were going, we wouldn't need an A–Z, a tube pass or my Kurt Geiger discount card. Where we were going, all I'd need were wellies and a weatherproof mac. We were heading to the Wild West of Scandinavia: rural Jutland.

The tiny town of Billund to the south of the peninsular had a population of just 6,100. I knew people with more Facebook friends than this. The town was home to Lego HQ, Legoland and ... well, that was about it, as far as I could make out.

'You're going somewhere called "Bell End"?' was a question I got from family and friends more times than I care to remember. '*Billund*,' I'd correct them. 'Three hours from Copenhagen.'

If they sounded vaguely interested, I'd elaborate and tell them about how a carpenter called Ole Kirk Christiansen started out in the town in the 1930s. How, in true Hans Christian Andersen style, he was a widower with four children to feed who started whittling wooden toys to make ends meet. How he went on to produce plastic building blocks under the name 'Lego', from the Danish phrase '*leg godt*', meaning 'play well'. And how my husband was going to work for the toymaker. Those curious to know more usually had a Lego fan in their household. Those without children tended to ask about opportunities for winter sports.

'So, Denmark, it's cold there, right?'

'Yes. It's Baltic. *Literally*.'

'So, er, can you ski or snowboard?'

'I can, yes. But not in Denmark.'

Then I'd have to break it to them that the highest point in the whole country was only 171 m above sea level and that you'd have to travel to Sweden for skiing.

'Oh well, it's all Scandinavia, isn't it?' was the typical response from those angling for a free chalet, to which I'd have to explain that, sadly, the closest resort was 250km away.

Many struggled to get their heads around precisely which of the Nordic countries we were moving to, with various leaving cards wishing us the 'Best of luck in Finland!' and my mother telling everyone we were off to Norway. In many respects, it may as well have been. The downshift from London life to rural Scandinavia was always going to be a shock to the system.

Once the removal men had gone, all we had left was a suitcase of clothes and the entire contents of our drinks cabinet, which apparently we weren't allowed to export due to customs laws. We convened an ad hoc 'drink the flat dry' party in response to this, but it turns out that drinking three-year-old limoncello from a plastic cup in a cold, empty room on a school night isn't quite as jolly as it might sound. Everyone had to stand or sit on the floor and voices echoed around the furniture-less space. There was no sense of occasion and it wasn't anything like the epic, cinematic send-offs that you see in films. For most people, life was carrying on as normal. Us leaving the country wasn't much of a big deal to anyone other than a few close friends and family. Some made an effort. One friend brought over mini Battenbergs and a thermos of tea (we had no kettle, let alone tea bags by this point). I was so ridiculously grateful, I could have wept. Thinking back, I may have done. Another made a photo montage of our time together in the capital. A third lent us a lilo to sleep on for our final night.

A damp, Edwardian terraced flat with no furniture, in winter, in the dead of night, is a very sad place indeed. We lay uncomfortably on the not-quite-double lilo and tried to stay still lest we bounce the other person off onto the hard wooden floor. Eventually, Lego Man started to breathe more deeply so that I knew he was asleep. Unable to join him, I stared at the crack in the ceiling in the shape of a question mark that we'd planned to fill in ages ago. It felt as though we'd lost everything, or we were squatters, or had just gone through a divorce, despite the fact that we were lying next to each other. Just for that night, we had nothing. I stared at the plaster question mark for what felt like hours until the street lamp outside the window went off and we were finally plunged into total darkness.

The next day we had lunch with family and a couple of close friends in a café near our flat. There were chairs! And plates! It was heaven. There were also tears (mine, my mother's, and those of a school friend whose alcohol tolerance had been severely diminished by the recent arrival of twins), as well as beer, gin and gifts of several more Scandi box sets to get us in the mood. And then, a few hours later, the taxi arrived to take us to the airport. I suddenly wanted to linger longer in London, to take in every detail of the city as we drove through it by dusk, to memorise every twinkling light along the river so that I could keep hold of it until I next came back for a visit. I wanted to Have A Moment. But the driver wasn't the sentimental type. Instead he turned on some hard-core US rap and unwrapped a Magic Tree air freshener.

We sat in silence after this. I kept my mind occupied by

going over and over my plan of action, 'keep busy, then you can't be sad!' being the mildly manic philosophy I'd adhered to for the past 33 years. My loosely thought-out plan was this: to integrate as far as possible in an attempt to understand Denmark and what made its inhabitants so happy. Up to this point, my typical New Year's Resolutions consisted of 'do more yoga', 'read Stephen Hawking' and 'lose half a stone'. But this year, there was to be just one: 'live Danishly'. Yes, I even invented a new Nordic adverb for the project. Over the next twelve months, I would investigate all aspects of living Danishly. I would consult experts in their fields and beg, bully or bribe them to share their secrets of the famed Danish contentment, and demonstrate how Danes do things differently.

I had been checking the weather in Denmark on an hourly basis during our last few days in London, prompting my first question – *how do Danes stay upbeat when it's minus ten every day?* Revelations about how much we'd both take home after taxes were also eye-opening. *Doesn't a 50 per cent tax rate really stick in everyone's craw?* Lego Man remained stoic in the face of possible penury and focussed instead on all the great examples of Scandinavian design that kept being featured in weekend living supplements. *Could the much-celebrated Danish aesthetic influence the nation's mood?* I wondered. *Or are they just high on dopamine from all those pastries?*

From education to the environment, genetics to gynaecological chairs (really), and family to food (seriously, have you *tried* a freshly baked pastry from Denmark? They're delicious. Why wouldn't Danes be delighted with life?), I decided I would set out to discover the key to getting happy in every area of modern life. I would learn something new each month and make changes to my own life accordingly. I was embarking on a personal and professional quest to discover what made Danes feel so great. The result would, I hoped, be a blueprint for a lifetime of contentment. The happiness project had begun.

To ensure that each of my teachers walked the talk, I would ask every expert to rank themselves on a happiness scale between one and ten, with ten being delirious, zero being miserable, and the middling numbers being a bit 'meh'. As someone who'd typically have placed herself at a perfectly respectable six before my year of living Danishly, this proved an interesting exercise. Despite having been commended for Julie Andrews-style upbeat cheerfulness in every work-leaving card I'd ever had, I soon learned that there's a difference between eager-to-please nice-girl syndrome and feeling genuinely good about yourself. I'd asked Christian for his score during our preliminary phone call, and he admitted that 'Even being Danish can't make everything absolutely perfect,' but then followed up with, 'I'd give myself an eight'. Not bad. So what would have made the professor of happiness even happier? 'Getting a girlfriend,' he told me, without hesitation. Anyone interested in a date with Denmark's most eligible professor can contact the publisher for more details. For everyone else, here's how to get happy, Danish-style.

1. January

Hygge & Home

Something cold and soft is falling on us as we stand in darkness on a silent runway, wondering what happens next. Before we'd boarded the flight it had been muggy, bright and noisy. We'd been pushed and barged by other passengers, ushered onto buses and shuffled around by ground staff. Mid-air, we'd been looked after by stewards in smart navy uniforms, plying us with miniatures and tiny cans of Schweppes. But here we are on our own, left standing on the frosty tarmac in the middle of nowhere. There are a few people around, of course, but we don't know any of them and they're all speaking a language we don't understand. The whole place glistens like it's made from soda crystals, and the air is so cold and thin that it catches in the back of my throat when I attempt to fill my lungs.

'What now?' I start, but the sound is muffled by snow. My ears already hurt from the chill so I cover them with my hair in lieu of a hat. This is surprisingly effective, though now I can hear even less. Lego Man's lips are moving but I can't quite make out what he's saying, so we resort to hand signals.

'This way?' he mouths, pointing to the white building up

ahead. I give him an 80s high school movie-style thumbs up: 'OK.'

A woman with a wheelie bag appears from behind us and moves decisively towards a small rectangle of light up ahead, so we follow, crunching compacted snow as we go. There's no shuttle bus or covered walkway here – Vikings, it seems, make their own way.

My husband squeezes my near-frozen hand and I try to smile, but because my teeth are chattering so much now, it comes out as more of a grimace. I knew it would be cold here, but this is something else. We've been exposed to the Baltic air for all of 90 seconds and the chill is gnawing at my very bones. My nose threatens to drip but then the tickling sensation stops and I lose all feeling in the tip. *Oh God, does even snot freeze in Denmark?* I wonder. I'm relieved to get inside to passport control and my toes and fingers burn with relief at the relative warmth.

We pass a giant sign advertising the country's most famous beer that reads: *'Welcome to the world's happiest nation!'*

Huh, I think, *we'll see.*

We know no one, we don't speak Danish, and we have nowhere to live. The whole take-a-punt, 'new year, new you' euphoria has now been replaced by a sense of: 'Oh shit, this is real'. The two-day hangover from extended farewell celebrations and our boozy leaving lunch probably isn't helping either.

We emerge from arrivals into a frozen, pitch-black nothingness and go in search of our hire car. This isn't as easy as it might be since all the number plates have been fuzzed-out by frost, like in a police reconstruction. Once the correct combination of letters and numbers has been located, we drive, on the wrong side of the road, to Legoland. After several wrong turns due to unfamiliar road signs, partially whited-out by snow, we reach the place we're to call home for the next few nights.

'Welcome to the Legoland Hotel!' the tall, broad, blond-haired receptionist beams as we check in. His English is perfect and I'm relieved. Christian had assured me that most Danes were proficient linguists, but I'd been warned not to expect too much in rural areas, i.e. where we are. But so far, so good.

'We've put you in The Princess Suite,' the receptionist goes on.

'"The Princess Suite"?' Lego Man echoes.

'Is that at all like the presidential suite?' I ask, hopefully.

'No, it's *themed*.' The receptionist swivels around his monitor to show us a pastel-coloured room complete with a pink bed and a headboard made from plastic moulded castle turrets. 'See?'

'Wow. Yes, I see...'

The receptionist goes on: 'The suite is built with 11,960 Lego bricks—'

'—Right, yes. The thing is—'

'—and it's got *bunk beds*,' he adds, proudly.

'That's great. It's just, the thing is, we haven't got any kids...'

The receptionist looks confused, as though this doesn't quite compute: 'The walls are decorated with butterflies?'

I fully expect him to offer us a goblet of unicorn tears next and so try to dissuade him gently: 'Really, it sounds lovely, but we just don't need anything quite so ... fancy. Isn't there anything else available?'

He frowns and taps away at his keyboard for a few moments before looking up and resuming a wide smile: 'I can offer you The Pirate Suite?'

We spend the first night in our new homeland sleeping beneath a giant Jolly Roger. There is a dressing-up box and all manner of parrot and pieces-of-eight paraphernalia. In the morning, Lego Man emerges from the bathroom wearing an eye patch. But things seem better by daylight. They always do. We draw the curtains to reveal a bright, white new world and blink several times to take it all in. Fortified by an impressive breakfast buffet, which includes our first encounter with the country's famed pickled herring, we feel ready to begin ticking off the various items of 'life admin' necessary for starting over in a new country. And then we step outside.

The snow has shifted up a gear, from gentle, Richard Curtis film-style flakes into snow-globe-being-shaken-vigorously-by-angry-toddler territory. The sky empties fast, dumping its load with urgency from all directions now. So we go back inside, put on every item of clothing we have, then emerge an hour later, looking like Michelin Men but better prepared to start the day.

In the hire car, I try to remember that the gear stick isn't on my left and that I need to drive on the right, while Lego Man reads from the to-do list that his new HR manager has thoughtfully emailed over. This comprehensive document extends to an alarming ten pages and is, we are informed, only 'phase one'.

'First off,' Lego Man announces, 'we need identity cards – otherwise we don't *technically* exist here.'

It turns out that the ID card scheme that Brits railed against for years before it was scrapped in 2010 has long been integral to Danish life. Since 1968, everyone has been recorded in a Central Population Register (CPR) and given a unique number, made up of their date of birth followed by four digits that end in an even number if you're female and an odd number if you're male. The number is printed on a yellow plastic card, which is 'TO BE CARRIED AT ALL TIMES' (the HR man has emailed in shouty capitals). Our unique numbers are needed for everything, from opening a bank account and healthcare to renting a property and even borrowing books from a library. (If only we could read books in Danish. Or knew where the library was. Or the word for 'library' in Danish.) I will even have a barcode that can be scanned to reveal my entire medical history. It all sounds very efficient. And I'm sure it would be relatively straightforward, too, if only we knew what we were doing, or how to get to the bureau where we're supposed to register. As it is, this task takes all morning. Even so, we count ourselves lucky – new arrivals from outside the EU have to wait months for their residency cards and these need renewing every couple of years. Being an immigrant is not for the admin-phobic.

Next, we need a bank account. A smart-looking man with closely cropped hair and distinctly Scandinavian-looking square glasses in the local (and only) bank greets us warmly and says that his name is 'Alan', before pointing to a name badge to reiterate this. I notice that it's 'Allan' with two 'l's, Danish-style. Allan with two 'l's tells us that he will be managing our account. Then he pours us coffee and offers us our pick from a box of chocolates. I'm just thinking how civilised and friendly this is in comparison with my dealings with banks back home when he says:

'So, it looks like you have no money in Denmark?'

'No, we only arrived yesterday,' Lego Man explains. 'We haven't started work yet, but here's my contract, my salary agreement and details of when I'll get paid, see?' He hands over our documents and Allan studies them closely.

'Well,' he concedes eventually, 'I will give you a *Dankort*.'

'Great, thanks! What is that?' I ask.

'It's the national debit card of Denmark, for when you have some money. But of course it will only work in Denmark. And there can be no overdraft. And no credit card.'

'No *credit card*?'

I've been batting off credit card offers in the UK since leaving school without a penny to my name. Global financial crisis or otherwise, credit cards have been akin to a basic human right for my generation. Putting it on plastic is a way of life. And now we're being made to go cold-hard-credit-card-turkey?

'No credit card,' Allan restates, simply. 'But you can withdraw cash, when you have it,' he adds generously, 'with this!' He brandishes a rudimentary-looking savings account card.

Cash! I haven't carried actual money since 2004. I'm

like the Queen, only with a blue NatWest card and a penchant for impractical shoes. And now I'm going to have to operate in a cash-only world, with funny green, pink and purple notes that look like Monopoly money and strange silver coins that have holes in the middle? I don't even know the Danish numbers yet! But Allan with two 'l's will not be moved.

'With this card,' (he waggles the plastic rectangle in front of us as though we should be very grateful he's trusted us with anything at all) 'you can log on to internet banking and get access to government websites.' This sounds very high-powered. I wonder whether we're talking CIA-Snowden-style info before Allan clarifies: 'You know, to pay bills, things like that.'

Bank account in place (if empty) we can now officially begin looking for somewhere to rent. A relocation agent will be assisting us with our search but with a few hours to kill until we meet her, Lego Man suggests a recce around the nearest normal-sized town in case we decide that toy town isn't for us.

Driving through Billund's uninspiring streets of identikit bungalows, like some sort of play-inspired military base, I have already decided that toy town is not for us and so I'm hoping that the next place is an improvement. Things start encouragingly enough with attractive red-brick mansion blocks and municipal buildings, cobbled streets and interesting boutiques nestled between big high street stalwarts. The place looks a lot like a Scandi version of Guildford. But after a couple of laps of the 'high street', we're left wondering whether perhaps there's been some sort of nuclear apocalypse that's only been communicated in Danish, meaning we've missed it.

'We haven't seen a single soul for...' I consult my watch, '...*twenty minutes*.'

'Is that right?'

'Yes,' I say. 'In fact, the only things resembling human forms we've encountered are the life-size sculptures of naked bodies with horses' and cats' heads on them in that weird water feature a few streets back.'

'The sort of porny pony version of Anita Ekberg in the Trevi fountain in the "town centre"?' Lego Man makes a bunny ears gesture to indicate that he didn't think much of the thriving metropolis.

'Yep. That's the one. The porny pony and the cats with boobs.'

'Huh.'

This particular statue, we later learn, was intended as a tribute to Franz Kafka. *He must be very proud*, I think. We pass more shops that are all either closed or empty and houses that look unoccupied save for the dim flicker of candlelight burning from within.

'This isn't normal, right? I mean, where is everyone?' I ask.

'I ... don't know...'

I check the news on my phone: there have been no atomic incidents. World War III has not been declared, nor has any alarming viral outbreak been announced. The threat of imminent death having been ruled out, Lego Man suggests going for a drink to wait for the place to warm up. Only we can't find a pub. Or a bar. Or anywhere that looks

a) open and b) isn't McDonalds or a kebab joint. Eventually, we locate a bakery that also sells coffee and I suggest to Lego Man that we order 'one of everything', in the hope that carbohydrates might cheer us up.

The place is empty, so we stand expectantly, waiting to be served. But the woman behind the counter remains expressionless.

'Hi!' I try, but she averts her eyes and busies herself rearranging a crate of buns. Lego Man tries pointing at various things with his eyebrows raised (the universal symbol for 'please may I have one of those?') until eventually the woman cracks and makes eye contact. We smile. She does not. Instead, she points to an LED display above her head that shows the number 137. Then she points at a deli-counter-style ticket dispenser behind us and says something we don't understand in Danish.

I'm not trying to buy ham from a butcher in the 1980s. I just want buns. From her. In an empty shop. Is she seriously telling me that I have to get a ticket? Or that 136 people have already passed through here today? Or that there even *are* 136 people in this town?

Bakery woman has now folded her arms resolutely, as if to say: 'Play by the rules or no buttery pastry goodness for you.' Knowing when I'm beaten, I turn around, take three paces to my right, extract a small, white ticket with the number '137' on it from the machine, then walk back. The woman nods, takes my ticket, and uncrosses her arms to indicate that normal service can commence.

Once we've ordered, Lego Man gets a call from his overly keen HR liaison officer. He steps outside to talk, away from the racket of the milk frother, and I pick a table for us and our gluttonous selection of pastries. 'Don't start without me,' he says sternly, hand over the mouthpiece.

His caution isn't unfounded. I have form in this area and can't be trusted within a hundred-metre radius of a cake. I can feel my stomach knotting with anticipation and don't know how I'm going to keep from taking a bite until Lego Man is back. To distract myself, I Google 'new country, Denmark, culture shock' on my phone and drink coffee furiously.

I learn that Danes drink the most coffee in Europe, as well as consuming eleven litres of pure alcohol per person per year. Maybe we'll fit in just fine after all. More helpfully, I also come across the website of cultural integration coach Pernille Chaggar. Deciding that a cultural integration coach is just what I need to start my year of living Danishly and buoyed up by a second cup of strong Danish coffee, I call and ask Pernille to take part in my happiness project. She kindly agrees – and doesn't make me take a ticket to call back later.

After expressing surprise that we've moved from London to rural Jutland, she offers her condolences that we've done so in January.

'Arriving in winter can be really hard for outsiders,' she tells me. 'It's a private, family time in Denmark and everyone hides behind their front doors. Danes are very wrapped up – literally and metaphorically – from November until February, so don't be surprised if you don't see many people out and about, especially in rural areas.'

Marvellous.

'So, where are they all? What's everyone doing?'

'They're getting *hygge*,' she tells me, making a noise that sounds a little like she has something stuck in her throat.

'Sorry, what?'

'*Hygge*. It's a Danish thing.'

'What does it mean?'

'It's hard to explain, it's just something that all Danes know about. It's like having a cosy time.'

This doesn't help much.

'Is it a verb? Or an adjective?'

'It can be both,' says Pernille. 'Staying home and having a cosy, candlelit time is *hygge*.' I tell her about the deserted streets and seeing candles burning in many of the windows we passed and Pernille repeats that this is because everyone's at home, 'getting *hygge*'. Candlelight is apparently a key component and Danes burn the highest number of candles per head than anywhere else in the world. 'But really, *hygge* is more of a concept. Bakeries are *hygge*—' *Bingo*! I think, looking at the spread of pastry goodness in front of me. '—and dinner with friends is *hygge*. You can have a '*hygge*' time. And there's often alcohol involved—'

'—Oh, good…'

'*Hygge* is also linked to the weather and food. When it's bad weather outside you get cosy indoors with good food and good lighting and good drinks. In the UK, you have pubs where you can meet and socialise. In Denmark we do it at home with friends and family.'

I tell her I haven't got a home here yet, nor any friends. And unless something radical happens and my mother decides that Berkshire is overrated, I'm unlikely to have family here any time soon either.

'So how can a new arrival get *hygge*, Danish-style?'

'You can't.'

'Oh.'

'It's impossible,' she says. I'm just preparing to wallow in despair and call the whole thing off when Pernille corrects herself, conceding that it 'might' in fact be feasible *if* I'm willing to work at it. 'Getting *hygge* for a non-Dane is quite a journey. Australians and Brits and Americans are more used to immigrants and better at being open to new people and starting up conversations. We Danes aren't great at small talk. We just tend to hole up for winter,' she goes on, before offering a glimmer of hope. 'But it gets better in the spring.'

'Right. And when does spring start here?'

'Officially? March. But really, May.'

Brilliant. 'Right. And, taking all this into account,' I can't help asking after the bleak portrait she's just painted, 'what do you think about all these studies that say Denmark is the happiest country in the world? Are you happy?'

'Happy?' She sounds sceptical and I think she's going to tell me the whole 'happy Danes' thing's been blown out of all proportion until she answers: 'I'd say I'm a ten out of ten. Danish culture is really great for kids. Best in the world. I can't think of anywhere better to be raising my family. Do you have kids?'

'No.'

'Oh,' she says in a voice that implies, '*in that case, you're really screwed...*' before adding: 'Well, good luck with the *hygge*!'

'Thanks.'

Lego Man returns from outside, lips now a blueish hue and shivering slightly. He announces that the toymaker and his elves are all ready for their new arrival and that he'll start work as planned in a week and a half, once we've settled in. I tell him that this last part may not be as easy as it sounds and relay my conversation with Pernille.

'Interesting,' he says, when I've downloaded. We sit in silence for a bit, staring at the fully loaded plate of glistening carbs in front of us. After a few moments, Lego Man raises himself up, removes his glasses and places them on the table, stoically. Then clears his throat, as though he's about to say something of great import.

'What do you think,' he starts, '*Danes* call their pastries?' He holds one up for inspection.

'Sorry?'

'Well, they can't call them "Danishes" can they?'

'Good point.'

In the great tradition of British repression, we ignore the potential futility and loneliness of our new existence and seize on this new topic with enthusiasm. Lego Man gets Googling and I crack open the spine of our sole guidebook in search of insight.

'Ooh, look!' I point, 'apparently, they're known as "*wienerbrød*" or "Vienna bread" after a strike by Danish bakers when employers hired in some Austrians, who, as it turned out, made exceedingly good cakes,' I paraphrase. 'Then when the pastry travelled to America—'

'—How?'

'What?'

'*How* did it travel?'

'I don't know – by *ship*. With its own special pastry passport. Anyway, when it made it to the US, it was referred to as a "Danish" and the name stuck.'

I don't read any more as I realise that Lego Man has been using the opportunity to get a head start on stuffing his face and I don't want to miss out.

'This one's a "*kanelsnegle*" or cinnamon snail,' he points at the curled, doughy, cinnamon-dusted delight that he's just eaten half of. I pick up what's left before he gets the chance to polish it off and swiftly sink my teeth in. It is a revelation. My taste buds spring into action and dopamine starts surging around my body.

'This is *outstanding*...' I murmur through my first mouthful. It's nothing like the part-dry, part-soggy, artificially sweetened 'Danishes' I've had back home. This tastes light and rich all at once. It's zingy yet sweet, with intense, complex flavours that trickle in one by one. The pastry is crisp, then soft, then gooey in turn. I am momentarily transported into another world where everything is made from sugar and no one gets cross, or has to work or do the washing up, or stubs their toes, and smiling is mandatory. I gobble down the rest of it before sitting back in wonder at this remarkable new discovery.

'I know! And that's only the basic one,' Lego Man tells me. 'They also do chocolate ones. And they get much fancier down that end of the counter,' he points.

'That was only a *gateway pastry*?' I slap a buttery hand to my forehead. 'Oh God, I'll be in elasticated waistbands by Easter.'

'Forget the post-Christmas detox,' I tell him through

pastry number two, 'if this is what living Danishly is all about then we'll be fine. And I don't care what Pernille says, we're going to get *hygge*, come what may.'

'I still have no idea what that means,' Lego Man replies, 'but I'm in.' He crams another *snegle* in his mouth to seal the deal.

We roll out of the bakery several thousand calories up and set off to meet our relocation agent – a slim woman with bleached blonde hair in an obligatory Scandi topknot, a black leather jacket underneath a thick, goose-down affair, and trousers that look distinctly flammable. She's set up several appointments for us to nose around Danish houses and we're fascinated to discover that they're all incredibly similar, with white walls, bleached wooden floors (complete with under-floor heating) and not a single item of clutter in sight. They're also hot. Jutlanders, it seems, like to lounge about in just a T-shirt at home – even in January. On every threshold, we peel off scarves and winter coats while perspiring as we attempt to adjust from the snowy outdoors to tropical interiors. We've lived in a poorly insulated Edwardian terraced flat for the past five years and having grown up with the mantra of, 'if you're cold, put another jumper on until your arms can no longer touch your sides', such centrally heated extravagance seems close to criminal.

'Too ... hot...' I mumble to Lego Man through a mouthful of merino wool as I start stripping off in the second home we visit.

'Yes, why is that?' he pulls at his collar to let out some hot air and wipes the steam off his glasses.

I wonder whether the Danes have gone in for hyper-heated homes historically because the climate is so cold. It always seems as though the colder the climate, the better prepared people are to deal with it. Perhaps the mildly chilly wet lick of your average British winter has meant we've been slow to catch on. I put this theory to Lego Man but the relocation agent, overhearing, cuts in.

'Danes are well known for their central heating, actually,' she tells us. 'We have very good doors and windows' – she points to an example of each in case we haven't quite got it – 'for thermal insulation. In England, I think, you have *drafts*,' she sounds disgusted at the very idea. 'Danes would not tolerate this.' She goes on to explain that an elaborate district heating system uses heat from burning waste, wind power and central solar heating to warm the pine floorboards of almost every house in the area. 'It's very efficient, so you don't need to turn it off!' is how she puts it. I'm not sure that's quite how a sustainable approach to energy consumption should work, but I'm impressed with her knowhow.

Each hot home we encounter is also rigorously neat, minimalist, yet full of designer touches. One proud renter, who boasts completely clear work surfaces and an ordered, Zen-like home, opens up her kitchen drawers to show off their soft-close mechanism and I see that her utensils are filed in the same impeccable order as the rest of her house.

'This isn't normal!' I hiss at Lego Man as we move on to the next room. In our kitchen back home, you couldn't open a cupboard without first protecting your face with your free arm, lest something spring out at you. The mismatched Tupperware drawer was stacked so precariously that it was just waiting to pounce on anyone who dared open it. But here, all the homes are ordered and spotless.

'These people are *renters*, right?' I ask the relocation agent. 'There's no incentive for them to do a big tidy-up before visitors come?' She looks confused.

'Tidy up? Before visitors? Is that what British people do?' She pulls a judgey face. 'Danes try to keep their homes nice *all* the time.'

I feel compelled to make it clear that we *try* to do this too. It's not as though we're smearing human faeces up the walls just for a laugh. Lego Man, sensing my ire, rests a gentle hand on my arm to warn me off this particular battle. Judgey Face also informs us that it's customary to remove your shoes before entering a Danish home, with all footwear stacked neatly on racks by the door. 'Just so that any dust or outdoor dirt isn't brought into the house,' she tells Lego Man, having clearly given up on his slattern of a wife.

Pretty soon it becomes clear that cleanliness is next to Danishness, and sleek, smart, wipe-clean design is everywhere; from wall-hung loos with tanks hidden in fake walls to universally built-in wardrobes and lighting that looks like it belongs in a gallery. On the downside, there are no baths. Judgey Face tells us that everyone in Denmark ripped out their tubs a decade ago to go for a more up-to-date look. ('Plus showering is more hygienic,' she asserts.) This is a setback to my happiness project.

How can anyone, let alone a whole nation, be happy without baths? Lego Man, understanding my pain, promises that we can always look online for a free-standing version à la *Downton Abbey* and adds this to his ever-growing list of things he's decided we need for our new Danish digs.

By the end of the great house hunt, day one, I start to wonder whether this great emphasis on having a clean, clear, sleek designer home plays a part in the Danes' chart-topping quality of life. Curious to find out more, I track down Anne-Louise Sommer, director of the Design Museum Denmark, and enlist her expertise. Anne-Louise has investigated the relationship between furniture design, cultural trends, national identity and ideology and come up with a few theories of her own.

'Denmark is very much a design society, and this plays quite a big part in happiness,' says Anne-Louise. She explains how the stylish Danish aesthetic was influenced by the German Bauhaus school and how good design has been a tradition here since the 1920s.

'In Denmark there was an economic recession and there were huge social challenges, but the government at the time decided that design was a high priority. They recognised that it was important for well-being and happiness,' she tells me. Danes, it seems, were ahead of their time. In 2011, scientists at University College London studied this phenomenon and confirmed that looking at something beautiful really can make us happier, by stimulating dopamine in our brains. (*Just like the pastries!* I can't help thinking.) Research shows that great art and design can even induce the same brain activity as being in love – something Denmark cottoned on to 90-odd years ago.

'For a young, socially democratic government, it was crucial to present quality design as part of the residential regeneration plan,' explains Anne-Louise. Big talents like architect and designer Arne Jacobsen (of the Egg Chair fame), lighting legend Poul Henningsen and furniture makers Hans Wegner and Finn Juhl made names for themselves and brought Danish design to an international audience. I ask if the average Dane appreciates how great their nation's design is. Anne-Louise thinks about this for a moment.

'If you stood in the street and asked someone, they might not have a reflective relationship with culture and design – but this is because they haven't *had* to. It's internalised in the consciousness. We are simply used to having nice surroundings,' she says. 'It starts from the very beginning of life. Children come to school and interact with quality architecture and furniture, and so from an early age they develop an understanding that functional yet beautiful design is essential to realising the good life. Then when they grow up and work in offices or public spaces, most Danes experience a high-quality environment combining function and design.' I can see what she means. The public spaces I've seen so far have been heavily invested in, with architectural flourishes and quirky design features everywhere (porny pony fountain aside).

'And of course, the weather plays a part too,' says Anne-Louise. 'We're inside so much during the long winters that we invest more in our environment. You're spending so much time at home, it may as well be nice!' And can having a designer home really make you happy? Anne-Louise thinks so: 'To my mind, there is a clear relationship between your aesthetic environment and how you feel.' Being surrounded by beautiful design all day long at the museum certainly makes her happy, she tells me. So how would she rate herself out of ten? 'I'd say I was a nine,' says Anne-Louise, before correcting herself. 'Actually, I can't think of anything else that would make me happier right now, so maybe I'm a ten!'

Feeling inspired to make a happy, Danish-design-inspired home, we now just need to decide which of Judgey Face's recommendations to go for. We've whittled the list down to two: a flat in 'The Big Town' near the porny pony (my choice), or a house by the sea (Lego Man's preference) in the grounds of an old red-brick institutional-looking building that Judgey Face informs us used to be a hospital.

Lego Man loves the countryside and vast sweeping landscapes marred by as few people as possible, something I put down to his upbringing in rural Scotland and the Yorkshire Moors. In contrast, my idea of getting back to nature is a stroll by the river in Hammersmith. Unsurprisingly, we're finding it hard to agree.

'Living here is never going to be like London,' Lego Man argues, 'so what's the point in living in a town that's rubbish in comparison to the world-class city we're used to? [People of Jutland, I apologise on his behalf.] We might as well make the most of this opportunity and live by the sea!' *It's all very well for him*, I think. *He'll be going to an office every day and I'll be stuck out here working from home with nothing but the dog and the waves for company*.

We'd talked about living by the sea one day, but in my head this was a) when we were about 100 and b) in a smart terraced house wedged between a chichi café and perhaps an artisan bread shop in Brighton or Hove or somewhere.

The sun would always be shining and we would have lots of visitors. Our seaside home was never, even in my most melancholy fantasies, a former hospital in rural Denmark. In winter.

And yet, somehow he wears me down. Or bribes me with the promise of a lifetime of pastries. Or gets me drunk. Or *something*. Because the next morning I find we've agreed and we get an email from the shipping company confirming that they'll be delivering all our possessions to Sticksville-on-Sea next Tuesday.

Four strapping Vikings unload 132 boxes from a shipping container before taking their shoes off and laying down rugs to protect the wooden flooring as they unpack our belongings, passing judgement on them as they go. Of a vase, 'I like this. The other ones, not so much' and of a painting, cryptically: 'Was this expensive?' 'No.' 'Good.'

The boxes have been coded according to what room they came from and I'm delighted to find that the contents of my London wardrobe have been labelled 'Lady Russell Dresses' (I'm hoping more people will address me by my official title in future). These are taken courteously to the bedroom where I later discover that, less courteously, the contents of my pants drawer has been liberally spread over the newly assembled bed and my navy lace bra is missing. But other than potential lingerie pilfering they are the most polite, articulate, over-educated removal men we've ever encountered and ask us multiple questions about coalition politics, what we think of David Cameron's hair (which, I learn, is a source of great hilarity over here) and our attitude towards the EU.

Once they've left, we both make resolutions to be better informed about the state of EU politics so we don't get shown up in future, and start rearranging our possessions and finding homes for things we'd forgotten we owned. It's then that I realise with horror how filthy everything is.

'Do you think it's from being in transit?' I ask hopefully, trying to buff the murky, grey tinge out of our white bookcase.

'Could be,' Lego Man looks sceptical. 'Or it could be that living in a lower ground floor flat we just never noticed how dirty everything was.'

I tell him I prefer my version and we set about soaping down visible stains, wondering whether we'll ever measure up to the standards of house-proud Danes. After a few hours of scrubbing, we have semi-clean furniture, but there isn't nearly enough of it to fill the new space. It turns out that the kind of space you can afford when you live in central London only necessitates about half as much furniture as your average Danish home. As the sun starts to set at around 3pm, we discover that we're also being plunged into darkness. It's customary to take not only your light bulbs with you when you move in Denmark, but also the *fittings*. There's not a ceiling rose in sight and I haven't a clue how to begin to tackle the wriggle of live wires that appear to be poking out from the ceiling at various points.

So we make tea by torchlight and resign ourselves to the fact that we're going to have to go shopping. Lego Man is delighted. For an outdoorsy, DIY-handy Yorkshireman, he has always been surprisingly obsessed by interior design. After years of 'passing' and allowing everyone to presume that the *Livingetc* subscription and our attractive home were down to me, he finally came out – mood boards, scrapbooks, the lot – and admitted his secret passion. Now he's hoping that a year of living Danishly will allow him to express this more fully, so that he can be out, proud *and* stylishly lit. He's already very taken with the Nordic aesthetic and decides he wants to populate our new home with all manner of eye-wateringly priced designer items. Concerned that we may never be able to afford *snegles* again if I let Lego Man go all-out, I call up an interior design expert to get a better idea of the essentials worth buying to make our new home *hygge*.

Charlotte Ravnholt, of Denmark's biggest interiors magazine, *Bo Bedre*, suggests keeping it simple. 'There's no need to go crazy buying lots of things to start with to get the Danish look,' she says. 'The more typical thing here would be to start with a few key items and mix and match them with what you've already got.'

This is encouraging. So what do we need first?

'Well, we use a lot of natural materials in Danish homes, like wood and leather, and we tend to have lots of lamps. In most of the world, lamps tend to be in the middle of the room, but here we loop the cords to position them and create pools of light or new areas of *hygge*, or cosiness. Then there are also pendant lamps, floor lamps and table lamps that you need to think about.'

I scribble all this down on a Post-It. Lego Man, who is craning to hear our conversation, leans in closer so that I have to swat him away before writing:

'She says we only need A FEW KEY ITEMS.'

I set down the pen to give Charlotte my full attention again. When I glance back at the pad, I see Lego Man has added a '☹' to the end of my message and wandered off in a huff to find more ways to spend money we don't yet have on things we don't really need for the home we don't own.

I ask Charlotte about *hygge* and she tells me that Danish homes typically have throws or blankets on the sofa for extra cosiness, as well as lots of cushions.

'Danes even have separate summer and winter cushions,' she tells me. 'There's a big market for them here – when money's tight and you can't quite stretch to a new piece of furniture, you can spend 500 kroner on a great cushion that will make your room look fresh.' Upwards of £50, or $90, for a *cushion*? This still seems pretty steep to me, and I wonder whether I'm too tight for this oh-so-stylish country.

'So does the average Dane spend a lot on their home?' I ask.

'I think we probably do prioritise spending on design,' says Charlotte. 'Figures from before the financial crisis showed that we were the nation that spent the most money on furniture in the world, per capita. Plus Danes really value good design, craft and quality. We want to buy something we can use for many years and pass down to our children.' She mentions a few of the big names in Danish design, from Arne Jacobsen to Finn Juhl and Poul Henningsen – names I'm vaguely familiar with having spoken to Anne-Louise and from the pages of Lego Man's deco-porn. I'd struggle to identify their work or pick a Poul Henningsen lamp out of a line-up at this stage, but Charlotte tells me that most Danes are pretty clued up on their designers.

'Everyone in Denmark knows who Arne Jacobsen is and about his work – not just design fans,' she says. The idea that design is part of the national consciousness helps me to understand why the Danish homes we've seen look as though they're straight out of a newspaper lifestyle supplement. I learn that Poul Henningsen's lamps are so popular here that 50 per cent of Danes have *at least* one in their home. 'People feel good about supporting Danish brands,' Charlotte explains. 'They want something that's been handmade here. Our design is something we celebrate and can be proud of, so yes, we do spend on it. And since the 1960s when more Danes began owning their own homes and both men and women worked, we've been able to *afford* to spend more money on furniture and design.'

Conscious of Lego Man listening in and champing at the bit to bring our 'emergency' UK credit card into play, I ask Charlotte to recommend five key Danish design touches that will sate my in-house Scandophile and help make our home *hygge*. She rises, stylishly, to the challenge.

'I'd start with a great wooden dining table for your daily meals, as well as talking and relaxing around,' she begins. I'm just feeling smug about the oak six-seater we already own when she adds, 'And in Denmark this should normally have at least eight chairs so you can have lots of people round.' Shit. We're clearly not sociable enough. 'Two more chairs,' I write down, 'and possibly a bigger table.' Lego Man's eyes light up.

'Then I'd invest in a hand-crafted chair like an Arne Jacobsen or a Hans Wegner or a Børge Mogensen,' Charlotte goes on. 'Your average Danish home might also have a designer lamp like Poul Henningsen's PH or an Arne Jacobsen AJ from Louis Poulsen. Then there's the Kubus candleholder – this is typically Danish and a lot of homes have this. And then finally, well, I'd probably go for some Royal Copenhagen dining plates,' she adds. I look over at our off-white Ikea crockery in a pile next to the dishwasher and see that we have work to do.

'Right,' I reply brightly, resolving to un-Ikea our home. 'And all this great design really makes Danes happy?' I ask. Lego Man already has an arm in a coat and is searching for the car keys to begin his retail therapy.

'I think so, yes,' says Charlotte. 'When we surround ourselves with quality design, it influences our mood. If our surroundings are nice, we feel cosy and safe. It makes us happier.'

I ask if she's happy herself. 'Oh yes, I'd say a nine out of ten – there's always a little room for something more.'

'Like what?' I can't help asking.

'That's personal,' she replies. I worry I've offended her by prying but she soon relents and reveals all. 'I'd like to live by the ocean and I'd like my boyfriend to propose. Then I'd be a ten.'

I thank Charlotte and say goodbye. Then I look at my husband, now wrestling a boot onto a foot, silhouetted against a panoramic view of a picture-perfect, dusky pink seascape. *Maybe I should start my happiness project by trying to be more grateful for what I've got*, I think, fondly. Then Lego Man writes *'HURRY UP!!!'* on a Post-It and sticks it to my forehead. The bubble bursts and I swiftly dismiss the idea of spending the next twelve months cherishing his every wet-towels-on-the-bed and inability-to-locate-the-laundry-basket foible. Instead, I grab my coat and go.

We Shop. With a capital 'S'. In spite of Allan with two 'l's from the bank. Lego Man is already happier once his new purchases are installed, and over the next few days our house starts to look more like a home. I try to think positively, too, but my own Pollyanna project suffers some setbacks.

I make my first Danish faux pas by putting paper into the wrong recycling bin. This leads to my inaugural interaction with our new neighbours, when two bearded gents call round at eight o'clock on Monday morning. I'm not yet dressed and haven't even had a chance to turn on the coffee machine, meaning I'm in no state to receive visitors. But Mr & Mr Beard aren't going anywhere. They ring the doorbell insistently until, living in a glass house where there's nowhere to hide, I have no choice but to answer. Huddled in anoraks and blinking behind surprisingly non-Scandi milk-bottle glasses, they start to speak in Danish before I explain that I haven't yet learned their fine tongue. Eventually they relent. Mr Beard I tells me in halting English that 'the neighbours' (collective) have noticed that the recycling bin has been more full than usual and so have been through the rubbish to discover the culprit. Mr Beard II holds aloft a tea-stained utilities bill addressed to Lego Man as evidence. Once I get over the weirdness of the fact that my new neighbours have been going through our bin (or *their* bin, as it turns out), I politely ask where it is they'd like me to deposit my waste paper. They point to an identical bin to the one I had been using, only a few feet further to the left.

Chastened, I promise to do better next time and get a free lesson in waste separation. The Danes, it turns out, are admirably obsessive about recycling. Almost 90 per cent of packaging is recycled and paper, cans, bottles, food and organic waste all have separate recycling homes. Sorting out what goes where is an art form I have yet to master, but I do work out that the Tardis-type booth at the local supermarket is for bottles. We pop one in on the off-chance one afternoon and marvel at the ad hoc laser show that commences. The bottle is scanned for its reuse value before the magical machine spits out a voucher, paying us the equivalent of 12p or 20 cents towards our next shop. I am disproportionately excited by this.

It's not just Prius drivers, hemp-fans and hipsters who are passionate about the environment in Denmark. Being eco-friendly here is seen as a basic duty and something you do to be a part of Danish society. Inspired by the fervour of my neighbours, I go on a fact-finding mission and discover that Denmark was the first country in the world to establish an official environment ministry, back in 1971. Today, the Danish clean power industry is one of the most competitive in the world and the country gets 30 per cent of its electricity from wind. In 2013, Denmark won the World Wildlife Fund's most prestigious award, Gift to the Earth, for inspiring leadership with the world's most ambitious renewable energy and climate targets. It has also been voted the most climate-friendly country by the United Nations' Climate Change Performance Index for the past two years. The Danish government aims to reduce CO_2 emissions by 40 per cent by 2020 and the environment ministry has a collective goal for a 'Denmark without waste' by 2050 – when they hope that everything will be reused or recycled. At a time when most countries are reneging on their environmental promises, Danes are setting themselves tougher and tougher targets, and they're on course to meet them.

Impressed, I resolve to perform my civic recycling duties rigorously and with pride in future, and am keen to inform Messrs Beard & Beard of this when they call round a week later to check I've been putting my cans in the correct bin. They nod in acknowledgement of my environmental epiphany then shuffle off again as fast as they can.

Other than this, no one speaks to us. If I was expecting the happiest country on earth to be welcoming, I was mistaken. I miss London. I miss noise. Instead of working to the sound of 747 engines whirring their way along the Heathrow flight path, or ear-piercing sirens speeding past to pick up London's criminal not-so-elite, I now hear birdsong, tractors or, worse, nothing. The place is so still and silent that the soundtrack to my day is often the ringing of long-forgotten tinnitus, acquired during an adolescence spent at bad gigs. Our dog finally arrives from the UK but gets so spooked by the deer, hares and foxes currently inhabiting our garden that he immediately retreats to the laundry room. Here, he whimpers and can only be comforted by a full load on spin cycle. Then, once we've finally got him settled, we're kept awake three nights running by *owls*.

I miss my friends, and find that moaning about owls to them over FaceTime isn't nearly so much fun as moaning to them about owls over wine. I was prepared for the fact that we'd be starting over. We'd convinced ourselves that this would be 'liberating', forcing us to try new things and meet new people and broadening our horizons. But this doesn't seem quite so appealing when we find ourselves sitting at home, alone, *again*, wondering how to kick-start our Danish social life.

'If Denmark has a population the size of South London,' I tell Lego Man, 'and we reduce our catchment area to, say, a twenty-kilometre radius of where we live and narrow it down to people within a two-decade age bracket, the number of people we may *actually like* gets even smaller. In other words, if the friendship pond is already tiny, we're not going to like all the pond life we meet.'

'Right,' says Lego Man, looking unsure. I wait for him to counter this and tell me that everything's going to be all right. But he doesn't. Instead he says: 'You should also bear in mind that they might not like *us*. They might have enough friends already, like we did back home.' *Great. Now I feel much better...*

'It'll be OK,' Lego Man says eventually, shuffling closer towards me on the sofa and putting his arm around me. 'We just need to get to know the place better. You should get out and about more, meet people.' He's probably right. Working from home and socialising via Skype and FaceTime isn't good for a girl. But then neither is Sticksville-on-Sea's public transport system. Having suffered frostbite and fury at the mercy of infrequent buses and trains since Lego Man started commuting to work with our sole mode of transport, a leased Lego-mobile, I decide that the time has come to buy my own car out here.

Coming from the UK, I have it relatively easy in terms of hitting the Danish roads. Most internationals from outside of the EU are forced to take a test before they can drive here. Regulations came into force in 2013 allowing new arrivals from countries deemed to 'have a level of road safety comparable to Denmark' to simply swap their licences, but there are conditions attached. Applicants have to have taken their test after the age of eighteen (ruling out most Americans who take their tests at sixteen) and need to have had a clean driving record for the past five years.

In common with everything else in Denmark, motoring isn't cheap. New cars have a sales tax of 180 per cent, making them cost about three times the amount that they would back home. This means that a simple hatchback that might fetch £10,000 in the UK (or $17,000 in USD) retails at the equivalent of £30,000 in Denmark ($50,000) – and the inflated costs trickle down to used car prices.

'Is this why most people drive matchboxes?' I ask Lego Man, when these alarming new discoveries have sunk in.

'I suspect so. Are you going to be OK out there? Car shopping, I mean?'

'Sure,' I tell him, sounding not at all sure but feeling as though this is probably something a grown woman in the 21st century should be able to handle.

Feeling courageous, I venture to the nearest car dealership. Having discovered that a return flight to London is cheaper than a twenty-minute cab ride anywhere in Jutland, I'm resigned to taking the bus again. Two hours later and relatively unscathed, I arrive in the showroom and am rewarded with the aroma of pleather, car air fresheners and cheap aftershave.

My price threshold rules out every car in the place bar two. The first is a scratched-up tin box on wheels that looks and smells like a family of feral cats have been living in it, relieving themselves regularly. The second, a cheery, tomato-red number, reminds me of a mobility scooter. I'm not instantly enamoured, but after a pootle around the block I find that a) the thing goes and b) my lofty driving position means that I can look down on other motorists. A novelty for a 5′3″ Brit in a land of Vikings.

'I'll take it,' I tell the dealer, who hands me a nine-page document – in Danish. I ask if I can take this away with me to interpret it or at least have some quality time with it in the vicinity of a Danish-to-English dictionary. But instead, he offers to translate for me. I'm not convinced that this is normal, but having been assured by my guidebook that there are fair trading rules for second-hand car dealers in Denmark and that salesmen don't get paid commission, I figure I'm unlikely to get ripped off. The guy has little to lose by being straight with me. *In for a penny, in for a krone*, I think.

So I thank him and he runs me through the deal. But it includes several more zeros than expected.

'What's *this* for?' I point at an alarming row of virtual hugs on page four.

'Oh, that's for the winter tyres.'

It's not just cushions that get a seasonal update in Denmark, it turns out. Winter tyres, though not mandatory, are advised. Shelling out a further 5,000 DKK (roughly £580 or $850 USD) for wheels that won't send me headlong into a ditch on unfamiliar roads in sub-zero temperatures seems like money well spent. I point at another line of digits and ask what it relates to.

'This is for fitting your summer tyres and storing your winter tyres in the tyre hotel from spring.' *The tyres get their own hotel in Denmark? My God, living standards really are through the roof.*

'And do I really need this?' I ask.

'We recommend that tyres are stored somewhere secure and fitted by someone who knows what they're doing,' is his reply.

'Right...' I wonder whether I might be able to make a saving by using a) Lego Man and b) the shed. I decide to risk it.

Sales Man points out another number: 'Then this is for the number plate—'

'—The number plate's not included?'

'No!' he sounds faintly amused. 'Otherwise everyone would know how old your car was!'

'Are you serious?'

His smile drops, leaving me in no doubt that he is entirely serious. 'Every driver gets new plates with numbers and letters generated at random.'

Equality, it turns out, is so important in Denmark that the authorities don't even want anyone judged by the age of their car. This seems commendable, but I'm pretty sure that anyone with half a brain will guess that my mobility tomato isn't the latest in high-end automotive design. And I rather resent having to pay to pretend otherwise.

'Then there's also registration tax, green tax, countervailing tax...' I can almost feel Allan with two 'l's' disapproving glare and imagine him shaking his head with disappointment as I sign swiftly and leave.

Over the next few days, I discover that the mobility tomato rattles if it goes above 70km per hour, makes a high-pitched bleeping noise unless I have Danish public radio tuned in and has windscreen wipers that merely move the dirt from side to side, smearing it across my field of view. But it's mine. All mine. The adventures start here.

Things I've learned this month:

1. Denmark is really, *really* cold in January
2. Money may not buy you happiness, but it can buy you cars, candlesticks and exceedingly good cakes
3. Owls are LOUD
4. Being an immigrant is not for sissies

2. February

Forgetting the 9–5

One of the advantages to going freelance, everyone told me, was that I could work in my pyjamas and wear slippers on the commute from bed to the laptop. After a decade of four-inch heels and dry-clean-only dresses, this seemed a bizarre and alien concept – a strange new world that I was interested to hear about but had no real intention of visiting. A bit like Las Vegas. And yet, just four weeks into my new life, I find myself merrily tapping away at the keyboard in a printed silk two-piece with an elasticated waistband at 2.30 in the afternoon. I tell myself it's not so bad because a) it's Friday; b) it's pretty much dark outside All THE TIME here in winter, so nightwear seems appropriate; and c) I'm doing phone interviews with people in the US and it's *morning* there. But basically I am a disgrace. I vow that when the clock strikes 4.30pm I'll shower, dress and maybe even brush my hair. *Like a proper grown-up*. Half past four has become the cut-off point for any kind of slovenliness that I wouldn't want anyone else to see. This is because Lego Man has taken to arriving home around about this frankly ludicrous hour.

He'd caught me off guard to begin with. A couple of

weeks before as I was tapping away at my laptop in my pyjamas, a rush of icy air surged through the front door as it swung open and there, barely distinguishable against the soul-destroying darkness, stood a figure.

'Hello?' I asked, alert lest an intruder was entering the house or the Mr Beards were back.

'It's me,' Lego Man replied.

'What are you doing here?' *Was he sick? Had he lost his job? Had Lego HQ been evacuated under missile attack?* (My motto: Why think rationally when you can add a little drama?) 'And shut that door! It's bloody freezing!'

'Thanks for the warm welcome,' was Lego Man's response, before dropping his man-bag and explaining that the office was virtually empty by 4pm. 'Most people with kids had cleared their desks to go and pick them up from school or daycare by 3pm.'

'*Three*?'

'Uhuh.'

'Everyone just leaves work really early? No one competes to be the last at their desk? Or gets takeout to pull an all-nighter?'

He shrugs: 'Not that I've seen.'

This was mind-blowing. In London, if we were both home by 7pm in time for *The Archers*, it was a cause for celebration. More often than not, we only saw each other at weekends or encountered the other as a warm body in bed in the small hours, having worked late or been out with friends.

But here, 4pm is the new 7pm. 4pm is *rush hour*, in Denmark. I haven't usually begun the meat of my afternoon's work by 4pm, having at least another few hours left in me. And yet he was back at home, wanting to put on loud music, chat and clatter things.

I've just about got my head around this new state of affairs and Lego Man's early arrivals when I hear a car crunch onto the drive at *2.30pm*. The sound of the door handle turning gives me such a shock that I knock over a glass of water while speaking to a time management expert in New York. I have to pretend to her that the resultant cursing is coughing and that the madly barking dog is interference on the transatlantic Skype line.

'Well, thank you *so* much for your time,' I say as I scribble some final notes in poor shorthand. 'I won't keep you any longer!' I add slightly manically in order to be heard over the din of the dog, whimpering with excitement at the return of his master, and Lego Man, bringing his characteristic drafts and *noise* into the house. He is affectionately mauled by the dog, buying me a few moments to consider my decidedly dressed-down look. *Perhaps I could pull off the early-afternoon-PJ-lounging-outfit as an homage to Hugh Hefner...?*

'You're home early!' I couldn't sound guiltier if he'd caught me in flagrante with Sarah Lund's series three love interest. (Google him. A treat.)

'Yes. Turns out everyone leaves even earlier on a Friday.' He sticks his head around the door and takes in my dishevelled state. 'You're not dressed! Are you OK? Do you feel ill?'

I think about faking something non-life-threatening and fleeting, then buckle under the pressure. 'No,' I reply, sheepishly. 'It's, er, for a feature.' This is a lie.

Lego Man looks around at the chaos of plates, mugs and evidence of bakery-based snacking all around me. 'What's the feature? "How slob is the new black"?'

'I'll have you know these pyjamas are Stella McCartney,' I say, weakly, before trying to change the subject. 'So how was your ... *morning*?'

'Good, thank you. I've been learning about Danish "work–life balance".'

'Haven't you just – you're home at *lunch time*!'

Lego Man ignores this. 'Apparently on a Friday, you don't need to be in until half eight and then there's—' here he makes a strange guttural sound, '*Moooaaaarrrnnnsssmullllll*.'

'I'm sorry, what?'

'It's written "*morgenmad*" and means "morning food",' he explains. He's already mastered some key food-based vocabulary and we haven't even started Danish lessons yet. I'm a little envious. 'Everyone in the office takes it in turns to bake and bring in rolls and pastries. One of the guys was up at 4am to bake today's buns.'

'Good grief! And there are such good bakeries here...' I can't help thinking that there's very little I could add to the world of Danish baked goods by getting up two hours earlier.

'Yeah. So *mooaarrnnssmull* went on for an hour, then we had a meeting where we agreed that we needed another meeting before we could make a decision, then I had another meeting where there were more buns and coffee, then we all went for lunch at 11.30, then, well, when we'd finished eating, it was someone's birthday so we had cake. After that, most people started clearing their desks for the weekend.'

'Busy day…' I mutter sarcastically.

'Yep, I'm stuffed,' he says, straight-faced, flopping on to the sofa and flicking through an interiors magazine.

As far as I can make out, a good chunk of the Danish working day seems to be taken up with refreshments. Lego apparently banned vending machines and *all sugar* on the premises some years ago, but now provide workers with free baskets of rye bread, fruit and carrots instead.

'So the world's largest toymaker is fuelled by nothing but betacarotene, whole grains and a childlike zest for life?'

'Nail your five-a-day and you can achieve anything,' shrugs Lego Man.

Lunch is a communal affair, taken at around 11–11.30am each day when everyone deserts their desks to eat together in the staff canteen. This is a bright, white space with Lego-brick-primary-colour furnishings and plenty of pork, herring and all the components for *smørrebrød* (the traditional open rye-bread sandwiches), but not a pudding in sight.

'Well, you can't have everything,' I tell him.

He explains that because sugar's so scarce, *morgenmad* and any other occasion involving the arrival of sweet goods is A Big Deal. He witnessed his first Danish birthday celebration this week when a colleague's desk was covered in flags and the extended team gathered around to sing something rousing.

'I wasn't quite sure what the song was about, but there were a lot of actions. It's hard to join in when you don't know what's going on, but by the last verse, I'd guessed it had something to do with trombones…' He does a quick mime to illustrate his point and I tell him that I've just read that the Danes are ranked as the most shameless nation in the world.

'They're meant to be practically immune from embarrassment.'

'That makes sense,' he nods. 'There's been a lot of singing, actually.'

'Really?' This is like catnip to me. 'You never said! Tell all! You know I love an awkward team-building sing-song…'

'All right, all right, I'll tell you about it,' Lego Man says, somewhat reluctantly. 'But promise you won't write about it somewhere or use it as a funny anecdote?'

'Of course I won't!' I lie.

'Well, there's actually an office band…' (at this, I clap my hands with glee) '… they play at every available opportunity and—' (he looks at me disapprovingly) '*—no one sniggers*.' I can already tell that I will never, ever, get an invitation to see the office band in action. 'And they also like making up songs about the team to the tune of popular hits…'

'No!' He's spoiling me now. 'Like what?'

'Well, this week, someone made up a song about our department to the tune of ABBA's "Mama Mia". My favourite part went something along the lines of, "We've been working so hard, to meet our KPIs" – oh, that stands for "Key Performance Indicators",' he adds, 'just in case you didn't know…'

'Of course I know,' I fib. 'Don't stop!'

'Sorry, well, after this comes the "de de de" bit…'

I join in, helpfully, to hurry things along: 'De de de de de de de, de de de de de de…' before Lego Man comes back in with the next line:

'And we all can agree, we're still a fun bunch of guys...'

'De de de de de de de, de de de de de de...'

'And then ... and then ... I can't remember the rest.'

'*Try*!'

Lego Man scrunches up his face and tries to remember before shaking his head and unclenching. 'I can't, sorry.'

'Oh well, the first two lines were amazing...'

'Thanks,' he says, as though taking credit for the composition himself. 'There's also a lot of drumming,' he adds, walking out of the room.

'What?' He can't just drop this percussive bombshell and saunter off.

'In meetings and workshops,' he calls out from the kitchen, 'there's often drumming. On buckets. Or boxes. Or bongos. Whatever you can hit a beat on really.' He says this as though it is the most normal thing in the world. Like fetching new staples from the stationery cupboard.

'And ... *everyone* joins in?' I'm on my feet now, following him around for further details.

'Oh yeah. Everyone joins in with everything. We're all equal, remember? Although you can tell who the most important people are – they tend to go for the biggest bongos.'

'Wow!' I'm unbelievably disappointed not to be witnessing the delights of office drumming first hand. 'And are some people just really musical? Do they end up competing to be the best drummers?'

He knows what I'm thinking. He knows that I would instantly become competitive about how my drumming measured up to other people's and start showing off.

'No,' he says very firmly. 'It doesn't matter how good a drummer, singer, or trombone-mimer you are, bragging about *anything* is bad form. They have a mantra in the business – "Lego over ego" – and people follow it.' He tells me that he and his fellow non-Danes have been guided towards the writings of a 1930s Danish-Norwegian author, Aksel Sandemose, for a better understanding of how best to 'integrate' into the workplace in Denmark. Sandemose outlines ten rules for living Danishly (otherwise known as 'Jante's Law') in his novel, *A Fugitive Crosses His Tracks*. These, as far as Google Translate and I can make out, are:

1. *You're not to think you are anything special*
2. *You're not to think you are as good as we are*
3. *You're not to think you are smarter than us*
4. *You're not to convince yourself that you are better than us*
5. *You're not to think you know more than us*
6. *You're not to think you are more important than us*
7. *You're not to think you are good at anything*
8. *You're not to laugh at us*
9. *You're not to think anyone cares about you*
10. *You're not to think you can teach us anything*

'Crikey, you're not to do much round here, are you?'

'Oh, and there's another, unspoken one.'

'Yes?'

'"*Don't put up with presenteeism*". If anyone plays the martyr card, staying late or working too much, they're more likely to get a leaflet about efficiency or time management dropped on their desk than any sympathy.'

'Blimey!' This makes a change from London life. Back home, answering an email at midnight or staying at your desk until 8pm was considered a badge of honour. But in Danish work culture, this implies that you're incapable of doing your work in the time available. Desks are all fitted with hydraulics so that staff can work standing up if they prefer, something that's been proven to be better for your health (according to research published in the *Journal of Social Psychological and Personality Science*) as well as facilitating swifter, more dynamic informal meetings or 'stand ups' as they're called. Instead of asking a colleague if you can 'have a sit down' to chat, you have a 'stand up' instead. 'And we're done in half the time,' says Lego Man.

He also tells me that no one uses titles and no one wears a tie – in fact you're more likely to see executives mooching about in hoodies, Facebook-style, than in suits. Somehow, I manage to persuade Lego Man to let me visit him at work for lunch (after promising to adhere to several conditions, namely not to mention the ABBA sing-song or ask for any drumming demonstrations). There's a laid-back Silicon-Valley-meets-Google-HQ vibe from the moment I step inside the glass-fronted head office in Billund's sleepy residential centre. I get comfy on the circular sofas, moulded to look like the relief of the iconic Lego brick, and contemplate whether or not it would be bad form to have a play with the giant pool of white bricks in the reception area. Lego Man meets me and escorts me through the office and we pass meeting rooms, all named after toys. This is something I find reassuring after a few weeks of hearing my husband on the phone talking about a 9.30am in *Tinsoldaten* – 'Tin

Soldier' – followed by a session in *Bamse* – 'Teddy Bear'. Each room has a vast glass bowl of Lego in the middle of the table to encourage employees and guests to build as they talk. 'I can barely hear a word in some meetings for the noise of people raking through bowls for the right brick,' Lego Man tells me.

Lego isn't just another business in Denmark – it's a way of life. A cultural beacon inspiring a cult-like dedication. Danes are proud of their country's most famous export, which now has parents in socked feet cursing as they stand on upturned blocks in 130 countries worldwide. There is a massive online community of adult fans of Lego, or AFOLs as they like to call themselves ('Not "geeks who can't get girlfriends"?' I ask Lego Man, doubtfully. 'No,' he tells me, sternly. 'I'll have you know that David Beckham and Brad Pitt have both come out as AFOLs so I'm in prestigious company, *actually*...'). *The Lego Movie* broke box office records in 2014 and its message of creativity, teamwork and the 'power of play' made such a splash that it garnered more column inches than any children's film to date and even attracted accusations of anti-capitalist propaganda. 'Trotskyite' Lego execs were delighted with the extra ticket and toy sales this free PR engendered, and a few younger minds were inspired to try living a little more Danishly.

After lunch (rye bread, salad and pork, as promised, with not a whiff of sucrose), I wangle myself a tour of the factory to see what all the fuss is about and am joined by some tourists from Japan who've flown in especially for the honour. I see where the minifigures are made, from their yellow smiling faces to their u-shaped hands and clip-on helmet hair.

A couple of misprints are brutally discarded, with only the most pristine toys allowed to pass through to the boxing area to be packed by elves ... I mean 'workers'.

Lego isn't the cheapest toy on the shelves, but quality is prized above all else. The founder, Ole Kirk Christiansen, once scolded his son, Godtfred, for announcing proudly that he'd managed to save money on paint by applying a thinner coat to each toy. Ole instructed him to recall the whole consignment and repaint each one, saying, 'only the best is good enough' – a phrase since adopted as the Lego motto.

Today, the company is estimated to be worth $14.6 billion (or £8.6 billion) and is the biggest toymaker in the world. There are 560 billion Lego pieces in existence, or 86 for each person on the planet (though having never been much of a Lego fan growing up, I can't help wondering who's got mine...). Lego produces 400 million tyres a year for its vehicles, making it officially the biggest tyre manufacturer in the world. Oh, and seven Lego sets are sold *every second*. There goes another one. And another. And another.

Ole Kirk Christiansen's grandson, Kjeld, now owns the company, making him the richest man in Denmark. But he eschews tropical tax havens or the bright lights of Copenhagen and chooses to live in Billund, the tiny town where it all started. Lego HQ is still based in the Jutland backwater and high-flying folk from all over the world are encouraged to meet with the toymaker in the rear end of *actual* nowhere. The Kirk Christiansens haven't just made Billund their home, they've paid for the town to have its own airport (the second biggest in Denmark, in a town of just over 6,000 people) a church, a community centre, a school, a youth club and a library. There's a lot of love in Jutland for Lego's Kjeld, who mysteriously changed the spelling of his surname to Kirk *K*ristiansen with a 'K' and is now referred to affectionately (if ill-advisedly) as 'KKK'.

It's safe to say that Lego Man is pretty pleased with his new job. Which is good, as otherwise we'd have uprooted our lives for nothing. No pressure... I ask what he enjoys most and he says that, aside from the food, the singing and the staff discount at the Lego Shop, the best thing is that the work is actually interesting. 'A lot of people say that out here, people don't bitch about work like they do at home. They don't choose a profession based on how much they're going to earn. They choose it based on what interests them. Education is free so anyone can train in whatever they want. You know you're going to get taxed a lot anyway, so you may as well just focus on doing what you love, rather than what's going to land you a massive salary.'

'So there's less incentive to sacrifice career fulfilment for the almighty dollar?' I ask.

'Precisely – because the more you earn, the more tax you pay.'

He tells me about a word he's been taught that encapsulates the Danish attitude to work: '*arbejdsglæde*' – from '*arbejde*' the Danish for 'work' and '*glæde*' from the word for 'happiness'. It literally means 'happiness at work'; something that's crucial to living the good life for Scandinavians. The word exists exclusively in Nordic languages, and hasn't been found anywhere else in the world. By contrast, the tourists I meet on my factory tour tell me that the Japanese have their own word that sums up their country's approach to work: '*karoshi*', meaning 'death from overwork'. There's no danger of that in Denmark.

Later that day, Lego Man and I are comparing diaries for the week ahead when he tells me he'll be away for two days. 'It's a team retreat. We've got to take loose-fitting clothes and an open mind, apparently, to "explore engagement through yoga".'

'Sorry?' I splutter. Lego Man has never saluted the sun in his life.

'That's what the email says…' he points at his computer screen, slightly defensive now.

'What does "engagement through yoga" even mean?'

'I don't know,' he shrugs, 'but it looks like you won't be the only one working in their PJs next week.'

Lego Man's work-life balance seems to be in pretty good shape. But then, a family-owned toy company in the business of making kids happy and developing creativity was never going to be the most cut-throat of environments. I can't help wondering whether Lego Man's experience is unique. Could there really be something similar happening in all Danish workplaces? I decide to branch out and investigate other fields of working Danishly.

I do some digging and discover that public sector workers don't do too badly, either. America's ABC News anchor Bill Weir brought Denmark's binmen to international fame a few years ago when he took a trip to Copenhagen and met Jan Dion. Jan told Bill how he loved collecting rubbish for a living because he worked just five hours a day and could then spend the rest of his time at home with his family or coaching handball at his children's school (53 per cent of Danes do some kind of voluntary work, a Ministry of Culture poll found – something else that makes them happier, according to recent research from the University of Exeter). Jan told the world how no one in Denmark judged him on his career, and how he felt happy every day because he met friends along his route and old ladies would bring him cups of coffee. Inspired, I attempt to strike up conversation with my own refuse collector but he's a) in a hurry, b) not great at English and c) not keen on coffee (possibly the only Dane in the country who isn't). He lets me know this by making an '*eurgh, yuck*' face when I show him a cafetière and offer to make him a cup. There's to be no bonding over caffeinated beverages for us. But he is smiling and we establish, through a complicated series of hand gestures, that he likes his job.

'Happy?' I ask, wrapped up in a totally impractical cerise cocoon coat on my doorstep, trying to keep the dog from making a break for freedom into the snowy wilds of Sticksville-on-Sea. My refuse man looks at me quite rightly as though I am a lunatic, then nods and tries to make his escape.

'Happy? Out of ten?' I hold fingers up.

At this point, the postwoman arrives on her scooter and offers to translate. Feeling more than a little foolish, I explain that I'm trying to ask my refuse collector how happy he is out of ten.

'Ok-ay...' she also looks at me as though I'm deranged, then says something very fast to the bin man. They look at each other for a few seconds, then do the Danish equivalent of the winding-your-finger-around-one-side-of-your-head to denote that you think someone's mental.

'Otte?' Bin Man finally replies.

'Eight!' I yelp, before the postwoman has a chance to translate. 'That means eight, right?' I look to her for approval and feel pleased that I am now capable of counting to ten (or rather, eight) in Danish. Postwoman nods, pulls another 'this woman is batshit crazy' face, and then zooms off on her bike.

Buoyed up by my 'research', I start seeing evidence all around me. I meet a yoga teacher for a feature in Aarhus, our nearest Big City, and canvas her opinion. Ida is a fresh-faced, healthy, tanned, toned Viking. *If this is what yoga does to you then I want in*, I think. I tell her about my happiness project and she says she thinks Danes do have a good work-life balance on the whole. 'And if we don't, we usually do something about it. You ask yourself, "are you happy where you are?" If the answer's "yes" then you stay. If it's "no", you leave. We recognise that how you choose to spend the majority of your time is important. For me, it's the simple life – spending more time in nature and with family. If you work too hard, you get stressed, then you get sick, and then you can't work at all.' She tells me that she used to work as a political spin doctor in Copenhagen until she found she was getting so stressed that her hair started falling out. 'I had big chunks missing, I felt tired all the time, and then I fell off my bike quite badly one day on top of it all and thought, "this is crazy, I need to make changes".'

Ida quit her job the very next week and began training as a yoga teacher. Because the welfare state offers a safety net,

Danes can change career relatively easily. After a five-week 'quarantine period' following a resignation, you're entitled to all the same benefits as someone who's been made redundant – 80–90 per cent of your salary for up to two years. The Danish labour market has a 'flexicurity' model – a flexible yet secure labour market that means it's easier to make someone redundant, but that workers are protected and looked after until they find something else they like, and it's all financed by tax revenue. According to statistics, 25 per cent of the Danish workforce gets a new job every year and 40 per cent of unemployed workers find new jobs within the first three months. Denmark also spends more on lifelong training than any other country in the Organisation for Economic Co-operation and Development's group of 34 developed countries (the OECD), with the government, unions, and companies paying employees to attend training and pick up new skills. This helps workers stay up to speed in a changing job market. And since moving jobs has no effect on pension entitlements or earned holiday time, there are no barriers to changing employer in Denmark. You can hop around and still accrue the same benefits and number of days off. The system seems to be working, with the current unemployment rate at just 5 per cent. With around two-thirds of Danes belonging to a trade union, there's also muscle on hand to fight for the preservation of workers' rights and privileges should anything go wrong – so it's very much power to the people.

'It means that in Denmark, we all have a choice,' says Ida. Now she works how she wants and when she wants to in a candlelit haven of a yoga studio. 'I'd say I'm an eight out of ten in terms of happiness these days. It would be a ten but I still haven't met the love of my life – though I'm hopeful! Right now, I'm so grateful for the changes I've made. I feel like I'm really *living*.' She makes it all sound so simple. Not easy, but simple: life wasn't feeling right so she made changes and now, things are good. I'm not sure I've ever made any major decisions without a hefty kick up the arse. But then, I've never lived Danishly before.

I start to wonder whether Danes are just braver, or more confident in their own decisions. Martin Bjergegaard thinks so. A businessman and entrepreneur, Martin is Denmark's poster boy for happy working practices since his book, *Winning Without Losing*, was published in 2013. He had a stressful spell working for an American company for fifteen months until, he says, he couldn't sleep any more. 'I don't know if you've ever tried not sleeping, but when you do it for too long, things go downhill pretty fast. By the end of night number three wide awake, I just thought, "I need to make a change". I had to stop being in a work environment that was making me unwell. The day I quit, I slept like a baby and I've felt amazing ever since.' Martin is also a runner, travel fanatic and father to seven-year-old Mynte. Tall, tanned and youthful-looking for his 38 years, Martin insists that each day should be 'fantastic' and ensures that he always spends a part of it recharging his batteries, playing sports and having fun. Oh, and he rates his own happiness out of ten at 'a pure ten'.

'Denmark is really at the forefront of this movement towards more happiness at work,' Martin tells me, once he's woken from his power nap one drizzly Wednesday afternoon. 'I think this is down to equality and our great security system. It's really hard to be happy if you feel insecure, but Danes know that even if they lose their jobs, they're not going to end up on the streets. They'll be looked after. And this means they work more efficiently and are less stressed and happier in their jobs. In the US, no one has any support. Everyone is on their own. And yes, they have the chance to make it big without such high taxes, but they also have to look after themselves. If anything happens and you don't have insurance, then you're...' he searches for the right word and finds it. '...you're *fucked*. But in Denmark, we have this "work-life balance" thing pretty well sorted.'

The symbiosis between work and play in Denmark appears to have come about by accident. After the Second World War, industry overtook agriculture as the primary employer and growing cities needed more workers. The government advertised overseas for workers to join the Danish labour market and for the first time, women from all backgrounds were given a shot at the nine-to-five (or 'eight-to-four' in Denmark). The Danish workforce increased by a million between 1960 and 1990 – and women accounted for 850,000 of these, I find out from Denmark's Centre for Gender, Equality and Ethnicity, KVINFO. During this period, it became acceptable for married, middle-class women to work, whereas previously only the unmarried or hard-up had taken paid employment. With women in the workplace, parenting solutions became a priority. Working hours, childcare and maternity leave were standardised and the idea of balancing work and leisure time became entrenched. Now, it's just something that Danes have come to expect. People leave early on a Friday because they want to spend time with their family. Parents get a day off work, fully paid, to stay at home with their children if they get sick. As a result of these practices, Denmark comes top of the pile for work-life balance according to the OECD, closely followed by the Netherlands, Norway and Belgium. The UK and the USA limp in at 22nd and 28th place respectively.

The official working week in Denmark is 37 hours, already one of the shortest in Europe. But calculations from Statistic Denmark suggest that Danes actually work an average of just 34 hours a week. Employees are entitled to five weeks' paid holiday a year, as well as thirteen days off for public holidays. This means that Danes actually only work an average of 18.5 days a month. This blows some newcomers' minds so much that a few American expats on secondment insist on working from 8am to 6pm every day so it's not too much of a shock when they go home.

Danes may spend ridiculously few hours in their place of work, but they're enjoying the time that they do put in. A study by Ramboll Management and Analyse Denmark showed that 57 per cent would carry on working even if they won the lottery and could afford not to work for the rest of their lives, and research from Denmark's Aalborg University showed that 70 per cent of Danes 'agreed or strongly agreed' with the statement that they would prefer paid employment even if they didn't need the money. Danish workers are the most satisfied in the EU, according to a recent European Commission survey, and Denmark also comes top in terms of worker motivation, according to The World Competitiveness Yearbook.

The latest Eurobarometer survey found that Denmark has the happiest workforce in the EU and another study from Randstand.com showed Danish employees to be the happiest *in the world*. Oh, and workers are 12 per cent more productive when they're in a positive state of mind, according to research from the University of Warwick. In fact, Denmark ranked third in the OECD's study into worker productivity. They may not be working long hours, but they're getting the job done. The country also came ninth on the UN's global innovation barometer and the World Bank named Denmark as the easiest place in Europe to do business. It's lucky Danes don't like to brag.

But it's not all *smørrebrød* and sing-songs in the Nordic workplace. Despite all the obvious advantages to being an employee in Denmark, workplace stress – as Ida discovered – is becoming more common.

The Department of Occupational Medicine at Herning University Hospital ran a study suggesting that one in ten Danish employees considered themselves to be frequently stressed. Their findings were supported by research from the Danish National Institute of Social Research, the National Institute of Public Health and the National Research Centre for the Working Environment. But individual trade unions report more alarming results, with the Confederation of Salaried Employees and Civil Servants in Denmark, the Danish Association of Lawyers and Economists and the Financial Services Union putting the proportion of their members suffering from stress at 30 per cent.

I'm surprised to learn that the country with the best work-life balance in the world also has a stress problem.

But just as there are no definitive statistics on how many Danes are signed off with stress, there's little consensus about *why* workers are suffering. Danish workplace happiness expert Alexander Kjerulf of woohooinc.com believes that the increased prevalence of smartphones, laptops and remote working may be to blame.

'It's becoming more common to have to check messages in the evenings,' says Alexander, 'which isn't good, as you never relax and recharge.' This is backed up by some unions, with the Danish Association of Lawyers and Economists even reporting that 50 per cent of its members work when they're supposed to be off on holiday.

The landscape of big business in Denmark has also changed. Over the past two decades, there's been a 500 per cent increase in highly skilled foreign workers arriving in Denmark, according to the Danish Immigration Service. Because so-called 'educated immigrants' pay high taxes and arrive in the peak of their working life and health, they place little burden on the welfare state and contribute handsomely to the country's coffers. This increases the feeling of competition in the workplace for native Danes – something that can send stress levels soaring, according to some of the Danes I speak to. It feels strange to be on the receiving end of a 'bloody foreigners, coming over here, stealing our jobs' cliché, but in this instance I can't deny that we have. And it's making many native Danes anxious.

Danes also have high expectations of working life. 'We know our jobs are secure and that there's a safety net,' one woman who works in middle management for a major Danish company tells me on the sly, 'so if I'm not happy at work, I think, "what's my boss going to do about it?" We realise we have it pretty good, compared to the rest of Europe. But if we're not having it *great*? Well, then we think something's wrong. I know several people who've been signed off for stress because of this.' In keeping with the idea of *arbejdsglæde*, most Danes want to enjoy themselves at work. To many, a job isn't just a way to get paid; they expect far more. And this can make them demanding employees. At Lego, a spy tells me, there was a recent mutiny when the toymaker changed their coffee supplier.

'The internal message boards went nuts,' my secret agent says. 'The guy who makes the coffee decisions got trolled. People went mad! There's a culture of entitlement because we've had it so good for so long now. If we don't get everything we hope for from work, people can get depressed – or at least think they're depressed.'

Another theory is that because stress has been on the agenda in recent years, Danes get asked about it more often and so are inclined to think, 'actually yes, I am stressed'. Researchers from Denmark's National Research Centre for the Working Environment recently expressed concern that the preoccupation with stress might be leading survey respondents to report being stressed even though they weren't, with some Danes going on stress leave as a 'preventative' measure.

Workplace happiness tsar Alexander has another hypothesis: 'I don't think there's really more stress in Denmark than in other countries, it's just we take care of people better here,' he says. Local municipalities can fund absences of up to a year before suggesting reduced working hours and offering job counselling for Danes diagnosed with stress. 'Whereas in the US or the UK you'd be expected to soldier on, in Denmark your employer and your doctor will listen if you say you're stressed – and they'll do what they can to help.'

'So, are you saying Danes are *a bit soft*?' I suggest.

'We're *caring*,' Alexander corrects me. 'We get people well again, and then they're really productive.'

This is beginning to sound plausible. Denmark is still coming top of the list for happiness, worker motivation, work-life balance *and* productivity. OK, so things aren't perfect, but I'm pretty sure there are still lessons to be learnt from work-life balance, Danish-style.

After another hard day at the coalface of happiness research, I pour myself a medicinal glass of wine at 6pm and think about whether there's a way I can apply the principles of Danish work-life balance to my own laptop-tied existence. I've given up a good position to come here and freelance – something most Jutlanders can't get their head around, with numerous people asking me when I plan to get a 'proper job'. Instead of being known by my name here, I am referred to as 'Lego Man's wife'. My work feels like the only thing that still defines me as 'me', rather than as a small yellow minifigure with a click-on ponytail. My work has always been my identity. So the idea of doing *less of it* is terrifying.

I get the whole money-can't-buy-you-happiness thing. Having chosen a career as a journalist, I know all about picking a career that sounds interesting but will in no way bring you wealth/yachts/a champagne lifestyle (unless it's on a press trip). I understand that success and happiness should be measured by something other than money. That you can work and work to build up your bank balance and then end up spending it all to outsource your life, buying back your sanity and bribing yourself to keep on going. Over a certain basic threshold, it's simple life maths: *Fewer new shiny things = fewer hours overtime = happier life.*

So why do I find it so hard to say no to work? Even when I'm too busy to eat/breathe/wee? I was like this when I was a staffer too, but now it's worse. The curse of the freelancer is never knowing where your next pay cheque is coming from or when they might stop – so it seems foolish to take my foot off the pedal and stop working evenings, weekends, and those bleak, lonely hours in the middle of the night when you wake up stressed and steeled to tackle a deadline. But then, that's part of the reason we're here. Doctors in the UK warned us that an out-of-whack work-life balance was probably one of the reasons I haven't been able to get pregnant. Having spent the last two years bloated on hormones and acting as a virtual pincushion for various different types of fertility treatment, I'd promised to try and relax a little more out here. To take a break from worrying about baby-making and from working quite so hard, if I can.

'*If you work too hard, you get stressed, then you get sick, and then you can't work at all*,' Viking goddess Ida's words come back to me as I take another slug of wine (did I mention the 'on a break' part? No judging). By glass number two, I'm feeling bullish. Fuelled by bravado and Beaujolais, I move the cursor of my laptop to the silhouetted apple symbol on the top left-hand corner of the screen. *I'm going Danish*, I think. *No more being a slave to my inbox all night*. It's 6.25pm Danish time. That's only 5.25pm UK time. A whole 35 minutes before the commissioning editors in the offices of the newspapers and magazines I write for will even think about logging off. A whole 2,100 seconds of email communication or last-minute additions or deadlines or commissions I might miss until morning. And that's assuming that the London folk are clocking off on time. Which is unlikely. Feeling a rush of something resembling adrenaline mixed with bile, I hover the cursor over '*Shut Down*' and click. There is silence. The whirring sound I'd assumed was just part of the general hum of my new, all-mod-cons Scandi house, dies down. LED lights dim to nothingness. And the world does not end.

Nobody calls me on my mobile to shout at me for not answering an urgent email. Nobody lets off a flare gun from London that can be seen all the way over in Jutland to alert me to the fact that my services are required. No bat-light goes on over the North Sea to summon my expertise. I have a startling realisation that I am not nearly as indispensable as I think I am. My natural reaction is to panic that my career must therefore be in tatters and assume that I'll never work again. But then I try breathing. And not being a massive idiot. And this, it transpires, is a far more effective strategy.

I have 'an evening', despite putting in two more hours of work than the average Dane. I walk the dog in the forest and feel as though I'm in *The Killing*, about to discover a shallow grave at any moment. I watch TV. I *talk* to my husband. Life goes on. And in the morning? Other than the glut of emails offering to enhance my manhood and a few PR memos, my inbox is empty. Lesson two of living Danishly, learned.

Things I've learned this month:

1. Someone out there has my share of Lego bricks
2. Jante's Law can be strangely liberating
3. If I'm going to be stressed anywhere, Denmark's the place to be
4. I am not important. If I take a break, no one dies. And this is A Good Thing.

3. March

Leisure & Languages

Now that Lego Man and I have all this free time, we need to work out how to fill it. At home, this wouldn't have been a problem. At home, we had a social life, as well as an extended circle of friends and family we kept meaning to see but didn't have the time because we were always so busy. Now we have the time, just not the friends or family. We go back to the UK for a weekend and see lots of people all in one go. It feels a little like we're celebrity guests making a cameo appearance – for one night only in a gastropub near you. But then we come back to Sticksville and realise that we have to start over again. Some friends from home make plans to visit. Some send care parcels of Cadbury's Creme Eggs and British magazines. I am immensely grateful to them all. But we've got another nine months of living Danishly to go, and we can't keep going home every other weekend to carry on a social life across the North Sea. If we want to make this work, we're going to have to get out there, make some *actual* Danish friends and find things to do. This is somewhat scary.

'So, what happens now?' Lego Man asks. It's a Thursday evening and he's restless. I can tell he's restless because he's just emptied the dishwasher, unprompted, and is now moving his expensive Danish designer candlestick from one end of the dining room table to the other and back again to assess where it looks best.

'What do you mean "what happens now"?' I look up from a book, holding my finger at end of the sentence I've just read so that I don't lose my place and hoping this interruption won't last long.

'Well, we've cleaned the house. We've walked the dog. We've watched *The Bridge*, and it's only 7pm...'

'So...?'

'So, what do we do now?'

'Oh, I see. Why don't you read something?' I nod vaguely in the direction of the bookcase.

'Done that,' he says, tapping his head as though every book we own is now safely memorised within his skull.

'Right...' I cast around for a bookmark. *This could take a while*.

Since getting our heads around this strange new 'work-life balance' concept, Lego Man has been at a loss. He's like one of those National Lottery winners facing a lifetime of leisure and luxury who doesn't quite know what to do with it. As Danes work just 34 hours a week, we're left with an alarming 134 hours to fill. I'm happy to boxset/read/eat the extra time away for a little while longer, but Lego Man is not. Nor does he feel it's 'healthy' for me to be stuck inside all the time.

'Well?' Lego Man is waiting patiently. 'What do you think *they* all do?'

'*They*?'

'The Danes. Of an evening, I mean?'

'I don't know,' I say, getting up from the sofa and noticing that I have left a deep indentation. This suggests that I may have been there for some time. *Damn it, maybe Lego Man is right...* 'We could ask around, I suppose?' I say, reluctantly. I can tell that I'm about to be bullied into doing something other than lazing around reading books. 'We could find out what normal people do, I suppose—'

'—We *are* normal people!'

'—*other* people,' I correct myself swiftly, 'I mean *other* people.'

'Right. Yes. Good plan. Let's both do that.'

And so the very next day I begin to investigate how the good people of our newly adopted homeland fill their free time each week and whether the pursuit of leisure can have an impact on happiness levels. I look up the leading authority on leisure in my new hood – Danish sociologist Bjarne Ibsen – to get a bit of background on leisure in Denmark and why it's such a big deal around these parts.

'Danes, in common with all Scandinavians, love a club, an association, or a society of some description where they can pursue a hobby,' says Bjarne. 'It all started with gymnastics.'

'*Gymnastics*?' I hadn't expected this.

'Yes, we have a long tradition of gymnastics in Denmark. It was considered good for the health of society after the modernisation of the farming class in the second half of the 19th century—'

I translate this into laywoman's terms: 'So farmers were encouraged to do backflips and roly-polies and things?'

'*I think they're called forward rolls*,' Lego Man mutters as he rifles through the detritus on the desk to find his glasses.

'Sorry, *forward rolls*. So, why gymnastics?'

'Well,' Bjarne goes on, 'it's a form of exercise you can do inside as well as out, and you don't need any special equipment. It was more about calisthenics than competitive displays back then. "Sport for all" became a goal for Scandinavian societies post-war,' he tells me. This sounds wonderfully worthy. Studies show that moderate exercise has been proven to lower the risk of depression and boost long-term mental health. So could getting active and getting out there also be contributing to the Danes' happiness levels?

Bjarne thinks so. 'It's definitely something that we recognise has a positive impact on people,' he says. 'It started with sports clubs but now there are groups for all sorts of things.' The Danish government has a long tradition of supporting hobby societies, offering free premises and facilities as well as subsidies for under-25s who want to start an association or join one. The individual municipalities – the Danish equivalent of counties or states – will often provide facilities for free for those over 25 as well. There are approximately 80,000 associations in Denmark and around 90 per cent of Danes are members of societies, with the average Dane a member of 2.8 clubs. Bjarne tells me that they have a saying here: 'When two Danes meet they form an association'. 'We form associations for things we don't even *need* an association for. And because there's such a consensus culture and Danes don't like conflict, if there's the slightest disagreement, we'll often split into smaller clubs.'

'Like leisure splinter groups?'

'Exactly.' He tells me that in the town of Rønne in Bornholm, the small island off the coast of Zealand, they started up a roller-skating club but the organisers couldn't agree on one of the rules for the club. 'So they split,' says Bjarne, 'and now there are two roller-skating clubs in the town.'

'And why are the Danes so keen on clubs?' I ask.

'It fits in with the Scandinavian countries' ideas about unity, harmony and equality. The theory is that being a part of a club helps you to be an active person, involved in community life and with a sense of responsibility for the collective. This is important for developing a society of trust. There's lots of research to show that being part of a club helps develop trust as it encourages us to live a connected, *associational* life – which is good for us and makes us happy.' Clubs in Denmark also transcend any class barriers – as happiness economist Christian had told me before I set off on my quest, everyone is considered equal in a Danish club or society, so you'll find a CEO playing football with a cleaner.

Hobbies have long been proven to boost levels of well-being, and research from the Australian Happiness Institute found that having a pastime outside of work also improves quality of life, productivity and likelihood of career success. So clever Danes combine individual passions and pursuits with a feeling of community by doing them as part of a club or association. And having a sense of belonging and a ready-made social circle just makes Danes even happier. I ask Bjarne whether he counts himself among Denmark's happy hobbyists and he tells me that he does. His score? 'Nine out of ten.'

Determined to get myself a slice of the happy action, I start by trying to find out what my options are, hobby-wise, in Sticksville. The Mr Beards haven't been seen since our altercation over the recycling bins but the woman who lives next door has taken to giving me a semi-friendly wave whenever we're out at the same time. She looks alarmingly like Sarah Lund from *The Killing* but so far I've only seen her in a caterpillar-like duvet coat so I'm yet to discover whether she also favours a Faroese jumper. Last week, I tentatively tried a '*Hej!*' ('Hi' in Danish) and felt disproportionately jubilant when she responded in kind. We then had a cursory conversation – in English – about where we were both from and what on earth we were doing in Sticksville and I discovered that Friendly Neighbour was originally from The Big City of Aarhus in Jutland, that she was single, aged 40 and fond of designer chairs (along with every Dane, it seems). Today, I take things further.

'So, er, what do people do around here in their spare time?' I start, sounding very much like I'm trying to pick her up. This is not my intention so I try another tack: 'Are you a member of any, er, *clubs*?' I ask casually.

'Oh yes,' she tells me. 'I do t'ai chi, handball, hunting, then there's the normal fitness classes like interval training and Zumba, of course.' *Of course*. 'And you? What do you do?'

'*Weeeeeeell*,' I make the word last as long as possible to buy some time before admitting, 'we haven't quite signed up for anything yet…'

'Oh,' she looks at me as though I've just told her that I don't floss (I do, FYI). 'So, what did you do in London?'

'Erm…' I scroll back through the past decade. The only extracurricular activity that I can remember fitting in between an exhausting work schedule and an excessive social calendar for the past twelve years is a life-drawing class Lego Man and I signed up for in 2009. It was part of a hopelessly optimistic New Year's resolution to 'better ourselves' but the results were below poor. The whole affair culminated in a Tony Hart-style gallery presentation where I made one of the older models cry because my portrait of her looked uncannily like Noel Edmonds. (Me: 'Honestly, I don't know how it happened, I couldn't even draw Noel Edmonds if I tried! Look.' I tried. And failed. Surprisingly, this didn't help.) Lego Man developed a signature style of heavily etched pubic areas but wasn't so hot on faces or hands, which always ended up looking like garden trowels. We stopped attending after week five.

'Well,' I tell my neighbour, 'we both just worked a lot in London. I mean, *a lot*.'

'Right. So have you signed up for Danish language classes yet?'

Damn! I knew there was something I should have been doing rather than curling up with Ian McEwan every night.

We've had our official documentation through for weeks now and I still haven't enrolled for evening classes, kindly funded by the government for all immigrants for up to three years. ('But I'm sure it won't take us that long!' Lego Man and I laugh when we're sent the automatic application form. Fools.)

'It's on my to-do list. In fact, I'm phoning them this afternoon!' I shuffle off to inform Lego Man that we have our first leisure-time assignment. A University of Edinburgh study suggests that learning a second language has a positive effect on the brain and though there's no direct proof that it'll make us happier, it feels like something we should be doing to try to integrate and understand more of the secrets to living Danishly. So I sign us up, determined to give it a go.

The local municipal language centre runs evening courses twice a week, so on a cold, dark (surprise!) Tuesday, we bowl up for lesson one. It doesn't begin brilliantly.

'*Hvor hedder du?*' A skinny woman with too-long hair barks at us.

'Oh, hi! Sorry, we're here for the beginners' Danish class?'

'*Hvor hedder du?!*' She's insistent now.

'Sorry, we haven't started learning Danish yet, I just wanted to check – are we in the right room?'

'*HVOR HEDDER DU?!*' the strange woman is now screaming at us.

'I'm sorry,' I bleat feebly, 'I don't know what that means … is it … Danish?' *Well done, genius.*

The strange skinny woman now begins to shout some other phrases ('*HVOR KOMMER DU FRA? HVOR ARBEJDER DU? HVOR GAMMEL DU? ER DU GIFT? HAR DU BØRN?*'). As a cool panic trickles down my collar, I'm transported back to tellings-off in the headmistress's office circa 1994.

Finally, a Ukrainian woman takes pity on us and explains that the teacher is asking our name, where we come from, where we work, how old we are, whether we are married and whether we've got any children.

A large part of me wants to shout back at the teacher, 'it's none of your bloody business!' but instead I try being reasonable: 'As I said, we haven't had any lessons yet, so I'm afraid we don't know what this means and how to answer in Danish…'

But Mrs Bad Teacher ignores me and instead turns around and begins writing choice phrases up on a white board in shouty red capitals.

'I think she's screening us,' whispers the Ukrainian.

'What?'

'I think she's looking at our natural ability. To work out what level class we should all take.' The Ukrainian is clearly picking up a lot more of this that we are.

We end up in a class with a few Polish men, the kind Ukrainian woman, and half a dozen Filipino girls. Kind Ukrainian works in a '*fiskefabrik*' – something that sounds far more glamorous than it actually is (a fish-processing factory). The Poles all work as cleaners and handymen in hotels and the Filipinos work as au pairs. I can't help feeling surprised by this.

'Isn't everyone supposed to be equal in Denmark? Aren't Danes supposed to do their own cleaning and child rearing?' I mutter to Lego Man during break time.

'I thought so too,' he admits. But it turns out that the lure of Denmark's quality of life has as much appeal for our Polish and Ukrainian classmates as it had for us. Enough, in fact, to outweigh the upheaval of relocation, career changes and being far from friends and family. One of the Filipino girls tells us that she and her friends earn more in Denmark as au pairs than they did at home as a nurse, a physio-therapist and a psychiatrist respectively. It's interesting to be in a group with people we might never normally have met or spent time with and I find that being an immigrant is a humbling experience. I'm ashamed of the fact that my classmates all speak perfect English on top of their mother tongue and a smattering of other languages, when all we can do is ask where the nearest train station is in French. It turns out that attempting to learn a new language as a mid-thirties monoglot is no mean feat – and subtlety is everything.

When the teacher asks us whether we've been practising our Danish in our spare time, I tell her I've been watching *The Killing* in preparation for class. She looks confused.

'Have I pronounced it wrong? The "*Killing*"?' I try again, more slowly

'You *watch* killing?' She sounds baffled so I try another pronunciation.

English speakers' guide to learning languages, lesson #3: If in doubt, try saying the same thing again in a different accent (lesson #1 being 'say it louder' and lesson #2 being 'say it more slowly').

'*Koolling*?' I try again. She looks doubtful. I try one more time: '*Kelling*!'

The teacher's eyebrows shoot up like pointy hats and hover somewhere around her hairline. 'Or maybe not...' I mutter, as Lego Man gets busy on Google Translate. Kind Ukrainian is also leafing through her Danish dictionary and intervenes.

'I think you have that wrong, look,' she points, helpfully, to the appropriate entries in her dictionary and then reads out loud: '"*Killing*" means "kitten". "*Kylling*", pronounced "*kooling*" means "chicken" and "*kælling*", pronounced "*kel-ling*" means ...' she tails off.

'Yes?' I strain to read the tiny print over her shoulder but am beaten to it by the Polish man sitting next to her.

'It means "bitch"!' he reads out with relish as I feel my cheeks redden.

Excellent. Week one of language school and I've already called my teacher a bitch. I stay remarkably quiet for the remainder of the class but pick up some other surprising vocabulary, including the fact that '*slut*' means 'ends' or 'finished'. *So my new washing machine hasn't been abusing me all this time when it stopped and flashed the word 'slut' at me in bright red lights!*

Language can tell you a lot about a country, and we learn that there is an extensive vocabulary to describe Denmark's variable weather but no word for 'please'. I've just about got over the hilarity of '*fart kontrol*' ('speed limit') and '*slut spurt*' ('closing down sale'), when we're taught, helpfully, that the Danish for nipple is '*brystvorte*', which translates as 'breast wart' and that '*gift*' means 'married', as well as 'poison'.

'Coincidence?' remarks another of the Poles, who's currently going through a tricky divorce. 'I think not.'

I'm concerned about how I'm ever going to get my head around the language – the ninth most difficult in the world according to the United Nations Educational Scientific and Cultural Organisation. In the hope of some reassurance, I seek out Søs Nissen, deputy head of Jutland's Kolding language centre. With Scandi-issue square glasses, a sparkling silver batwing jumper and a glossy bob, she looks like a rather glamorous owl. I try to explain my predicament and resist the urge to share my bird of prey observations.

'I don't think I'm very good at this Danish malarkey,' I say instead. 'Do you think I'll ever crack it?'

Søs sits me down and tells me it was never going to be easy. 'The biggest problem that native English speakers face is that we have nine vowels in Danish, and outsiders often can't hear or pronounce the differences between these.'

'I learned this the hard way,' I tell her, explaining all about bitch/chicken/kitten-gate.

'Brits and Americans need to work on their motor skills to become aware of the shapes their mouths are making, especially with our 'g' and 'r' sounds. It's the same as learning football or piano – you have to physically do it, over and over again. You can't just read about it or hope to pick it up by observing other people.'

Depressingly, I learn that only 20 per cent of English speakers moving to Denmark ever master Danish. 'But it is possible,' Søs insists. 'You just need to practise more. One reason that English speakers struggle is that all Danes speak English to them. We aren't used to hearing our language spoken with a foreign accent – it's weird for us. If we encounter a foreigner, we're used to switching to German or English or Spanish.'

'And how come the Danes are so flipping good at speaking other languages?'

'We just have a strong tradition of learning them,' she says simply. English is taught in schools from the third grade (at around age eight or nine) and foreign films and TV programmes are subtitled, rather than dubbed into Danish. This all adds to the presence of foreign languages, especially English, in Danes' everyday lives. As Søs puts it: 'If you're Danish and no one in the world understands you outside of your tiny country of 5.5 million people, then of course you have to take up another language. Even my dad who's 90 can speak fluent English and German.' *Oh great,* I think, *I've been out-gloted by someone in their tenth decade…*

'It keeps our brains working and challenges us – there's a sense of achievement to lifelong learning.'

Studies show that this might help the Danes on their way to the number one spot for happiness, too. Continuing to learn throughout life helps improve mental well-being, boosts self-confidence, gives you a sense of purpose and makes you feel more connected to others, according to the Office for National Statistics.

Søs tells me that Danes love learning so much that many pensioners spend their winters learning Spanish or Italian at evening classes so that they can ask for a beer and get around on their next summer holiday. 'We like to study and we like to travel, so it's the perfect combination. Whereas I get the impression that English-speaking people don't know much about learning languages – that there isn't such an evening class culture?' I tell her she's right, and I don't mention the Noel Edmonds sketching incident. 'You should try to enjoy the learning as well,' says Søs. 'That's what will keep you coming to class. It'll help if you interact with more Danes socially. Join some clubs – it's a great way to improve your Danish.'

Has she been talking to my neighbour? I wonder. *Is there some sort of hobby-lobby operating in rural Jutland?* I attempt to turn the tables and ask Søs just how content lifelong learning and extracurricular activities make her.

'How happy am I? Out of ten? I'd say eight.' I feel a little relieved that there's still room for improvement – I can't believe evening classes can make anyone *that* happy. But then she corrects herself: 'Or maybe a ten, actually.'

'Ten?' *How can this be?*

'Well, thinking about it, I couldn't find a way to be happier,' she tells me. I wonder whether this is because she has already mastered what I'm starting to suspect is in fact *the* hardest language in the world.

'But keep practising your Danish and you'll get there!' she offers as her final pearl of owl-like wisdom before I hot-foot it out of her office and down the corridor.

'Apparently we have to join clubs to really try living Danishly,' I tell Lego Man on the way home. He nods and thinks for a while about the various hobbies we could take up.

'What about a bike club? We've already got bikes,' he points out. 'I know you don't use yours much...' I'm about to protest that this isn't true when I realise that the last time I strapped on a cycle helmet, George W. Bush was in the White House and boot-cut jeans were in. '...but you'd soon get back into it.' He goes on, enthused, 'You know what they say – you never forget.'

'Because riding a bike is *just like riding a bike*?'

'Yes! And besides, Denmark is famous for its bikes.'

He's right about this – biking is practically a religion here, no matter what your age or occupation. Denmark is covered with over 7,500 miles of bike paths and Danes will cycle come rain or come hail. The government recently introduced a 'National Cycling Strategy' to get even more Danes on their bike. Danes are so bike-obsessed that you can even opt for a tricycle hearse to end the cycle of life. Half of all commuters in Copenhagen go to work by bike and *Forbes* magazine recently reported that cyclists save the city £20 million

($34 million) a year in avoided air pollution, accidents and congestion. There are also safe lanes, where you can still ride home after a glass of wine, and taxis are obliged to have a bike rack to take you and your bike home if you have two glasses. Or a bottle. This strikes me as inordinately civilised. Because Danes cycle everywhere, the one-upmanship of cars as a status symbol is also diminished so that managing directors and dish-washers will wait at the traffic lights side by side on their bikes on their way to work. There's no social stigma to biking, and cycling is seen as another of Denmark's great equalisers. It's also said that 30 minutes of daily biking adds an average of fourteen months to life expectancy, according to a report published in the Environmental Health Perspectives journal. And a study from Harvard Medical School found that cycling boosts cognitive well-being, too. No wonder Copenhageners all look so hot and smug.

Danish cyclists, as far as I can make out, ride their bikes during the week wearing whatever they've been dressed in all day. But weekend cyclists tend to go full-on Lycra, complete with liquid energy pouches in case of a low blood sugar emergency. I promise Lego Man that I'll give it a go, but tell him that I prefer the casual 'weekend' approach. 'I'm not going all-out Lance Armstrong.'

'What, taking EPO then going on *Oprah*?'

'More like "wearing shorts with gel in the bottom",' I clarify. 'I'm only going if I can wear normal clothes that don't look and feel as though I've soiled myself.'

'OK...' Lego Man holds up his hands and gives me a look that says '*it's your loss*'. Minutes later, I find him ordering some kind of alarming Lycra onesie for himself online.

The following weekend, Lance and I set off. Me, wobbling on a hybrid that's far prettier than I remember from the last time I was in the saddle (as it were); Lego Man, on a seriously souped-up mountain bike that I'd no idea had been lurking in our shed.

Our inaugural voyage into the Danish countryside begins well, until a farmer stops us in his tractor to say that we haven't got the right headlights. He tells us this in Danish first, before sighing, rolling his eyes and realising he's going to have to interact with a pair of stupid Brits who still haven't mastered his mighty language, despite intensive lessons at the taxpayers' expense. At least, that's what I sense he's thinking.

'The right *headlights*?' I ask, incredulous. 'It's midday! The sun's—' I want to say 'shining', but this isn't strictly true, so I settle on, '—not going to set for hours!'

'That does not matter,' he shakes his head. 'This is the *rule*.'

I'd always been under the impression that *any* headlights marked you out a responsible cyclist. When I was growing up, all we had on our bikes were the free reflective strips from the Texaco garage and plastic Kellogg's cereal packet clackers in our spokes to alert passers-by of our impending advance. And we survived. Admittedly with a few cuts and grazes and one particularly painful arm fracture. But I digress.

'Head and tail lights must be permanently installed and emit light straight forwards and straight backwards,' Officious Farmer uses his hands to mime this and ends up doing a very passable charade of The Bangles' classic, 'Walk Like An Egyptian'. 'Headlights should be installed with a small inclination, to avoid blinding oncoming traffic,' he goes on, 'and lights must not—' he makes a floppy motion with his wrist and then gestures to my bike, '—*dangle*.' I feel offended on my bike's behalf.

Lego Man assures him that we'll get this seen to at the next available opportunity but Officious Farmer isn't done yet. He turns his attention to my husband's vehicle.

'Lights should also have 120 flashes per minute!'

'I'm sorry?' *There are rules on how often your flashing, properly attached, correctly positioned, Danish-standard approved lights should flash? What, in case we come across an epileptic badger?*

Officious Farmer-slash-keen-amateur-cyclist (I'm assuming) shrugs: 'That is the rule *in Denmark*.' He says the last two words as though to make it quite clear that he's not sure what sort of slapdash cycling standards we're used to in our own country, but that here they like to do things properly.

'Right. OK. We'll get it sorted. Thank you.'

We press on, but even Lego Man feels that some of the fun has been sponged out of the expedition. After an hour, I am cold, I've got oil from the chain up the leg of my Sweaty Betty yoga pants, and I have a very sore bottom.

'We'll get you some special shorts for next time,' Lego Man starts as I hobble off. 'They do some good padded ones now. I could buy you some for your birthday.'

I say nothing, horrified at the idea of technical outerwear as an acceptable gift for your beloved. Lego Man mistakes my silence for encouragement. 'In fact, I read about some new abrasion-resistant, antibacterial ones you can get. Apparently they're good for preventing thrush...' I glower at him. Lego Man looks confused, then, sensing he's losing me, tries one final push: 'They've got silicone grippers?'

'As tempting as all this sounds,' I tell him, 'I might leave the biking to you. I'm not sure I'm cut out for a Danish cycling club. Plus I'd like a proper birthday present, please.'

Watching me walk off like John Wayne, Lego Man doesn't argue and instead starts researching alternative hobbies (and, I hope, gift-appropriate shiny things).

'Swimming!' he announces, waving an iPad in front of me an hour or so later. 'Did you know,' he reads from the screen, holding it in both hands as though giving a lecture on something important, 'that just 20 minutes of swimming sends signals the body to release euphoria-producing endorphins? Boosting well-being and sending you home buzzing, according to human kinetics research.' Lego Man knows that I'm a sucker for a health-related fact.

'Is that right?' I reply.

'Yes! What do you think? There's a pool not far from here,' he gestures out to the world outside Sticksville-on-Sea. 'They have teams, and club nights, or you can just go along for an introductory session, you know, to see if you like it. In fact, they have a late night, kid-free swimming session tonight.' Lego Man is brimming with enthusiasm. *Again*. It's exhausting.

'I think I'm too broken for one day,' I start.

'But swimming,' he swipes the screen to show me the municipal pool's website, 'can help. All that warm water. And they have a steam room – that'll help loosen up your muscles!'

I can already tell this is happening: we're going.

A few hours later, we step into a large, chlorine-scented

leisure centre. We buy two pool passes and the receptionist grins at us, before adding in a rather knowing tone: 'Have a *really* great night!'

'What was that about?' I whisper as we move away from the desk.

'She was just being friendly,' Lego Man says, sounding not entirely convinced himself. We push open the fire door into the '*bad*' or 'baths' area and I start to feel a vibration under foot. *Weird*, I think, but keep moving. As we walk towards the changing rooms, I begin to make out a melody.

'There's music, coming from ... in there,' I point.

'From the pool?'

'Must be.'

'Huh.'

We continue a few paces in silence until Lego Man says, 'Is ... that ... *Barry White* playing?' We pause and listen.

'Do you know, I think it might be.'

We go our separate ways to change and I'm faced with a stark communal changing and shower situation complete with wall-mounted illustrations of the key areas that must be thoroughly scrubbed, sans swimming costume, before I enter the pool (head, armpits, groin and feet, in case you're wondering). I'm half expecting a swimming pool matron to arrive and stand over me to check I'm doing it right but manage to complete my ablutions unsupervised. *At least my fellow swimmers will be clean*, I console myself.

Having scoured my epidermis, I push open swinging doors and emerge poolside. To my astonishment, I'm faced with a candlelit sea of bodies, moving slowly to the strains of 'Love Serenade' by the Walrus of Love.

'Oh my...' I mutter.

'Oh shit...' whispers Lego Man, appearing beside me and looking pale.

'When you told me it was "no kids night",' I speak in low, deliberate tones, 'what did the website *actually* say?' There is an audible gulp.

'Well?'

'It might...'

'Yes?'

'It *might* have said, actually, now I think about it, "*adult* night".'

'Right.'

'Sorry.'

'So what you have in fact brought me to, is some sort of 1970s porn pool party?'

'It's looking a little like that, yes.'

'Brilliant.'

'Well, we're here now...'

Lego Man is a practical sort of chap. Rationalising that we might as well attempt to swim now that we're here, we try doing some lengths but keep having to divert our course to avoid canoodling couples.

'The entire upsies and downsies system has gone to pot,' I hiss at Lego Man through a mouthful of suspect chlorine.

'"*Upsies and downsies*"? Is that actually a system?'

'Isn't it?' I'm not a regular swimmer (can you tell?). 'Or is it roundsies and roundsies?'

'If you mean anticlockwise, then yes, that's the "system". But,' he squints without his glasses on to see the far side of the pool, 'it looks like there might be some heavy petting going on in the shallow end so I'd stick around here for now.'

I try a few more lengths before my path's blocked once more by an amorous couple face-sucking to Marvin Gaye's 'Sexual Healing'.

We think about trying the Jacuzzi instead, but as we wade over to it, a sulk of teenagers sit bolt upright and a dozen or so hands appear above the water from wherever they've been beforehand.

'Oh dear god … how about we call it a day?' I ask Lego Man, hopefully.

'Yeah, see you on the other side.' He's out of the pool faster than a performing seal and already halfway to the changing rooms by the time I've navigated my way around a pair of sexagenarians dry humping (were it not for the water).

'You're leaving? Already?' The receptionist asks as I emerge, bedraggled.

'Yes, we've had plenty of excitement for one day,' I mumble as I pass her.

She addresses Lego Man who's been hovering uncomfortably by the leaflets for aqua aerobics, waiting for me: 'There's a wellness evening for men next Monday, with beer tasting, pulled pork, sauna and steam room. Only 199 DKK for the whole evening [around £20 or $34]. Shall I sign you up?' She proffers a wooden clipboard with a pencil dangling from a piece of string.

'Er … I'm sorry, I can't make it,' he stammers and backs out through the leisure centre's revolving doors as fast as he can.

'How about Sunday?' she calls out across the reception as we're leaving, 'Sunday is family nudist night!'

'Um, I think we're busy ... but thanks!' I reply politely as Lego Man is already revving the car. I do an attractive half-jog to join him and we screech out of the car park.

At a loss as to what to try next, I initiate 'hobby week', resolving to try a different hobby club each night, and then at the end of the week decide which ones to join. I'm also hoping that this might be a good way to meet people and make some Real Life Friends.

Lego Man says he'll play along too and lines up an array of sea-based pursuits to make the most of the fact that we live by it. Our newly adopted homeland, I discover, is made up of 406 islands (even more than Greece – stick that in your pub quiz trivia folder) and 7,314km of coastline – so you're never more than 50km from the sea. Aside from Denmark's Olympic sailing success, Danes are also fond of sea kayaking, windsurfing, sailing, water-skiing, and sea swimming.

'In *March*?' I ask doubtfully, pulling my jumper sleeves down over my hands for warmth.

'All year round, apparently,' he says. 'The club told me that 20,000 Danes swim in the sea during the winter, even when the water's frozen over.'

'How is that even possible?'

'I'm not sure,' he admits, sounding anxious. 'I'm hoping I won't need to find out.'

After some ringing around, cajoling and general begging to see if any of my new acquaintances mind me tagging along with them to their various pursuits, I too manage to amass a week's worth of activities. By the end of the week, my diary looks something like this:

MONDAY: Volleyball followed by handball with fellow expat American Mom [who I met after hearing her speaking English in supermarket and then stalked]. Embark on adrenaline-fuelled, aerobic double whammy with poor results. Hand-eye coordination hasn't improved since age of eleven, when gave up on team sports because they were after school and clashed with *Neighbours*. Wrists get bruised during VB, then palms battered during HB. Coach in no hurry to sign me up (even for 'fun team'). Arnica tablets before bed. Suspect will have to wear sling tomorrow.

TUESDAY: Danish language evening class, then local choir with Lego Man's colleague in The Big Town. Songs all in Danish. No clue what I'm singing about. Choir mistress attempts to give me some direction in English but suspect something is lost in translation. Highlights include: 'Think like a fish!', 'Remember, you have potatoes in your mouth!' and 'Pretend your bottom is bigger!' But overall, fun. Find out that singing releases endorphins and slashes stress, plus doing it with other people boosts mental well-being, according to Harvard and Yale studies. Sold, I sign up. Am officially member of my first Danish club!

WEDNESDAY: Local yoga class in Danish (would have preferred Viking goddess Ida's class but a three-hour round trip to The Big City to get my Zen on might have reverse effect). Yoga apparently improves well-being and increases serotonin levels. Only it turns out that meditation isn't so relaxing when you don't yet speak the language and the teacher only knows one English phrase: 'Feel your rainbow!' She shouts this, repeatedly, for 90 minutes. No clearer on where my rainbow actually is by end of class. Fail.

THURSDAY: Danish lessons again. I still suck. Kind Ukrainian gets moved up to the top group. Polish Divorcee and Filipino girls stay in dunce class with Lego Man and me.

FRIDAY: Cooking club with Friendly Neighbour. Learn that even casual suppers here are An Event with competitive napkin folding, three courses, and an implicit understanding that if you go home after fewer than six hours, you've had a terrible time and insulted your host for evermore. Make venison burgers from a deer that one of the members shot last week at 'hunting club'. Hunting, gathering, and entertaining = high on happy-hobby list for many Jutlanders.

SATURDAY: Sign up for Stitch & Bitch session in The Big Town in attempt to get crafty. Learning a new skill supposed to make you happier, according to researchers from San Francisco State University. Caveat: not if you get lost en route, arrive late, then discover you've forgotten to bring any fabric and so spend three hours rearranging bobbins. Any bitching there may have been was all in Danish so missed most of this but apparently there are rival sewing clubs that all hate each other. Like the Sharks and the Jets but with needles. Terrifying.

SUNDAY: Supposed to be day of rest but woken at 8am by loud roar followed by smell of burning rubber. Motorbike season has begun. Friendly Neighbour tells us winter is so treacherous that insurance is only affordable once the weather lets up, so bike clubs hit the roads at first opportunity. Catch up on Lego Man's week. He's surprisingly less keen on sea-based pursuits after sea swims in temperatures of minus one. Going back to biking and running.

Exhausted from our exploits, the remains of the day are spent pottering. I'm excited about joining the choir and fully intend to persevere with language classes. But I'm not sure I've quite cracked the whole Danish leisure time and club culture.

'Wouldn't it be nicer to just be spontaneous?' I put it to Lego Man. 'Playing a game of tennis if you felt like it? Or going for a run when the mood takes you? Why does it all have to be so formal?'

He puts down his new gel-bottomed black cycling onesie that makes him look like a stretched seal and thinks about this.

'I don't know. I was chatting to some of the guys at work and they all say they really like *knowing* what they're doing, weeks in advance. The way it was explained to me was that it just makes people feel better this way.' He relays a discussion he and his fellow Lego minifigures had over *morgenmad* last week. 'It's like the structure helps you feel secure, you know what you're doing and when – your social life is sorted weeks in advance, so there's nothing to think about or worry about. Plus there's so much spare time, it's nice to know you have something constructive to do with it.'

I'm a fan of a timetable as much as the next girl but I can't help feeling that rules take some of the fun out of free time. But I get the idea that being part of something – that feeling like you *belong* – can make you happy. It gives you an identity, beyond just your job or your marital status or, in our case, nationality. Already, getting involved has made me feel more at home in Denmark. I'm no longer just 'Lego Man's wife' or 'that weird new English girl that's moved here' – I'm now an alto in The Big Town's premier (OK, 'only') choir. I'm that weird new girl who called her teacher a 'bitch' in Danish language class. I exist outside of my work and my wifeliness. And it feels good.

Things I've learned this month:

1. Living somewhere new makes you realise who your friends are
2. Danes love a rule
3. I am not a linguist
4. I am also not a cyclist
5. Or a swimmer
6. You can dry hump in water
7. Filling an entire week with extra-curricular activities makes you really appreciate a Sunday lie-in (and really angry when this is denied you)

4. April

Great Danes & Other Animals

'What are you doing tomorrow?' my new *official* pal Friendly Neighbour asks, wiping a crumb of soil from her face with the back of an arm and smearing it across her forehead in the process.

It's a Saturday afternoon and Lego Man and I are walking the dog. This mainly involves trying to make sure he doesn't defecate in anyone's garden and following him around with hands encased in black plastic bags just in case, ready to pounce. With the arrival of spring and a reduction in the number of mornings I've needed an ice-scraper to get the car going, our sleepy seaside town has come to life. Suddenly, there are *people* in the local shop. Boats are being unloaded from trailers in the marina and the trees look as though they're *thinking* about sprouting greenery. Our neighbours *smile* at us, their brusque wintery exteriors sloughing off with the new season as they unfurl like the beech leaves on the bushes surrounding our house. New shoots appear from the earth as flowers contemplate putting in an appearance and Jutland's gardeners come out to play. There is a *staggering* amount of double-denim on display in Sticksville.

Friendly Neighbour is out digging something. She's kneeling in the grass, trowel in hand, sporting some heavy-duty gardening gloves that she takes off as she sees us coming.

'Tomorrow?' I survey her perfectly manicured lawn and newly planted bulbs and pray that the dog doesn't feel the call of nature just yet. 'No plans, I don't think...' This is a lie: I *know* we have nothing on tomorrow. Just like we currently have nothing on next weekend, nor the one after that. Despite our newly acquired extracurricular pursuits, our social life is still on the sluggish side since arriving in Denmark, so we're adopting the strategy of saying 'yes please!' to any invitation proffered. It's an interesting exercise in embracing the unfamiliar. So far this month, I've been to a Tupperware party (yes, these still exist), a drum and bass night, crab-racing (a popular pursuit in seaside Jutland) and line dancing (with mixed results).

'You're free then? Great!' Friendly Neighbour stabs her trowel into the earth like a stake and uses it to lever herself up. 'Do you want to come see the dancing cows?'

'*Sorry*?'

Lego Man eyes the empty bottle of beer and half-drained glass on Friendly Neighbour's garden table suspiciously. I shoot him a look that says, '*it's a free country, a woman can drink-garden if she wants to...*'

'This Sunday, it's Dancing Cow Day!'

She had me at 'dancing cow', but Lego Man still needs

convincing and so Friendly Neighbour goes on. 'It's tradition here – a special day for farmers. Every spring, they let the cows back out into their fields after a long winter inside. And then they dance. The cows, not the farmers,' she clarifies.

I'm reminded of my late grandmother who became utterly bemused every time the Anchor butter advert featuring quickstepping Friesians came on the telly. 'How *do* they make them to do that?' she'd marvel, blissfully unaware of the world of computer animation. *Jurassic Park* would have blown her mind.

'Cows can't dance,' Lego Man states categorically, bringing me back to the present. He's frowning now, as though someone is deliberately trying to bamboozle him.

Friendly Neighbour smiles patiently, in that way that parents do when explaining something painfully simple to a small child. 'Sure they can! Well, we say "dance" – they sort of jump. And run around a bit. Because they're so happy, see? To be back with the grass.' She gestures at her own grass as if to illustrate and the dog takes this as the go-ahead to make himself at home. He begins assuming the familiar, hunched-over position: knees trembling pre-release. Before I can pull him away, it's happened and I'm down on all fours with a plastic bag, apologising.

'Don't worry. It's no problem,' says Friendly Neighbour, though her wrinkled nose clearly suggests otherwise. 'So, shall I pick you up tomorrow to see the crazy cows?'

'Yes, thank you. And sorry about…' I tail off, giving the black bag and its still-warm contents a swing to avoid having to say '*sorry my dog crapped on your lawn*' out loud.

Friendly Neighbour nods before adding: 'Have you considered dog training?'

I assure her that I have, and that we'll be sending him to canine remand school just as soon as I can find one that will have him.

The next day's crazy cow party proves just as rock and roll as one might imagine. The ritual marks the start of the outdoor season for all organic cows in Denmark and we learn that a certified organic animal must be outside eating grass for at least six hours a day between April and November. We're joined at the local farm by crowds of children, all with their faces painted to look like cows (allegedly, though there's some very inexpert daubing on show). Parents with camera phones line up, poised to capture the moment itself and children tear around making mooing noises. It's a chilly day with a sharp wind nipping at any exposed flesh so everyone is muffled up in technical outer layers to ensure that they're well protected from the elements. Spring may have sprung in Jutland, but that doesn't mean the sun is necessarily ready to make an appearance just yet. Some children are even wearing snowsuits, which, combined with the Jersey-cow face painting, makes them look a lot like Oompa Loompas.

After a countdown in Danish (which, I'm pleased to report, I can now join in with) the barn doors are hauled open and several dozen cattle are released. As promised, Daisy and co. run, jump and skip excitedly out to pasture. Then there's some puzzled mooing and the cows stop dead. A few start to buck. There's an air of panic, and then one by one the animals turn around and run right back inside.

'*Ohhhhh*!' the crowd exclaim in disappointment, en masse, as an angry farmer does his best to shoo the cows back out again, without success. After spending five and a half months inside, it appears that the cows have forgotten about the climate in Denmark. They too are finding it a bit cold for their liking. A woman in waders tries enticing them out of their warm, cosy stable with fistfuls of fresh grass, but this fails to pique their interest. There is some shouting and stamping (the farmer) and laughing (us) before everyone decides to call it a day and go home.

'This is most unusual,' Friendly Neighbour assures us, sounding a little disappointed. 'Usually it's quite a good show. The cows are so happy!'

In lieu of any actual dancing, we spend ten minutes looking at YouTube footage of cows from previous years on Friendly Neighbour's phone. We make the appropriate '*ooh!*' and '*ahhh!*' sounds as we watch a herd hopping around and galloping gleefully and, despite his scepticism, even Lego Man has to admit that it's pretty remarkable stuff.

Before this, I'd thought of cows as fairly phlegmatic creatures. My only non-YouTube encounters with cows to date have involved them chewing the cud, lying down and forecasting rain, or accompanied by strips of fried potato and a glass of red in a French restaurant. None of which have given much indication of the presence of joy or strong feelings one way or another. But what if living Danishly could even make cows happy? And what about the non-organic cows that are always inside? The outdoorsy cows might experience a high at being turned out to pasture, but didn't that mean that they'd feel worse when they had to go back in their barns? And the cows that stayed in their shed all year round wouldn't know anything different. With no expectations of grassy euphoria and no idea what they were missing out on, might they not be more content with their lot? I think about all the studies saying that Danes are the happiest people on earth and wonder where they've been measuring dairy cow contentment instead. In the same way as the indoor cows might be content because they've never considered going out to graze (or dance), Danes pottering around Jutland might be similarly satisfied with their lot having never considered the possibility of jacking it all in to become a samba instructor in Brazil. *Is it*, as Alfred Lord Tennyson might have said had he been knocking around rural Denmark today, *better to have danced then stopped dancing than never to have danced at all*? Are Danes as happy as they are, not because they have a lot of great experiences compared with others, but because they live in a predictable and stable environment? Am I living among a nation of non-organic dairy cows?

I put this theory to Lego Man but he's distracted on his phone. Feeling cheated by the less-than-thrilling spectacle of cows being not-very-crazy, he has been seeking out other animal-tastic outings and proposes a visit to the local zoo. There, we inadvertently witness 'feeding time' in the lion enclosure and watch a recently slain horse get torn apart by a ravenous pride in front of a group of schoolchildren.

'It's like Aslan's turned on Mr Tumnus...' I mutter in horror.

Lego Man, who is now a queasy shade of green, suggests calling it a day. Our reaction makes me wonder; are we particularly squeamish? Or are Vikings just more practical than your average population when it comes to the harsh realities of life and death?

On the Monday I'm due to have lunch with one of the 'natives' I met at cooking club (not the one who shot Bambi), who is on the verge of becoming another *actual* friend (hurrah!). The scene of Mufasa and his mates gorging on the back end of a My Little Pony is still playing on a loop in my mind so I recount the episode, interested in his take on the spectacle. But my new *almost-actual-friend* is unfazed.

'So?' he takes another sip of coffee and stops the waitress to ask whether she recommends the pulled pork or the beef burger.

'But there were *children* watching!' I try to impress on him the Tarantino-esque horrors of the scene but The Viking is unmoved.

'And?' is his response. 'Danish kids are used to that sort of stuff.' '*Stuff*' being disjointed limbs and bloodbaths. 'When I was seven, we went on a school trip to see a wolf getting dissected.'

'Sorry?' I splutter cappuccino froth down my jumper and cast around for paper napkins to mop myself up.

'It's educational,' he shrugs. He explains that museums in Denmark have been doing public dissections for years, on animals ranging from snakes to tigers. I wonder whether this is something that only happened in the 1970s and 80s, before health and safety and political correctness were invented, but The Viking assures me that the practice is still alive and well. 'My nine-year-old niece is a huge fan. She asked to go and see a snake get slit open for her birthday this year.' The Viking's niece is not alone in her enthusiasm.

Animal autopsies are so popular in Denmark that museums often have to hold two a day in the school holidays to meet demand. Children gather around the operating table while a zoologist talks through what they're doing, from the knives and scalpels they're using, to what's inside ('which mainly looks like sausages,' The Viking assures me).

'And seeing these things didn't freak you out?'

The Viking thinks about this: 'The smell, I remember, wasn't great. But the rest was fun. And it's good for kids to learn. They need to know that nature can be rough and to learn about life and death.'

'At *nine*?'

'Why not?'

I tell him that this is a far more graphic introduction to life's harsh realities than we got when I was growing up. Even my class hamster's untimely demise at the hands of Melissa Vincent's cat was described euphemistically as a 'passing' and the nearest we came to seeing his remains was a Start-rite shoebox being covered with soil in the junior school garden. School trips in my day were to places like Anne Hathaway's cottage in Stratford-upon-Avon or Bekonscot Model Village. Never once did we hop on a coach stinking of sandwiches and chemical toilets to go and see the innards of a wild dog.

'Sounds like you missed out,' is The Viking's response.

He tells me about another outing during university where the whole class decamped to an abattoir: 'We were studying design in action and they have some really cool lasers to cut through the pigs and joint them and stuff...' He looks almost wistful as he reminisces about cleanly severed carcases before taking a big bite of his pulled pork sandwich. It's clear that there isn't much sentimentality when it comes to animals in Denmark. But this philosophy isn't always well received by rest of the world – as was shown in the case of Marius.

Marius was an eighteen-month-old giraffe living in Copenhagen Zoo. Though healthy, he was considered genetically unsuitable for breeding because his genes were too common, so it was decided by the zoo authorities to put him down. This provoked an international outcry and 27,000 signatures on an online petition calling for the zoo to rethink its decision. Several zoos worldwide offered to rehome Marius, but Copenhagen Zoo claimed that these institutions didn't have the same ethical standards that they did. Officials said that sending the giraffe elsewhere would mean that it could be sold to a circus or spend the rest of its life suffering in a 'substandard zoo'. Euthanasia, they claimed, was a kinder option. Copenhagen Zoo's scientific director told CNN at the time that his job was to preserve species, not individual animals.

So on 9 February 2014, the young giraffe was given a last meal of some quintessentially Danish rye bread before being shot in the head with a bolt gun. All in front of an audience of zoo visitors. After this, staff conducted a public autopsy, enthusiastically attended by crowds of Danish children and their parents curious to see the inner workings of the creature. Marius was dissected and fed to the lions – again, in full view of all who cared to watch. The world's press was perplexed at what they saw as the Dane's macabre callousness. One letter to the *Guardian* newspaper in the UK noted that 'the public execution of Marius and his equally public consumption by lions' made 'Danish noir crime easier to understand, psychologically...'

I talk to Peter Sandøe, professor of bioethics at the University of Copenhagen and former chairman of the Danish Ethical Council for Animals, to get his take on this. Peter was a key commentator on Marius-gate and in common with The Viking and all the other Danes I've met, he struggled to see what the fuss was about.

'Denmark was an agricultural society only two generations back, so we think of animals as *animals*,' he tells me. 'Most people with an agricultural background would feel the same way [about Marius] – the giraffe was a breeding male who was not going to be used in breeding, so then you slaughter it. It would be the same with sheep – you can't have more than one ram in a flock, otherwise they will fight. It was the practical approach,' says Peter.

He was surprised by the international media furore ('I even got a letter comparing me to Adolf Hitler after one BBC interview, which I felt was a bit much!') and suspects that it was the graphic aftermath that non-Danes found particularly shocking. 'People from overseas felt squeamish about the fact that the giraffe was cut up in front of an audience including children and that his bits and pieces were fed to other animals. But people should be able to face these things. If they don't like to see an animal being cut up but are happy to go to Marks & Sparks to pick up a packet of plastic-wrapped meat, then they're hypocrites.'

I tell him I'm guilty as charged on this one (though I'm also delighted by his cultural reference to my mother country's favourite fancy supermarket and pant purveyor). Danes, it seems, are happy to watch their animals be butchered before they eat them, and vegetarianism is practically unheard of. 'Most people eat meat here,' admits Peter, 'and there are significantly fewer vegetarians in Denmark – around 3–5 per cent – than in the UK, where the figure's 10 per cent.'

Danes don't feel guilty about eating animals, and their carnivorous diet may also contribute to their happiness levels. Vegetarianism has been linked with higher rates of depression and anxiety according to research from the Medical University of Graz, Austria.

'We don't tend to get as sentimental about animals here as people in, for example, the UK,' says Peter. I wonder whether this psychological distance protects Danes from distress when creatures inevitably get hurt or die. *If you don't feel pain when Bambi's mum gets shot or Simba's dad carks it in* The Lion King, *then of course life's less upsetting and it's easier to be happy*, I think. And if you can eat your beef burger without concerning yourself too much about how happy the cow was during its lifetime, well, then you've got one less thing to worry about.

But not all meat eaters in Denmark are cock-a-hoop. In 2014, Denmark's agriculture and food minister Dan Jørgensen decreed that all animals used for food should be stunned before they were killed. This effectively banned ritual slaughter as prescribed in Jewish Orthodox and Muslim laws, which both require animals to be intact and conscious when they're killed. In practice, the rule didn't change much. The final Danish slaughterhouse allowing animals to be killed without pre-stunning closed in 2004. Ever since then, Denmark's estimated 7,000 Jews have imported kosher meat from overseas. Most of the 210,000-strong Danish Muslim community still view animals stunned before slaughter as Halal, providing concussion wasn't the cause of their death (population figures from US Department of State – the Danish government doesn't officially record religious affiliations). But the principle of the case riled Jews and Muslims, who united in protest. They claimed that the legislation was less about animal welfare and more about the politics of immigration and integration.

For many Danes, the issue was clear: killing an animal should be done as quickly and as painlessly as possible and it's their belief that this can't be done if the animal is conscious when it's killed. Jewish and Islamic media outlets internationally accused the Danish government of Islamophobia and anti-Semitism, but high-profile figures from both faiths within Denmark avoided using either phrase. The Danish response was more measured, perhaps due to an understanding that a secular bias is just '*The Danish Way*'.

'It was an easy law to pass,' says Peter, 'as ritual slaughter without pre-stunning had not been practised in Denmark for about ten years anyway, so it was more about sending a signal without really getting into trouble with religious people. It was a clever political move. Like Tony Blair banning production of mink for fur in the UK – there wasn't much mink production in the UK anyway anymore so it just made him look good.'

Ah yes, fur. The Danes' relationship with fur has been

another thing I've been wondering about, and I was surprised to see a few grande dames in ankle-length animal pelts when we first arrived in bleak midwinter. I've since learned that Denmark is the largest mink exporter in the world and Copenhagen is at the centre of the fur trade, with China and Russia as its biggest clients. But surely this goes against most Danes' principles on animal welfare?

'Actually, fur production is quite sustainable,' says Peter. 'The mink have the same breeding cycle as they would in the wild, they're not transported anywhere [which can be distressing for animals], and they're fed fish leftovers and chicken pulp from old laying hens. Once the mink fur is removed, their flesh is used to make biodiesel.' This is used to power buses in The Big City. 'Not a bit of the animal is wasted,' Peter assures me, 'plus the industry creates a lot of employment, so the government isn't going to shut it down.' Denmark's 1,500 mink farmers can charge 20 per cent more for their pelts than for those bred elsewhere because of the prestige attached to Danish fur. This is credited to a carefully controlled diet producing a more lustrous fur and Danish designers championing skin in their collections. There aren't animal rights protestors attempting to shut down production in Denmark, as there would be in other European countries, and most Danes don't mind a bit of fur. As a liberal Brit raised during the era of Peta-inspired paint-chucking, who was once cautioned to ditch leather shoes and refrain from eating tuna before interviewing Stella McCartney (true story), this all comes as a bit of a shock.

Hunting, too, is perfectly acceptable and is a popular pastime in Denmark for folk from all walks of life. 'It isn't a class thing here like it is in other places,' Peter tells me, 'and people accept hunting provided the animals are shot and die quickly before being taken home and eaten, so there's no cruelty. I think fox hunting with dogs and horses, which was never practised in Denmark, has been an issue in the UK because it's considered an upper-class thing and the way the fox dies is cruel.'

Peter tells me that he thinks animals get 'put into boxes' in the UK and the US (metaphorically speaking), 'so that people care very much about a lost puppy or an animal at the zoo, but then they go home and eat pig. People get a bit touchy-feely and feel very strongly about kittens and giraffes and things. In Denmark, this tendency to divide up animals is less pronounced. The majority of people think that it's important to look out for an animal's welfare and we don't like them dying for no reason but we're not going to humanise them.'

Cruelty to animals is illegal in Denmark, but interestingly, bestiality is not. 'Anyone who engages in sex with an animal where this will hurt the animal physically or psychologically can be punished,' Peter explains, and so to date, Danish politicians simply haven't seen the point of going through the hassle of writing up a new law to ban bestiality outright. 'However,' Peter tells me, 'it should be said that opinion polls show that a majority of Danes want a ban. So this may eventually come.' (In fact, as this goes to print I learn that the Minister of Food and Agriculture, Dan Jørgensen, has announced that sex with animals will be banned in next year's Animal Welfare Act.)

There aren't many places left to go once you've covered

hunting, fur and getting biblical with a bull all in the space of an hour, so I attempt to bring things back to the rather more pedestrian by asking for his take on dog ownership in Denmark.

'Not sex with them,' I add hastily, alarmed to be in a situation where this even needs clarifying, 'just training and things...'

As someone with a vested interest and a poorly behaved pooch, I'm keen to find out how Danes feel about dogs and whether they're the one animal that my new countrymen and women might get 'touchy-feely' over. *Kristeligt Dagblad* newspaper recently reported that Danish households have more four-legged members than ever before, with 600,000 dogs owned by Danes and 70,000 new ones registered each year. There's also been a 300 million DKK (around £34 million or $58 million) rise in the amount Danes spend on their pets, according to Statistics Denmark. There are proven psychological benefits to having a dog, with owners having lower blood pressure, lower cholesterol and fewer medical problems than other pet owners or the rest of the population, according to research from Queen's University, Belfast. *Which must make Danes happier*, I think. I see a lot of dogs where I live and the whole of Jutland seems perfectly tailored for them, with handy hooks for tethering leads and regularly replenished water bowls outside many local shops and cafes. There are also designated beaches and 200 so-called 'dog forests' where you can let your dog run unleashed.

'Many Danes have dogs,' Peter tells me, 'and of course they care for them very much and they are part of the family. I suppose they may get "touchy-feely" about dogs. But a difference to UK and North America is that it is less fashionable to acquire a dog from a shelter. Most Danes still buy a pure bred or even a pedigree dog. People seem to like to know where their dogs come from.' And when Danes have invested in a pedigree pooch, they like to make sure that it's well-behaved, apparently. Training, it has now become clear, is key for our mutt – as well as for our standing in Danish society.

I ask whether Peter counts himself among the happy Danes I'm researching and he tells me that he's very happy indeed: 'I think people in Denmark generally are, although we do like to moan – we're spoilt! Personally, I'd say I'm a nine out of ten. Maybe ten out of ten professionally.' And there you have it. Even a man who spends his days defending giraffe deaths and getting hate mail comparing him to Hitler is happy in Denmark. Now that's job satisfaction.

Still bemused by all I've seen and heard over the past few days but determined to get my own animal behaving a bit more Danishly, I come home intent on finding a canine camp to teach him some manners.

'You're going to school,' I tell him.

'*yeowungggggg*,' he protests.

'It's not just me who has to give this living Danishly thing a go. You do too. We're four months in and I haven't seen any evidence of Danish integration...' I scold. 'It's time you started evening classes as well.' I sign him up and training starts the very next week.

Our first class involves a shouty woman in a utility waistcoat trying – and failing – to teach our dog how to fetch, sit, rescue a child from a forest and stand on top of an upturned washing-up bowl. No one's quite sure why. The next morning, I stumble out of bed to find that Lego Man has given the dog our washing-up bowl. The dog still isn't interested in using it as a podium. Instead, he's chewing it.

'The dog seems to be eating our washing up bowl,' I remark.

Lego Man looks at the dog, then points to the pile of envelopes that have just been delivered: 'Yes, but he's not eating the postwoman. Baby steps...'

Things I've learned this month:

1. Danes don't do squeamish
2. Animals are just animals in Denmark, unless they're dogs (and they're well-behaved)
3. *The Danish Way* is *The Only Way*
4. ...and outsiders will have a job on their hands convincing Danes otherwise
5. Cows can't dance

5. May

Traditions & Getting Told Off

Against a drizzly sky the colour of bleached slate, several strapping men are busy erecting white poles at regular intervals along the street as we make our way to the bakery. The dog takes the trouble to sniff a few of them before marking his territory on as many as he can manage. This makes for a far longer, wetter, walk than usual.

By the time we've selected our Sunday morning pastries (yes, this is our gluttonous life now – *snegles* all round…) and untethered the hound from the handy dog hook outside, we see that a Danish flag has been hoisted to the top of each pole. White crosses suspended on blood-red rectangles ripple and buckle in the breeze, transforming the road into a majestic sweep and making the place look far grander that we'd ever imagined it could.

'What d'you reckon's happening? D'you think we're in for a royal visit?' Lego Man asks, hopefully.

I can't help thinking that however down-to-earth Denmark's Queen Margrethe is reported to be, a Sunday morning jaunt to Sticksville-on-Sea probably isn't top of her list of royal engagements.

'Maybe…' I wonder how to let him down gently.

We start walking and the dog gets busy bothering my jealously guarded brown paper bag of baked goods. The rape is flowering all over Jutland this month and the fields around us have turned a vibrant yellow. As we round the corner and come closer to home, we're greeted by the familiar sight of our local church: a beautiful, stark, typically Scandinavian building surging up like a bright white rocket against the grey sky and citrine fields. The place is all lit up from within, despite the fact it's 10am, and there are several dozen cars parked in the field next door. This is not normal. Usually, the church is just *there*. Looking nice but not doing much or showing any signs of activity or purpose. Like a well-designed Scandi-style ornament. Only now there are signs of life. The dog stops in his tracks and lifts a paw, ears pinned back, tail straight out behind him, alert.

'I haven't seen anyone go in there since we arrived,' Lego Man observes, as the dog strains at his leash to get closer to the action. We're just contemplating the strange arrival of *actual human beings* to our village, when a low growl starts up, quiet at first, then getting louder. For once, it's not the dog. I can make out the sound of an engine, combined with pumping music and a throbbing bass. It grows to a deafening crescendo until we see, droning into view, an enormous, buffed, black Hummer. The windows are tinted, gangster-style, and it's followed by the long, glossy nose of a stretch limousine, edging its way around the corners of our country lane.

We're used to seeing tractors in these parts, or family cars towing trailers or boats. Once, Lego Man spotted a Beetle (a thrilling day...). But never, since our arrival in Denmark, have we seen anything like this. A few American muscle cars, a Cinderella-style horse and carriage, and another couple of limos arrive, looking incongruous in such a bucolic setting. The church car park starts to look like a snapshot of Leeds city centre on a Saturday night, or a hen do convention. Teenage girls in prom dresses plus a few boys in suits spill out and onto the grass, struggling to avoid getting mud or grass clippings on their finery.

The dog is beside himself. (*New people! To play with! Who might possibly have food! This is BRILLIANT!*) It's the most excitement he, or we, have had since moving here. With a small whimper and a shimmy of his tail, he makes a break for it, surging forward so forcefully that his lead is wrested from my pastry-laden hands. Before I can say, 'Well so much for sodding dog training...', he is gone.

In cinematic slow motion, we watch him bound gleefully towards the group of teens. It's like a miniature version of the opening credits to *Black Beauty*, only with a far messier outcome all-but-inevitable. Lego Man leaps into action like some sort of highly impressive dog-owning superhero, dropping his bakery bag and starting to give chase, hands slicing the air Usain Bolt style. I try a different tactic, inspired by our dog training classes. I tear off a morsel of pastry and hold it out, calling: 'Here boy! Come!' in the hope of luring him back.

But the dog is oblivious. Lead trailing behind him, tail wagging, tongue flapping out of the corner of his mouth, he bounds up to the petite blonde who's just stepped out of the latest limo. She makes the mistake of greeting the dog with what he takes to be encouragement and so he reciprocates. By leaping up and planting two muddy paws on the front of her pale, pink, *silk* dress.

'*Nooooooo!*' Lego Man cries out in horror.

But it's too late.

Limo Girl and her friends do some shrieking. I do some shrieking. Parents of Limo Girl remain astonishingly calm and do some patting down of the pink dress to assess the damage. There is much confusion as to where the dog has come from until the crazy English couple wearing wellies and clutching baked goods finally arrive on the scene, panting, perspiring, and muttering '*Undskyld!*' ('Sorry,' in Danish), over and over again. We're just trying to work out how to say something along the lines of, '*We are mortified! Please, let us prostrate ourselves, here in your fine Danish mud, and buy you a new dress, or at least pay to have that one dry-cleaned...*' in Danish, while getting the dog back on his leash, when Limo Girl's mother seems to magic a suit carrier out of the back of her car. The girl nods and unzips it to reveal an identical dress in pale blue. Holding the dog firmly by the collar now, we watch in amazement as the girl is then ushered into the back of the blacked-out limo. She emerges, seconds later, resplendent in baby blue following a quick costume change.

'Did that just happen?' Lego Man is asking.

'I think so,' I answer, unsure.

'Did she have a *back-up* dress? Just handy? In case of emergencies?'

I shake my head in general confusion as the girl gives us

a friendly wave and turns to make her way into the church followed by her friends and family. The surprisingly understanding crowd appear to dismiss us, and once there's no one left to apologise to, we start walking, slowly, back to the road as well.

I have no explanation for what we have just witnessed. It is bonkers. Along the rest of the route home, we notice gazebos and marquees being erected in different neighbours' gardens. Catering vans seem to be arriving in convoy and people in white chef coats begin to unload trestle tables and large crates of food.

'Is there some sort of enormous party going on that we're not invited to?' I wonder out loud. At this moment, a mobile DJ van drives by as if to confirm my suspicion.

'I'd say that's a fair guess,' Lego Man nods.

As we near home, we spot Friendly Neighbour. I say 'hello' and ask if there's something special going on today.

'Well yes! It's confirmation season! You don't have this where you're from?'

I explain that while we have confirmations, there isn't so much of a '*season*' for them, debutante-style.

'Oh, I see,' she says, pityingly, her head on one side in a look I've come to recognise as '*feeling rather sorry for anyone not fortunate enough to have been born in Denmark*'.

'We don't tend to go all-out on the cars, either,' adds Lego Man.

'The cars? Oh but that's *tradition*,' Friendly Neighbour tells us. 'You have to have a nice car for your special day!'

Of course you do, I think, *because everyone knows that Jesus loved a pimped-up limo...*

After assuring us that confirmation is 'kind of a big deal around here', Friendly Neighbour excuses herself. She's double-booked and has to wrap presents and get ready for not one but *two* confirmation after-parties that she's been invited to today: 'So there's a lot to do!'

After-parties? Gifts? Limos? The whole thing sounds light years away from my own experience of confirmation – a quick daub with oil and ash in the local Catholic church, aged twelve, before a ham sandwich at my gran's. I wore an ill-advised pair of floral culottes along with a matching scrunchie. There were no caterers, mobile DJs, or marquees. And my mum drove the three of us there and back in her navy blue Renault 5 (Turbo, mind).

Back at home, the rest of the morning is spent washing the dog while surreptitiously spying on the confirmation goings-on all around us. Floral displays get delivered. Balloons arrive. Lego Man even thinks he spies a chocolate fountain being wheeled in to the gazebo in our elderly neighbour's garden for some lucky grandchild or other. Consumed with curiosity and realising that I'm unlikely to score an invitation to attend a confirmation myself (this 'season', at least), I get back in touch with cultural expert Pernille, who helped us get to grips with *hygge* in January, to find out more.

'Confirmations are huge,' she tells me. 'It's tradition!' *Ah, that old chestnut again*. From dressing up and eating special cakes at '*Fastelavn*' in February to DIY paper doilies and special cakes at Easter and woven hearts, ugly elves, marzipan pigs and special cakes at Christmas, there's a ritual (and a special cake) to go with everything in Denmark. Traditions and the faithfully repeated customs and behaviours that go with them seem to give Danes a sense of security, stability and *belonging*, even. Having recently read a study from the University of Minnesota that found having rituals could make things more enjoyable, I can't help thinking Danes might be on to something. *It's like the hobby clubs*, I think, *only here it's not just your evenings and weekends that get planned in advance – it's your whole year!*

Danes find it reassuring to have these things taken care of – and the numerous traditions mean that things are done in the same comforting way, year in, year out. The unknown becomes known. 'It's like *tradition* is our religion,' says Pernille, 'something that's really important to the majority of Danes.' Confirmation, then, is no exception and comes with its own set of rules and rituals.

'Most Danes will get confirmed when they're around fourteen in a big church ceremony with up to 40 other teenagers. It's a really fun day for kids. Everyone gets new clothes, there are flags everywhere, and it's often standing room only in the church for friends and family,' says Pernille. 'Afterwards, there are a lot of photos taken, a big three-course meal with songs and speeches, then there's a party with entertainment and loads of presents. Danes get rather materialistic when it comes to confirmation these days – it was a different story twenty years ago when I did it!'

'Same here!' I tell her. I recount scrunchie-gate, we both agree that we were horribly deprived and that the youth of today don't know they're born. Then I get back to business: 'And how much gets spent on confirmations in Denmark now?'

'A lot,' she replies. 'With both parents working full-time and a lot of couples divorced these days, there's often an element of guilt spending involved as well. It's like, "*we can't spend much time with you but here's a big party! Here's a virtual plaster, let's patch this up*!" Plus a lot of Danish parents have a problem saying no. These kids are showered with presents, like it's a wedding or something.'

She tells me that it's traditional to give money as a gift – at least the amount that will be spent on entertaining you (including food and drinks). The closer you are to the family, the more you'll be expected to shell out. If you decide you'd prefer something you can gift-wrap, you'll still have to dig deep. Items topping teenage wish lists for the soon-to-be confirmed in Denmark include iPhones, laptops, watches, jewellery and holidays, and the average Danish teen will receive confirmation gifts worth 17,000 DKK (£1,980 or $3,200) according to a survey by Nordea Bank. *So much for Danish equality*, I think. The high streets capitalise on confirmation season with many stores putting up posters that read, '*Don't forget, you can exchange your confirmation gifts up until 1 June!*' and advertising confirmation cards, suits, dresses, shoes and, of course, special cakes. Any cold, hard cash gifts get put to use immediately by Danish teens on 'Blue Monday'. No, not the New Order song, but the day after the church service when the newly confirmed take the day off school to go on a shopping spree. Most buy clothes and gadgets before comparing hauls with their friends and drinking a lot of cider, I'm reliably informed.

'And what about,' I hazard, 'well, you know, the whole "God" bit? Does He (or She) come into this?'

'Well...' Pernille starts, in a tone that implies '*not so much*'. Confirmation in Denmark is, I learn, about God confirming His (or Her) promise to the individual – a promise to watch over them that was first made when they were baptised. In other words, a Danish confirmation service is God saying 'yes' to you, and not the other way around. Looking at it this way, it doesn't seem to matter too much whether or not you plan to be a committed churchgoer, or even believe at all.

'A fear of God isn't included in the Danish version of the Protestant religion,' explains Pernille. 'Confirmation's not a sacrament in the Evangelical Lutheran Church, but a rite of passage from childhood to adolescence – so everyone's included.' I can almost hear my grandmother tutting in her grave. 'Most Danish families view confirmation as a coming-of-age celebration. We aren't a very religious country on the whole. There isn't much pressure from parents [to be confirmed]. Some families say to their children, "if you don't have a confirmation, we'll throw you a big party anyway so you'll still get presents". This way, they can make sure the kids only get confirmed if they really want to.' This gets called a '*non*firmation' and involves just as much fanfare and gifting as the traditional version. Despite this, many teens opt for the church part. 'I think this is because it's an exercise in autonomy,' says Pernille. 'It's one of the first choices a Danish teenager can make for themselves, and encouraging children to make choices as individuals is considered very important in Denmark.' More important, it seems, than religion, at least for most Danes.

I take tea with Denmark's church minister, Manu

Sareen, to see if he minds this, but he too seems remarkably relaxed about the whole 'faith' business. 'Danes have an interesting approach to religion,' says Manu. 'There aren't many countries where such a high proportion of the population are members of a state church – we have 4.4 million members out of a population of 5.5 million, and yet most people probably take it for granted and don't worry too much about their faith.' Most Danes are signed up at birth, with parents registering their babies at the local church unless they've made a special request for a secular procedure. Many feel a civic obligation to pay church tax, up to 1.5 per cent of their salary depending on the municipality, as though this is just another tax that must be paid to keep Denmark the great nation that it is. As a result, the country has a Lutheran state church financed via taxes, but only 28 per cent of Danes believe in any kind of life after death, according to a survey by the country's Palliative Knowledge Centre (in the US it's 81 per cent). Just 16 per cent believe in heaven (the figure rises to 88 per cent in the US). A 2014 survey carried out for *Berlingske* newspaper found that almost every fifth Dane identifies him- or herself as an atheist.

I tell Manu that I find this fascinating. Lots of studies link religion with happiness and researchers from Columbia University found that faith can even ward off depression. Yet despite Denmark's top spot on the happiness index and its high levels of church membership, it's actually one of the *least* religious countries in the world, with low church attendance, secular schools and civic institutions and a population that regularly reaffirms its atheism (or at least agnosticism) in national surveys and polls.

'Most people don't use the church much apart from for baptisms, weddings, funerals and at Christmas,' says Manu. In contrast with the rest of the Christian world, Easter isn't a big draw in Denmark, with 48 per cent of Danes attaching importance to 'spending time with family' over Easter but only 10 per cent mentioning 'church' and 'the Christian message' according to the country's official website. Statistics Denmark found that just 3 per cent of the population regularly attend church services in a 2013 survey. As a result of this widespread apathy, congregations struggle to keep numbers up and churches are starting to close countrywide. A few that have changed with the times are still going strong and some city churches now offer 'spaghetti services' – mass followed by a bowl of pasta where you can be in and out in an hour. 'The church can just be there for you in Denmark,' says Manu. 'It's like our welfare system – it's there to catch you if you need it.' It's as though the country's safety net extends to faith as well, and it's The Danish Way, rather than regular attendance at church, that keeps the nation so buoyant. Manu assures me that this is what keeps him chipper: 'I'd rate my happiness at a nine and half out of ten. I've got everything I need, I couldn't ask for any more.'

Psychologists at the University of British Columbia in Vancouver, Canada, found that the better educated and wealthier a nation is, the less likely its population is to believe in a higher being. The Global Index of Religion and Atheism also assessed that poverty was a key indicator of a society's tendency towards religion – so that poorer countries tend to be the most religious. The one exception to the rule? America. But in the strongly religious USA, despite the country's wealth, there's no universal healthcare, little job security, and a flimsy social welfare safety net. This means that the USA has a lot more in common with developing countries than she might like to think. Researchers from the University of British Columbia suggest that people are less likely to *need* the comfort of a god if they're living somewhere stable, safe and prosperous. This helps to explain why Denmark and her Scandi cousins Sweden and Norway regularly rate among the most irreligious in the world. Scandinavians don't *have* to pray to a god that everything's going to be OK – because the state has this sorted. In other words, Danes don't have so much left to pray for. And because there isn't a big culture of churchgoing, the next generation are even less inclined to turn out in their Sunday best for mass. Research from St Mary's University in the UK found that there was only a 3 per cent chance that a child would be religious if neither parent was.

But because nature's not crazy about a vacuum, there's still an intrinsic human need to look for answers to the big, thundering life questions that religion attempts to 'clear up' for believers. For Danes, it's almost as though this need is met by the sense of shared values; a close, homogenous society, and a semi-religious, unquestioning *faith* in The Danish Way.

Manu is also the Minister for Gender Equality and so comes at church matters from a relatively progressive point of view. 'It is a funny combination, gender equality and the church,' he admits, crunching on a carrot stick from the array of crudités that have been set before us as an unusual accompaniment to morning tea. 'Gender equality is about being pro-human rights, but sometimes the practice of religion goes against human rights, for instance in the case of abortion. If there's conflict, I just have to take each situation as it comes.' Manu tested this strategy when pushing for Denmark's blasphemy law to be abolished, writing an op-ed in Denmark's *Politiken* newspaper arguing that: 'free speech and human rights are far more important than the danger that someone might feel offended if their religion is subject to mockery and derision'.

Because most Danes don't take their religion too seriously, they're surprised when others do (see ritual slaughter-gate from April). There's been freedom of religion in Denmark since the constitution was signed in 1849. Since then, everyone has been allowed to practise his or her faith, and discrimination is against the law. All Danish residents are free to wear religious symbols and dress, from the crucifix to the Hijab, in public spaces as well as in parliament and schools. Islam is the biggest 'minority religion', making up 3.7 per cent of the population (according to the US Department of State). There are 22 approved Islamic communities in Denmark with the right to deduct their financial contributions to a religious community from their taxable income. Everyone seemed to be rubbing along pretty well until 2005 when the Danish newspaper *Jyllands-Posten* famously printed twelve cartoons of the Islamic prophet Muhammad. This sparked international controversy as well as violent protests, a boycott of Danish goods in several countries and the burning of the Danish embassy in Damascus and its consulate in Beirut. The fallout mystified many Danes, who couldn't understand why anyone was getting so het up. As The Viking put it: 'They were just cartoons in a paper that most people would throw in the trash anyway…'

But conservative types keen on clamping down on immigration used the incident to launch a campaign 'defending Danish values'. Denmark's far-right Danske Folkeparti gained supporters as a result and has since called for a halt on immigration. The party has been growing steadily ever since and won nearly 27 per cent of the vote in the 2014 European elections, doubling its number of MEPs.

But these aren't the views of the majority. Social Democrat PM Helle Thorning-Schmidt has managed to hold on to the reins of the country since 2011 and present a strong front for the traditionally liberal nation's Scandinavian ideals. In her last New Year's Eve speech, Denmark's Queen Margrethe took the opportunity to caution the nation about the perils of being small-minded and urged respect for those from other cultures. 'Denmark is a country with many different people,' she said. 'Some have always lived here, some have come here. But we are a part of the same society and therefore we share the same conditions, both big and small, good and bad.'

Danes have a reputation for being a tolerant nation, as happiness economist Christian told me right at the start, and in 2013 Denmark was the focus of celebrations marking the 70th anniversary of the 7,000 Jewish lives saved during Nazi occupation. The rescue operation to smuggle Danish Jews to safety over the border to Sweden was almost completely successful with 90 per cent saved (to put this in perspective, only 30 per cent of Holland's 140,000 Jews and 60 per cent of Norway's Jewish population survived). For Danes, standing up to Nazism by championing democracy – an idea totally incompatible with anti-Semitism – was considered crucial.

Perceived tolerance is a great source of national pride. I find that the Danes I meet need the merest of excuses to come over all patriotic about their country. Being born in Denmark is seen as incontrovertibly fortunate and even having a tenuous association with the nation is perceived as A Good Thing. Lots of companies incorporate 'Dan' in their business's name, because being Danish here is equated with being generally fabulous and of a high quality. I join a Facebook group dedicated to recording this phenomena and finding as many 'Dan brands' as possible – 357 at the last count – including *DanAir*, *DanFish*, *DanCake*, *DanDoors* and my personal favourite, *DanLube*.

I start to wonder whether all this patriotism might also be having an impact on the nation's well-being. Could loving your country and continually reminding yourself of what a fabulous place you come from contribute to higher life satisfaction? I have a scout around and discover that feeling good about your country has been scientifically proven to make you happier, according to research published in *Psychological Science*. A European Values Study also found that the greater one's sense of national pride, the more likely you are to report higher levels of personal well-being. 'So no wonder the Danes are happy,' I tell Lego Man. 'Nearly 90 per cent of them say they're either "proud" or "very proud" of their country,' I read to him from my laptop. Another piece of research from the International Social Survey Programme asked how many Danes agreed with the statement, 'My country is better than other countries'. A staggering 42 per cent of Danes answered 'yes, my country is better'. In contrast, other liberal countries with strong welfare models reported far lower figures, with only 7 per cent of Dutch people thinking their country was superior and 12 per cent of Swedes inclined to shout about their homeland.

Flag waving – both literally and metaphorically – is nigh-on compulsory here. Regardless of your beliefs, waving that white cross against a red background is the one thing that unites everyone from Social Democrats to Danske Folkparti members, and Lutherans to atheists. Whether flying majestically in the background of any given TV broadcast or outside homes, decorating office desks, adorning food, being strung up to celebrate a birthday or used to sell something – anything that stays still long enough in Denmark will eventually get a Danish flag stuck in it.

The *Dannebrog* is one of the oldest national flags in the world and was, allegedly, first spotted falling from heaven in the 13th century. Legend has it that Danish soldiers were about to lose the Battle of Valdemar in June 1219 when they took a mini time-out to have a group huddle and pray for help. Lo and behold, instead of extra weaponry, manpower or world peace, God delivered unto them ... the *Dannebrog*. The red and white pennant fell from the sky and was deftly caught by the Danish king before it had the chance to touch the sodden earth. This divine offering was said to have brought the royal army to victory – but instead of worshipping the God who delivered it to them, today's Danes appear to invest more faith and loyalty in the flag itself.

Having found out more about the heavenly talisman, we're excited when we find a flagpole in various bits buried under cobwebs at the back of our shed (thank you, previous tenants). We take it out and assemble the thing before trying to hold it upright in the wind, like an inexpert re-enactment of the Amish barn-raising scene in *Witness* (Lego Man: 'Bagsie being Harrison Ford!' Me: 'Er ... sure...'). We manoeuvre the fifteen-foot-high pole, fully upright, to an area a safe distance from the car/our windows/the dog and find to our delight that it fits snugly into a conveniently lined hole, that until now we'd taken for an ineffective drain. Having never had a flagpole before (I know, it's a First World problem...), we only realise once it's up that the pulley mechanism could do with an oil so we take the thing down again. In a fit of adoptive patriotism, I order a Danish flag online. (Our predecessors didn't think to leave us theirs. Rude.)

'This could just be the start,' I tell Lego Man, getting excited. 'We could put up different flags for visitors! Or do a skull and crossbones and hold a pirate-themed party! We could *create our own coat of arms*!'

He gives me a look that tells me I've probably had enough coffee for one morning, before relenting and agreeing to let me buy a few more, 'just to have in'.

The following weekend, an old university friend is coming to stay. I'm touched when friends from home make the effort to visit and it means more to us than I suspect they will ever realise. Flights here aren't expensive – you can get a return from London on a budget airline for £30 (around

$50) – but I get that venturing outside your comfort zone and choosing to fly to Billund for a minibreak may not be everyone's first choice of getaway. For those adventurous enough to risk it for a biscuit, I want to make things special and reward our intrepid guests with as fun a time as possible. This week's guest of honour is coming for a couple of nights ahead of what we are instructed to refer to as 'his big birthday'; something he's been in denial about for some time now. He is originally from Switzerland and is very polite and very handsome and whenever we see him, he brings me a near-obscene sized box of chocolates. Swiss Friend is *always* welcome. So I feel we should do something special to mark his major milestone that's also non-specific enough to keep us on his Christmas list in case he's still planning to insist he is 'only 39'. I bake cakes and Lego Man buys booze. Then I have a brainwave.

'We could get him a flag!' I exclaim with glee, two coffees in, the following Saturday.

'What?'

'A Swiss one! Like the Danes do for their birthdays! And then we could fly it from our flagpole so it's the first thing he sees when he arrives!'

'Couldn't we just put up a Danish one? It's not far off—'

'—No!' I try to interject though a mouthful of muesli. Unable to say it rather than spray it, I point to a story on the BBC news website about how the Swiss president was greeted by Ukraine's prime minister waving a Danish flag. 'It's not the same thing at all,' I manage through a cheek full of oats, '—and no,' I pre-empt his next suggestion, 'not even with a bit of Tipp-Ex. We need to do it properly.'

I'm already programming the address of the flag shop into the satnav, removing Lego Man's half-drunk mug from his hands and putting an arm in the sleeve of a jacket when he realises that he has no choice but to agree.

Two hours later and we're unfurling the thing to winch up pre-arrival. The Swiss flag, as Ukrainian PM Arseniy Yatsenyuk discovered a little too late, is slightly different to the Dannebrog, with a fatter white cross in the centre of a bright red rectangle. We get it up there and admire our handiwork as it wafts in the wind.

'It looks like an enormous army knife,' Lego Man murmurs wistfully, harking back to his hunter-gatherer days in the scouts. He starts getting all misty-eyed about past jamborees before I remind him of the time and say we really must get going.

Lego Man pops the flag a solemn scouting salute then fetches the car keys and we drive to the airport to pick up Swiss Friend.

I'm high on social-interaction-plus-sugar (having cracked open the 'starter chocolate box' Swiss Friend gave me 'for the journey') when we arrive back at Sticksville. The first thing we see as we turn off the road toward our house is the flag, flapping smartly against a bright blue sky.

But before I can even hold out a chocolate-clagged finger and say, *'Look, look, we're flying your flag!'* we notice a gathering of elderly bearded gentlemen around our pole, so to speak.

'Is that my welcome committee?' Swiss Friend asks.

'Perhaps they're admiring *our new flag*,' suggests Lego Man, nodding towards the new installation, 'see?'

Swiss Friend clocks the tribute, holds a hand to his chest, and says he is deeply moved. 'Do the old men come with it? Is that some sort of Danish welcoming tradition as well?'

'Er, no.'

As we get out of the car, Messrs Beard & Beard and their follically gifted friends move towards us, en masse, like something out of a zombie film. Only slower.

'Hello?' Lego Man addresses them, trying to sound upbeat.

One of the beardies frowns and makes some guttural vowel sounds I can't quite decipher. I'm just about to give him my whole, '*Undskyld, jeg ikke forstår*' ('sorry, I don't understand') spiel when he utters another sentence and I catch the words '*Schweiziske*' ('Swiss'), '*forbudt*' ('forbidden') and '*Dansk flag*'. Then, the ringleader Mr Beard points upwards, his face quite puce.

'Do you think perhaps he wants you to take it down?' Swiss Friend asks.

I mime '*I'll just go and look up what rule we've broken and promise to take the flag down if we're contravening anything*' by pretending to type at an imaginary keyboard, then feeding rope through two hands stacked vertically (not bad, eh? Charades: one of my most useless talents) and we usher Swiss Friend over the threshold.

Safely inside, Lego man wonders out loud how on earth anyone can object to the Swiss flag. 'I mean, they're *neutral!*' he says as he flicks on the kettle and clanks mugs onto the kitchen counter. 'All they've ever done is produced great watches and chocolates!'

'And Roger Federer,' I chip in. 'Who can hate R-Fed? The man made *mandigans* cool, for god's sake.'

'*Mandigans*?' Swiss Friend looks blank.

'Man-cardigans.'

'Oh.'

'And then there's Ursula Andress,' Lego Man goes on, sloshing boiling water into a teapot as well as all over the kitchen work surfaces, before slinging in a couple of Yorkshire Tea bags.

'Ursula and who?' Swiss Friend asks. Lego Man sets down the teapot and stares at him in horror.

'White bikini? *Dr No*?' My husband is just looking as though he might be reconsidering his friendship with Swiss Friend when there's a knock on the door. Mr Beard is back. And this time he's brought back-up in the form of a third hirsute septuagenarian.

'Hi, sorry, we're just about to get on to this, er, flag issue,' I start, helplessly, as he holds up his hand, palm facing me, and closes his eyes. It is frustratingly impossible to have a conversation with someone who has their eyes shut. It's as though they've already zoned out and anything you may have to say is of no interest. I bite my tongue and wait.

'As you do not speak good enough Danish,' the original Mr Beard says, finally, 'we have taken the liberty of translating and printing out the rules for flags in Denmark.'

Mr Beard III proffers an A4 white sheet. I reach out to take it and am surprised to find it stiff and shiny.

'And you *laminated* it?'

Mr Beard III waves his hand as if to say, 'it's nothing'.

'He has a machine,' Mr Beard I adds, by way of explanation.

'You did that *just now?*'

'Yes. It is important to get this right,' Mr Beard III says gruffly.

'It is not your fault if you did not know the correct rules,' Mr Beard I adopts a more conciliatory tone. 'But now you will know. And this will not happen again.'

'No,' I find myself agreeing, like a disgraced schoolgirl or a British minister put on the spot by Joanna Lumley over Gurkhas.

'You will find that the Danish flag is very important here,' Mr Beard I goes on. 'If you have any further questions, just ask me.'

'Right. OK. And thank you. And you are?'

But he turns and leaves without letting me know his name. Again.

When Lego Man and Swiss Friend have finished laughing, I read the laminated rules out loud:

Ministry of Justice Flag Protocol

It is ESSENTIAL ☺* that flag rules are followed correctly.

It is generally forbidden in this country to hoist a flag other than Dannebrog (unless you are a foreign states ambassador, consul or a vice-consul).

You need prior authorisation from the police to fly the flags of foreign nations with the exception of the flags of the Nordic countries (as well as the UN and EU flags).

* The Danes, I've noticed, love an emoticon, especially to dilute the impact after saying something that could be construed as confrontational, critical or rude.

You should not be authorised to fly a foreign flag on days when Denmark commemorates special national events (like confirmation).

At other times, permits may be granted subject to flags being CO-FLAGGED with Danish flags of AT LEAST the same size and arranged in no less prominence. Otherwise it is considered an act of one nation's domination over another and can result in warfare—

I break off. 'That sounds awfully dramatic!'

'Just imagine the power you've been wielding without even realising it!' Swiss Friend takes a gulp of tea, amused and clearly enjoying himself now.

Permits are conditional and can be withdrawn at any time. Failure to adhere to the rules is ILLEGAL and should result in a FINE.

PS: It is also illegal in Denmark to desecrate the flags of foreign nations, but it IS allowed to burn the Danish flag—

'What?' Lego Man interrupts.

'—That's what the laminated sheet says…' I go on:

—it IS allowed to burn the Danish flag. This is because the burning of foreign flags could be understood as a threat to that country. The burning of the Dannebrog, on the other hand, does not fall under foreign affairs, and so remains legal. In fact, according to Danish tradition, burning is the proper way to dispose of a worn out flag.

'How do you *wear out* a flag?' Swiss Friend asks. 'Too much waving?' We are stumped.

> The Danish flag cannot be raised before sunrise or 8am (whichever comes first) and must be lowered before sunset.
>
> The flag should be hoisted briskly and lowered with ceremony.
>
> The flag must never be allowed to touch the ground, as this means war will break out in Denmark.

'Blimey, there's a big risk of starting a war with these flags…' Lego Man interrupts again. I tell him strictly that since the Danish defence budget is only 1.3 per cent of the GDP and military service is notoriously easy to evade, another war is the last thing we want on our conscience, before reading the remainder.

> We hope that you will enjoy flying the Danish flag ☺

'Extraordinary!' Lego Man is now retrieving three bottles of beer from the fridge, having decided that this afternoon's excitement calls for something stronger than tea. 'Who'd have thought we'd have risked legal action, and/or incited international military unrest, all in one day?'

'Still, it was a nice gesture, I was very touched,' Swiss Friend offers, taking a swig of beer. 'I guess there was just no way of knowing just how seriously Danes take their flag.'

In the UK, flying the St George's Cross has become a

bit of a joke – the preserve of the English Defence League or football hooligans. The Scottish flag, the St Andrew's Cross, screams affiliation with the Scottish National Party (or BDSM, depending on your proclivities...). The Irish tricolour means St Patrick's Day, Guinness and theme pubs. The Welsh dragon makes me think of rugby, or some sort of male voice choir. During the London 2012 Olympics, the Union Jack had a brief reprise as a symbol of pride rather than a suspect political statement. Suddenly, our flag meant Stephen Fry; French and Saunders; ginger nuts and Churchill. Overnight, it became OK to be proud of our nation – for a fortnight, at least. And it felt good. So I can't help thinking that the Danes might be on to something here with all their flag waving.

Lego Man and I carefully fold up the Swiss banner and we send our soon-to-be-40 bachelor home with this and a care-package of all things Danish to remember the weekend by. We won't be hoisting the Union Jack any time soon ('And you can forget about the Jolly Roger,' Lego Man tells me), but I'm considering adopting the Dannebrog as my own during our time here. We're five months into the experiment now and I'm starting to feel more settled – possibly, even *relaxed*. *Which has to be one step closer to becoming more contented*, I tell myself. And if national pride and traditions really can make you happier, then I want in. I may not be a born and bred Dane, but I'm doing my best during our year of living Danishly to go native. So maybe I can adopt some of the local customs and traditions and things worth shouting about while I'm here. Maybe I can be an honorary patriotic Dane. I resolve to live by the bastardised mantra of 1970s folk-rocker Stephen Sills and 'love the one I'm with'. For a year or so, anyway.

Things I've learned this month:

1. You can set fire to the Danish flag but a tardy hoist is criminal
2. Religion can't make you happy, but traditions and special cake can
3. Danish parents are remarkably understanding and generous
4. Patriotism is good for you
5. The dog needs more training

6. June

Just a Girl

The sea glistens invitingly, the sky is a cloudless cobalt and Lego Man has taken to wearing pastel-coloured shorts, like an extra from a Wham! video circa 1983. This can mean only one thing: summer has finally arrived in Sticksville-on-Sea. And yet surprisingly it's this month that my quest for happiness takes a blow.

Things start promisingly enough. Watching white triangles of sailboats meander from side to side as they wind their way out of the marina while we kick back on wicker loungers drinking iced spritzers, it feels as though we could be in the Côte d'Azur (*off season*, mind, let's not get too carried away...). To my astonishment, it gets warm here. Really warm. As though the lack of pollution (or any kind of drama, or excitement) allows the sun to beam down more strongly. The earth radiates heat and the whole of Jutland looks as though it's being viewed through an Instagram filter. We're forced to buy a parasol to keep from burning in the garden, but notice that the sun-thirsty Danes all around us prefer to oil up and *bask* until their skin turns to leather.

Living by the sea suddenly stops feeling bleak and takes

on a jolly holiday feeling. We wake up each morning and immediately calculate how many hours it is until we can go and play on the beach. And because we're so far north it's light until past 11pm, so there are a good seven hours of sun at the end of the working day. Our quiet beachside village is now bustling with barbecuers, swimmers, canoeists and sailors fitting in a second shift of leisure after a not-so-hard day at the office. Having never quite got over the shame of being officially cautioned for attempting to cook burgers on a disposable aluminium tray of coal on Clapham Common one summer, I can't quite get used to the fact that lighting a fire wherever you fancy seems totally OK here. Not only that, but the *kommune* (the local borough or state) lay on picnic tables, a gazebo and a regularly replenished store of chopped wood to help you on your way. Lego Man can barely believe this untold bounty – '*Free* wood? No wonder the Danes are happy!' – and I can't help agreeing that when it comes to embracing the good life, the smart folk of Jutland seem to have got things sorted.

Five friends from school come to stay and I bathe in the familiarity and concentrated dose of oestrogen they bring with them. We talk fast – not at the pace I realise I've been adopting out here, over-enunciating every word to try and make myself understood. We catch up on each other's news. We eat *snegles*. We take group pictures at the porny pony fountain in The Big Town. It's A Lot Of Fun. A couple of them have small children, so there are daily Skype sessions before toddler bedtimes, reminding me of how much I want that life too. I love being a godmother to two utterly edible small people back home, and delight in being a not-at-all-related 'special auntie' to several more, but it's not the same. And I still have to swallow down the lump that appears in my throat sometimes when I think about this. But I'm really happy to have my old friends with me for a while and when they leave, I feel lifted, reinvigorated, and ready to take on another month – or six – of living Danishly.

Midsummer Night is the big festival this month, though confusingly Danes shift this to the 23rd rather than the 21st of June to mark *Sankt Hans Eve* – the night before the saint's day of John the Baptist. It's celebrated with a big bonfire that Danes begin building a month in advance so that by the third week of June, Denmark's countryside is dotted with impressive twiggy mountains.

Lego Man, the dog and I traipse along the beach, wriggling our toes/paws in the sand on the way to our first *Sankt Hans* celebration. The air smells of woodsmoke and sausages and the dog, who lives for sniffs and snacks, is in heaven. The locals are out in force and I spot the Mr Beards (I–III). I give them a tentative '*Hej!*' as we pass and miraculously, they nod in response. And then they *speak* to us.

'We see you have been getting the recycling right…' Mr Beard I comments.

'…But your dog still seems pretty wild,' cautions Mr Beard II, lighting a sleek black Popeye pipe and giving it a puff.

I thank them for their input and we walk on, not hugely easy as the dog seems to have become mesmerised by fire, like early man.

We're meeting up with Friendly Neighbour, The Viking and my *new* Danish friend who looks a lot like a blonde

Helena Christensen (and she's nice – I know, life isn't fair). There's also an assortment of other waifs and strays that each of them have brought along, and I eye up the picnic supplies and copious quantities of beer contributed to see us through. Tucked into The Viking's surprisingly well-appointed picnic basket is a Tupperware container filled with dough that he tells us is for '*snobrød*' or 'winding-bread'. To celebrate the feast day of John the Baptist, Danes wind strips of dough around a stick (efficiently prepared in advance and well-soaked in water) to cook by the heat of the bonfire. Lego Man makes the mistake of asking why, to which we get the now familiar response, en masse, like an upbeat Greek chorus: '*It's tradition!*'

A man who looks a lot like Robert Plant starts making a speech over a PA system but he's interrupted by screeches of ear-splitting feedback. He taps the microphone a few times, which does nothing other than add a thumping noise to the cacophony, before finally giving up and shouting to be heard.

'Who's he?' I whisper to The Viking.

'Oh he's a local MP. In Copenhagen and places like that you'd have someone famous doing this bit, but here we usually get a politician or a local radio DJ or something.'

'How showbiz...' I murmur, as The Viking turns back to give Robert Plant his full attention. 'And, er, what's he saying?' My Danish still leaves much to be desired and random mumblings in a rural Jutland accent are beyond me.

'He's just telling everyone what's happening – next we're going to sing.'

'Oh good,' says Lego Man, as a lady in her later years

ambles over to hand out song sheets. 'And what are we singing about?'

The Viking sighs slightly and I wonder whether he's regretting befriending a couple of dumb Brits. He points at the song sheet in his hand: 'This one's called "*Vi elsker vort land*", which means, "We love our country".'

Of course it does! I think.

A woman who's clearly had too much sun in her time and now resembles a mahogany-hued marmoset starts to slam out a few chords on an electric keyboard with one hand while smoking a cigarette with the other. The crowd begins to sing and Marmoset Woman joins in, trying not to set the sheet music alight during page turns.

I try to concentrate on the song, despite no prior knowledge of the tune or the words, but get distracted by a young boy who starts climbing the man-made mountain, dragging some sort of Flamenco-dancer scarecrow behind him. Having positioned the unfortunate offering on top of the stick pile, he proceeds to punch it in the face. Once the small child has dismounted, a woman stuffs some extra straw around the base of the bonfire then sets light to it with a torch. Flames begin to crackle and lick their way up, illuminating the figure astride the pyre. I can make out a hat covering scraggly wool-hair and a cape of some description over the top of a frilly red dress. Some wit has also seen fit to draw an unhappy face on the papier mâché globe of a head.

'I haven't revisited my convent school copy of the King James Bible for some years,' I whisper to Lego Man, 'but I'm pretty sure John the Baptist was beheaded, not burned alive. And he wasn't *famed* for his Flamenco dancing...'

The Viking, overhearing, chips in: 'Oh, it's not Saint John up there. It's just the eve of his saint's day.'

'Right … so, who's *he*?' I say, pointing at the unhappy felt-tipped face as it explodes into flames, sending a cheer around the crowd.

'*She*,' he corrects me, 'is a witch.'

At this moment, the unfortunate creature's synthetic red frills catch fire and black plumes of smoke start billowing out to sea. There's whooping and clapping and a few of our party capture the moment on camera phones.

'You *still burn witches*?' I ask in horror.

'Just tonight,' he tries to explain. 'That's what the bonfires are for. It's tr—'

'—Don't tell me, "*it's tradition*"?'

'How did you guess?'

'Just a hunch.'

'And the punching in the face bit,' Lego Man asks, 'was that part of the tradition too?'

'No, that kid was just a brat,' replies The Viking.

'Right. And the Flamenco outfit?'

'Just whatever someone could find, I suspect.'

A gust of wind fans the flames and soon the crudely fashioned 'witch' is just a blackened chicken-wire mesh on a stick. There's some clapping and Brat Boy and his friends begin laughing uproariously. Another song starts up and we're encouraged to huddle around the dying fire to start baking our bread kebabs, but I've rather lost my appetite.

Friendly Neighbour, observing my consternation, attempts to console me.

'We have to burn the witch to ward off evil spirits,' she says, as though this is the most natural thing in the world.

'Right...'

'Witches are very active around Midsummer Night's eve. So we burn a few to make the rest go to Germany—'

'*What*?' This is getting weirder by the minute.

'To Bloksbjerg, in the mountains, where all the witches get together.'

'*Why*? Why would they go to Germany?' *For cheap lager and cheese?*

This is met by general shrugging before The Viking announces, audibly tipsy now: 'I don't know, it's *Germany*. Bad stuff happens there!' This, it seems, is the best any-one can come up with to explain away the mild xenophobia towards Denmark's powerful southern neighbour.

It's at this point that I'm given a semi-inebriated beach-side history lesson by The Viking, who studied the subject at university, occasionally corrected by Friendly Neighbour and Helena C, keen that we don't end up with a totally skewed impression of their country.

I learn that the burning of 'witches' in Denmark started in the 16th century when the church took great pleasure in convicting and sentencing women to death by flames. The practice officially stopped in 1693, when 74-year-old Anne Palles was burned as a sorceress for having 'enchanted' a bailiff, caused the sudden death of a woman her husband danced with and been responsible for a poor yield on a farm on which she had once taken a pee.

'Really? Is that last part true?' I ask suspiciously, only to be met with vehement nodding. At this wee-based revelation, the dog starts to whimper slightly, as though conscious that he's done far worse on many of the farms around here. He backs away from the dying embers and hides behind Lego Man's legs.

'So you see, we haven't burned *actual* women for ages!' The Viking ends his tutorial brightly. 'It's just been fashionable to burn *straw* witches since the 1900s.'

'We don't mean anything by it,' Friendly Neighbour tries to assure me, 'it's just tr—'

'"*Tradition*"?'

'*Yes*!' the chorus responds in now-drunken unison.

'But I thought Denmark was meant to be this great place for gender equality? With a long and illustrious history of promoting women's rights?' I am not drunk enough to let this go.

'Sure,' The Viking shrugs, 'but not *witches*' rights!'

'You do know witches aren't real, right?'

There is laughter and Lego Man goes into peacekeeping mode: 'Don't worry, we're talking about hundreds of years ago. And things have been pretty good since then, right?'

'Well...' Friendly Neighbour pulls a face that makes her look like a plasticine figure from *Wallace & Gromit*.

'What?'

'Well, you know all the big red buildings round here?'

'The old hospitals?' I ask, thinking she means the 1920s red-brick institutions that make up most of the village and are now populated by bearded retirees.

'Ye-es,' she answers, sounding a little unsure. 'Only they weren't quite *hospitals*...'

'They weren't? That's what the estate agent told us.'

'No. They were institutions. For the mentally defective.' I wonder whether to politely suggest a more politically correct term, but she goes on. 'These were the men's buildings,' she waves a hand at the looming institutions further up from the beach, 'set up by Christian Keller, the famous Danish doctor. The guy whose statue's up there on the hill, you know?'

'The one with the big 'tash?'

'That's him. But the women—' she takes a deep breath, '—well, have you ever noticed the island as you cross over on the way from Funen to Zealand?'

Funen is the island to the east of the Jutland peninsular, with Zealand the island even further east that's home to Copenhagen and, as I describe it to folk back home, 'all the fun stuff'. Even with my woeful sense of direction, I know where Friendly Neighbour is talking about. This is novel.

'Yes! I do! We've driven over it a few times. Why?'

'Well that's Sprogø, where the defective women were sent. Only there wasn't always much wrong with them…'

Sprogø, it emerges, was used for the containment of women deemed 'pathologically promiscuous', 'morally retarded', 'sexually frivolous' or accused of '*løsagtig*' (lewd behaviour). The institution founded by Christian Keller in 1923 was essentially a prison for women who'd had unmarried sex, lovers or a child out of wedlock. Not that locking them up on an all-female island necessarily prevented any further shenanigans. Sprogø often swarmed with men visiting it in the hope of meeting 'easy women', though nobody seemed to think that the men setting sail for sex were much of a problem.

'So when did this place shut down?'

'Oh, in the 1960s.'

I'm shocked. I know this sort of thing isn't exclusive to Denmark. London's Magdalene Asylum was active until 1966 and the last Irish Magdalene laundry didn't close until the 1990s. *But in Denmark?* I'd assumed that the Danes had evolved sooner – that things were a little more equal here. I realise that I don't know as much as I thought I did about what it is to be a woman in Denmark.

The partying goes on until the sun finally sets at 11pm and the moon appears, shining so brightly that it feels like midday. We walk up the hill to our house soon after and I look down at the remains of the bonfire, glowing and joining up with dozens of others smouldering away up and down the coastline, like a string of pearls.

That night, I'm plagued by dreams of semi-charred women on flaming tinder, weaving their way to Germany before being woken at 3am by a slice of sun that's made it past the outer edge of our blackout blind and is now scalding my retinas. Midsummer, Danish-style, means a mere four hours of darkness a day, and while the long summer evenings have been most welcome, I could do without the early wakeup call complete with dawn chorus.

Squinting and cursing, I scrabble around on my bedside table for the free aeroplane eye mask I've taken to wearing in the early hours. I put it on, flump back down onto my pillow and attempt to drift off again, but by now my brain's kicked into gear and instead of dozing off, I lie there fretting. About all sorts of things. I'm good at this.

Why do birds get up at dawn, and doesn't it mean they're knackered by sunset in summer in Denmark? I wonder where the best place to buy bras is round here? Who first decided waxing was a good idea? When did women even get the vote in Denmark? And finally, the biggie: *What if it's no better to be born female in the famously progressive Scandinavia than it is anywhere else?* Realising I don't have the answers to any of these questions, I make a plan to find out.*

Aarhus, Denmark's second city, is home to one of the world's few women's history museums. Although not quite up there with the Smithsonian, it boasts an interesting assortment of artefacts and archive material charting the lives of those born with the double-x chromosome over the years. On the muggy Monday morning, I chug up to The Big City in my non-air-conditioned red mobility tomato in the hope of reassuring myself about the fate of womankind in Denmark. A helpful lady in horn-rimmed spectacles joins me for a turn around the museum's dusty collection and gives me a quick oral history of Nordic woman. I learn that women were allowed into universities in Denmark in 1875 and that the Scandinavian countries were early starters in universal women's suffrage, with Finland kicking things off in 1906,

* Important stuff to follow but FYI, it turns out that birds sing first thing to defend their territory but power nap in summer to get through the long working day (according to research from the University of Western Ontario and the Max Planck Institute of Ornithology, respectively). Ancient Egyptians paved the way for waxing with sugaring (messy, don't bother) – and there's nowhere decent to buy bras near me.

followed by Norway in 1913, Denmark and Iceland in 1915, and Sweden in 1919. In Denmark, Sweden and Norway political parties introduced voluntary gender quotas in the 1970s, encouraging so many women to enter politics that the quota has since been abandoned in Denmark as no further stimulus is thought to be required. At the time of writing, women make up 40 per cent of Danish parliament as well as leading both coalition parties. I learn, too, that the Danes have always been pretty progressive on women's rights, with abortion legalised in 1973 and equal pay becoming law in 1976. As I discovered back in February, Danish employment policies place a strong emphasis on making work accessible for all and include generous parental leave.

Families get a whopping 52 weeks off to share between them for a new baby in Denmark. Mothers must take four of these before the birth and at least fourteen weeks after. This seems eminently sensible since a decent amount of maternity leave has been linked to healthier children and lower rates of maternal depression, according to research from the National Bureau of Economic Research in the US. Men take the first fortnight off too and then the rest of the leave is divided between parents as they see fit. Because most men take paternity leave in Denmark, they bond with their children more quickly and learn how to do all the parenting jobs that mothers have traditionally taken care of.

The next step is more mandatory paternity leave. Norway was the first country to establish a paternity leave quota for fathers in 1993. Before that, only 2–3 per cent of Norwegian fathers took any time off. Today, Norwegian fathers are given fourteen weeks of leave and 90 per cent of dads use it, with

15 per cent choosing to work a shorter working week after this to spend more time with their family. Studies show that increased paternity leave in Norway has made a real difference to attitudes to gender roles, with boys born after 1993 doing more housework than those born previously. In Sweden, fathers take two months of paternity leave, paid at 80 per cent of their usual salary.

If we were ever able to start a family, I can't help thinking, *Scandinavia would be a bloody good place to do it....*

There's also a family allowance from the state, paid directly to any mother with children below eighteen, regardless of income, as well as child benefits awarded to single parents and the children of widows or widowers.

Once they've had children, 78 per cent of Danish mothers return to work – far higher than the OECD average of 66 per cent. This is because childcare is subsidised by the government and the famed work-life balance of Danish workplaces makes it easier to balance career and family life here than it would be elsewhere. What has traditionally been defined as 'women's work' is valued as highly as traditionally defined 'men's work' here – and both sexes do a bit of each.

Being out and about during the day (the happy lot of the freelancer) is always an interesting exercise in anthropology, and in Denmark I notice more men around than I did back home. This is not because I'm specifically looking for them, you understand, but because they're just *there*, usually with a small person attached to them. There are dads wheeling around buggies in the middle of the day, pushing kids on swings, waiting to pick up their offspring from childcare at 3.30 in the afternoon or racing around the supermarket with a head of lettuce in one hand and a toddler in the other. Men doing just the sort of parental chores that you see women or put-upon grandparents doing for the most part back at home. And this seems like a Very Good Thing. Studies from the OECD confirm that Scandinavian men are more involved in childcare than ever before and do a higher proportion of domestic work than their British counterparts. So I'm delighted to discover research from the University of Missouri showing that men and women are happier when they share household and child-rearing responsibilities. I make a mental note to send this to all my mum friends, with a suggestion to print it out and pin it to the fridge.

As well as doting dads, I check out the shops in Aarhus. For research purposes, obviously. The women's fashion on show is fairly homogenous, coloured strictly between the lines of Scandi chic and all looking a little on the flammable side. But it's not, I'm interested to note, overtly sexual, or in a size zero. The women I see around me aren't stick-thin. Instead, they're strong-looking. Vikings, in fact. In my local bakery (aka my second home) a rare American tourist passing through recently told the girl behind the counter: 'You look like a Viking woman!' OK, so it was slightly creepy, but if anyone had said that to me back in England, I'd have thought they were calling me stocky. *Manly*, even. And that would have been seen as A Bad Thing. But here, the girl looked genuinely pleased and thanked him for the 'compliment'. Being seen as a strong woman in Denmark is an accolade. Even in the fashion-conscious capital, Copenhagen, I haven't observed anyone rocking the bow-legged, heroin-chic look I became accustomed to in London, nor the bony, over-Pilated physique of New Yorkers. Being too thin isn't seen as particularly desirable here. Women eat.

I pass children looking almost indistinguishable by gender, free from colour-coded clothing. I'm reminded that the latest catalogue from the country's biggest chain of toy shops, BR, made a refreshing break from convention by showing boys playing with Barbie dolls and girls playing with trains on the front cover. Kids are allowed to choose for themselves here, regardless of their sex.

Feeling reassured that Denmark is an OK place to be a woman, but keen to find out more, I canvas Helena C and American Mom for their views over coffee (and a *snegle*, naturally) the following day. I mentally prepare to bask in a warm bath of pro-sisterhood sharing about my new spiritual homeland, and things begin positively enough. American Mom commends the opportunities for women in Denmark who want kids as well as a career, telling me that when she had her first child in the US she was considered 'extremely lucky' to get three months off work, unpaid. 'Having my second in Denmark was a dream by comparison,' she says. 'I had a year off and I got a promotion at work at the same time.'

Helena C tells me that girls and boys are treated pretty equally and offered the same opportunities at school, and American Mom agrees that 'you don't get too many girly girls here. "*Jeg kan gøre det selv*", or, "I can do it myself" is something they learn from the age they can talk in

Denmark.' I'm impressed. But then, things take a turn for the less fabulous.

'So yeah, it's pretty good for mothers and kids, but you should hear some of the jokes that go around about women – in my office at least,' says American Mom.

'Such as?'

'Where to start?' is her reply. 'Yesterday a guy in my department made a "joke" about women drivers in this big external presentation. That kind of talk would never be allowed in most workplaces in the US. OK, so in America, women still don't get *paid* as much as men for doing the same job. Here, you can pretty much be sure that if you have the same job title as someone of the opposite sex, you'll both be paid the same. But it's as though the Danes think, "Well, we've got the big stuff figured out, so what's a little joke?"'

Helena C agrees with this evaluation of her countryfolk and tells me about a TV show on the Danish version of the BBC where women stand silently naked in front of fully clothed men who verbally dissect their bodies. 'They talk about everything from these women's pubic hair to their caesarean scars,' she tells me.

'Nice.'

The show's host is Thomas Blachman (also a judge on the Danish version of *The X Factor*), who justified his 'naked lady show' to Danish press at the time as a cultural service to get 'men discussing the aesthetics of a female body without allowing the conversation to become pornographic or politically correct'. Presumably, because most women have never been fortunate enough to have their appearance critiqued by strange men before ... oh no, wait, my mistake...

On the topic of objectification, American Mom tells me she was accosted by teenage girls in their pants putting on a pole dancing display in The Big Town last weekend in preparation for the national championship. 'They were handing out fliers saying, "*Families with kids, old, young, couples and singles – all are welcome!*"' – all the while writhing around like strippers!'

They've also heard reports that employers still discriminate against mothers and mothers-to-be in interviews in Denmark. It's not unusual for interviewers here to ask a candidate's age, marital status, and whether or not they have children – or plan to. The Equal Treatment Act states that there should be no discrimination based on sex, especially around pregnancy and family status, and if a job applicant or employee feels they've been treated unfairly, it's up to the employer to prove that no discrimination took place. But a few trade unions I call up for a UK newspaper feature tell me that Danish women who are pregnant or on maternity leave have regularly been let go by employers, with some even refused jobs on the off-chance that they *might* become mothers in future. In 2012, one in eight newly qualified nurses were asked at interview if they had, or planned to have, children, according to the nurses' union *Dansk Sygeplejeråd*. One was told: 'We can't hire you if you will soon be on maternity leave.' The union for retail and office workers reported that 17 per cent of its members have been questioned about baby plans in job interviews and for lawyers, the picture's bleaker still, with 20 per cent of women saying that their careers have suffered setbacks because of children. Some unions even reported employers 'letting go' women undergoing IVF.

I'm beginning to appreciate that all is not necessarily rosy in my Scandinavian idyll, and decide to recruit some experts to help me get to grips with the state of equality in Denmark. First up, is Sanne Søndergaard, one of Denmark's biggest comedians and an out-and-proud feminist.

'Most Danes feel lucky to have been born here and women in Denmark don't have to compromise as much as they do in other places in the world, like the US or the UK,' says Sanne when we meet for coffee and a setting-the-world-to-rights session. 'But it's not perfect. We don't talk about sexism much in Denmark but there is a sexist culture. We need to acknowledge this and bear it in mind, otherwise we just reproduce it – men *and* women.'

I mention pole dancing-gate and she tells me about the plastic surgery ads she's been spotting on buses in Copenhagen: 'These things just drive around all day long with totally naked, two-metre-high breasts on them, encouraging Danish women to "*get new boobs!*" My nine-year-old neighbour said to me the other day that she wished she was a boy so she wouldn't "have to get new breasts all the time". That's the message she and her friends have picked up from these ads everywhere – that to be a woman you need enormous yet perky fake breasts. That's so sad!' A few things like this have been creeping into liberal Danish culture over the past few years, Sanne tells me. 'It's as though people here *assume* that we're equal so they can be as sexist as they want. Because Denmark was first with a lot of equality issues, like gay rights and abortion laws, I think we're also getting the backlash first.'

The Danish branch of The Everyday Sexism Project launched in 2013 and has been recording the daily contributions from women in Denmark keen to share their experiences of sexism online – from inappropriate behaviour to gender-stereotyping and sexist ads. I ask Sanne whether there's been the same amount of trolling and abusive tweets directed at women who speak out about inequality as there has been in the UK, to which she laughs.

'Twitter is much smaller in Denmark so there aren't so many psychopaths on there yet – only clever, tech-savvy, media types. Which is nice. Normally when I get insulted on Twitter over here it's more patronising than threatening, though I don't know which I'd prefer…'

'Sorry?'

'Everyone can *see* that a rape threat is over the line and you can press charges – you can't do anything about someone patronising you in 140 characters.'

Good point.

I get in touch with Sara Ferreira from Everyday Sexism Denmark to ask her what the response has been so far.

'Our members describe it as a relief,' says Sara, 'to acknowledge that sexism is still a powerful force even in a country like Denmark, where the level of gender-equality from the outside seems enviable. We're not blind – we know that women elsewhere are much worse off than here. But still, women have only been able to vote in Denmark for the past hundred years. Not long ago, we were second-rate citizens. We have to stay alert and be aware not to fall into old patterns. It's a big problem when young women – and men – don't have the historical perspective and mistakenly think that they're "free" to do what they want, without seeing the structural and cultural forces that are still at work.'

One of the key structural problems coming to the fore is gender segregation by stealth. In spite of my not-at-all scientific survey of boys and girls in Denmark, it turns out that schoolkids are getting different careers guidance depending on their sex. At the moment, more boys get pushed towards engineering (79 per cent of Denmark's engineers are currently male according to the Danish Society of Engineers) with girls being encouraged towards the humanities.

I talk to Manu, the equality and church minister I quizzed about religion, and ask for his take on this. He's surprisingly candid, accepting that it's a problem and telling me that it's something he plans to address.

'My daughter had a careers talk at her school,' Manu says, 'and afterwards I asked if she'd talked about engineering as an option as I thought it might be something she'd enjoy. She said she hadn't – and that she didn't even know what it was! Schools careers counsellors really need to educate girls and boys about what options they have – as do we as parents – to break out of gender stereotypes.'

The appointment of a woman to the top job in Danish politics has helped with this, Manu tells me. Helle Thorning-Schmidt came to power in 2011, overcoming her detractors and some pretty scathing press. The newspaper *Politiken* wrote that she was, 'too well-dressed for the Social Democrats, too fresh to become the head of the country and too cool to win people's hearts' – a criticism you can't quite imagine being levelled at a male politician. She was swiftly awarded the nickname 'Gucci Helle' for her love of designer clothes and has also been attacked by her own party for her good looks. Helle maintained a dignified silence for some time before taking down one particularly odious heckler at a ministerial meeting with the line: 'We can't all look like shit.' I love the Danish PM.

'It's been important, having Helle as a role model,' says Manu. 'Just like me being the first brown minister [Manu's parents are from India] will hopefully help other migrants to see that a career in politics in Denmark is a possibility for them, having Helle in the top job gives young girls someone to look up to. We could always tell girls that they could rise to the top in politics, but until they could see it happening, it didn't always seem real. To know as a Danish girl that you can get to the very top is a strong message.'

This strikes a chord with me. Growing up the only child of a single mother with Queen Elizabeth II on the throne and Margaret Thatcher as prime minister, I took it for granted that women ruled the world. I remember expressing disbelief when I read about a male prime minister in a library book, aged ten, so sure was I that this was a uniquely female role, not even open to men. Growing up in a female-centric bubble of delusion was a distinct advantage – it never occurred to me that I couldn't do absolutely anything. Now, with Helle running the country and Queen Margrethe on the throne, thousands of little Danish girls will be experiencing the same sense that everything is open to them. I feel a thrill just thinking about this.

'It's almost taken for granted that men and women are equal here,' says Manu, applying a slick of lip balm and looking every inch the modern metrosexual. 'It's part of our DNA. Being a woman in Denmark means good opportunities and not having to choose between a family and a career.' Which is reassuring. But the 'taken for granted' part might be starting to cause a few problems, because the system's not working for everyone.

A study published by the EU agency for Fundamental Rights in 2014 found that Denmark was top of the list when it came to violence against women with 52 per cent of Danish women surveyed saying they'd been victims of physical or sexual violence – well above the EU average of (a still horrific) 33 per cent.

'The numbers in the report are shocking,' accepts Manu when I bring this up, but he's keen to point out the fact that Denmark's Scandinavian neighbours, also praised for their gender equality, scored highly as well. In Finland, 47 per cent of women said that they'd been victims of violence and the figure was 46 per cent in Sweden. By contrast, women in Poland reported the lowest levels at 19 per cent, with the UK at 44 per cent. 'This could indicate some structural and cultural explanations,' says Manu. 'Danish women are very active on the labour market. This is positive but unfortunately it can also make women more vulnerable. The silence surrounding violence against women in Denmark is also much less than it used to be. Violence is no longer a private matter. Danish women will no longer keep quiet, which might be different in countries where violence is still hidden and shameful.'

Despite Manu's assertion that speaking out about domestic violence is no longer taboo in Denmark, there was a conspicuous silence in the Danish press when the report came out. The only person to go on record and comment publically was Karin Helweg-Larsen of Denmark's National Observatory on Violence Against Women. She was quoted in most of the country's major media describing the report as inaccurate, saying that it was unhelpful to compare liberated Danish women to those from Croatia, Bulgaria or Southern Europe, where, she suggested, violence may be normalised.

I call Karin and ask her to expand on this and she explains: 'It's unusual to compare trans-national data on violence as definitions alter from country to country. Violence against women isn't tolerated *at all* here, and since the 2000s there have been anti-violence campaigns to make sure domestic violence isn't thought of as a private problem anymore. We've worked hard to change people's minds and perceptions so that everyone understands that violence is something that won't be tolerated under any circumstances. And the campaigns have worked – criminal statistics show that violence is going down.' The Danish government's own figures show that 26,000 women aged between sixteen and 74 years old report having been exposed to violence from a former or current partner – a decline from 42,000 when the figures were last recorded in 2000.

But does such a vehement denial of the EU report's findings really help women in Denmark? Might this not allow Danes to rest on their laurels and think, smugly, '*oh, it's OK, there's not really a domestic violence problem here*'?

'No,' Karin insists, 'it was important for me to dispute these figures because if we accept them, then it's too easy for the rest of Europe, like Croatia for instance, to say, "well, there's no point in even having a national action plan for gender equality or to reduce domestic violence because it's not working in Denmark or Scandinavia".' It's unlikely Karin will be holidaying in Croatia any time soon, but she may have a point.

'It's dangerous to use this EU data for politics,' Karin goes on, 'to, say, reduce funding for shelters for battered women. Instead, we need to take responsibility and be advocates for improvement.'

This is something that all the women I speak to in Denmark agree on. But there's another theory as to why Danes reported such high levels of violence. As Sanne puts it: 'There is a lot of violence *in general* in Denmark.'

This comes as a surprise, having never witnessed any sort of aggression since I moved here. But this, Sanne explains, is because I'm not a Danish youth tearing up the town of a Saturday night.

'Men get punched in the face on a night out,' Sanne tells me. 'There are fights – and if you try to stop a fight, you get hit too. We just punch each other more. And we drink a lot. Because there's this idea that we're all equal, maybe some men think, "*oh well, it's probably not so bad to hit a woman*". There isn't this idea that women are the weaker sex in Denmark. We hit everyone. I got in fights growing up in Jutland – females too would just hit each other.'

I ask The Viking whether his experience of growing up in Jutland also involved using his fists a fair bit and he answers in the affirmative: 'There were always fights. There was usually alcohol involved, but yeah, there's hitting.' So where does this impulse comes from?

'No one's quite sure,' Sanne tells me. 'It's been against the law to smack kids here for twenty years, but we do have quite a violent culture,' she admits. 'We are *Vikings*. I'd be really interested to see if they did a study looking at whether we Danes are just more violent in general. Otherwise, I think it's difficult to compare violence towards women in Denmark with other countries. Violence towards women is horrible, but violence towards men is too. So if violence towards men is also worse in Denmark compared to other countries, then we need to work on the macho Viking culture.'

There aren't any studies looking specifically into whether Scandinavians are more violent than the rest of Europe (yet), but the Danish government's own figures suggest that violence against men isn't uncommon. The most recent report shows that 8,000 men between the ages of 16 and 74 have been victims of physical violence, a number that's increased by 25 per cent since 2005.

'No matter what, violence is a gender problem,' says Sanne, 'because the root is the macho culture. The aggression is rooted in a very specific idea of manliness. And when this idea is combined with the overall sexist idea that what men do is *right*, sadly some women are going to copy that behaviour.'

This glimpse of the darker side of life in Denmark has made me feel a little lost. Instead of living in 'Denmark: the country of equality, perfect pastries, an enviable work-life balance and a generous welfare state', I've found myself living in 'Denmark: just as troubled as everywhere else in the world and possibly peopled by above-average aggressive types'.

I've been around the block enough to know that even paradise has its flaws – but this seems like a fairly big one and I don't know quite how to get over it. It's like finding out that a lovely great aunt is a massive racist – the nice bits of them can never make up for the offensively crappy parts.

I ask Sara how she handles it and she points to the great strides that Everyday Sexism has taken: 'A sense of community and empowerment makes you feel stronger and less alone. Structural and cultural inequality is still very much an issue in Denmark – it just may not be as obvious as in other countries. But fortunately, as we have experienced, there are lots of women and men of all ages who want to challenge this.'

Sanne too is optimistic about the future of women here: 'It's like we may finally be getting a long-overdue new wave of feminism here. Denmark just needs to get its balls back – or rather, its ovaries – and make some changes to stay ahead in terms of gender equality.' She's noticing more and more men at her stand-up shows who identify themselves as pro-woman. 'I'm also meeting a lot of feminist guys at shows in Copenhagen and Aarhus, and Odense and Herning when I perform.' So is Sanne a happy Dane, despite all the gender-equality work that still needs to be done? 'I'd say I'm an eight out of ten,' she tells me. And Sara? 'I'm probably eight, too,' she tells me. OK then.

I can't forgive the racist great aunt, or forget what I've learned this month. But if Sara and Sanne can stay positive, then I suppose I can too. I sign up to Denmark's Everyday Sexism Project and resolve to do what I can to help, writing about as many injustices as I come across and telling any Danes I hear being rude about women drivers to desist. Immediately.

'Are you OK?' Lego Man asks, carefully, once I'm back home. He rubs at the stubble on his jaw the way he does when he's anxious, aware that this month has really got to me.

'I think so,' I tell him.

'Are we still on?'

'Sorry?'

'Are we still doing it, our year of living Danishly?'

I look at him, wide turquoise eyes looking up at me from underneath a crinkled forehead, wrinkles disturbed by a Harry Potter-esque scar between his eyebrows that he got from a scouting accident. (Other injuries sustained in service of Baden-Powell include a partially sawn-off finger, broken teeth and a dislocated shoulder. My poor in-laws lived in fear of the phone calls from A&E to say, 'We've got your son here. Again.') Now, I reach out and stroke his arm in the direction of the white-blond hairs on it, the way one might a cat. And I tell him I'm not about to pull the plug on our adventure just yet.

It's at this fairly fraught moment that Lego Man chooses to tell me his contract has been extended. He knows it's not great timing, he says, but how would I feel about staying in Denmark longer?

'Like, say, for another year…?'

I raise my eyebrows and give him a look that says: '*are you kidding me? You're asking now?*' He assures me that we don't need to decide just yet. That we've got a few months to think about it. And that he's made me something special for supper. And that there are ramekins involved.

Things I've learned this month:

1. Denmark isn't quite the gender-equality utopia it's sometimes made out to be
2. Feminists in Scandinavia still have work to do
3. ...but fortunately there are some ace ones doing their damnedest to make things better
4. And there are laws in place to make it better to be a woman in Denmark than it is in many other countries around the world
5. I live in a lunatic asylum. But then, perhaps I knew this already...

7. July

Going Away & Playing Away

It's still hot here. Really hot. It's 5.30pm and I'm driving home from an interview when I'm nearly blinded by the sun and struggle not to veer off the road. Searing white rays are beaming down while simultaneously being reflected back up from an immense liquid mirror of sea, coming at me from all angles and rendering sunglasses useless. I bead up with sweat as my car puffs out tepid air from its fans before wheezing to a stop outside our house. There are wavy lines coming up from the tarmac and the heat has left me dizzy.

Levering open the molten hot door, I'm met with a wall of humidity and waft of honeysuckle, out in abundance this month. Mr Beards I, II and III are pottering about in their gardens and wave a '*hej!*' as I pass. I note with interest that the residents of Sticksville have taken to sporting short shorts for high summer. I've never seen so much septuagenarian flesh before. They're also not shy of a medallion. It's all gone very Costa del Sticksville.

Inside the house, it's just as warm and the thermostat in the hallway registers a blood-boilingly balmy 33 degrees

Celsius. Scandi-issue glasshouses, it turns out, may just be *too good* at thermal insulation. I find Lego Man already home from work and stripped down to his pants. He's surrounded by guidebooks, G&T in one hand and scrolling furiously on the trackpad of his laptop with the other.

'What *are* you doing?' I ask, slightly horrified at how our standards have slipped. He doesn't look up, so I steal what's left of his aperitif and take a big swig before realising it's not going down as well as it normally would and giving it back.

'We need to leave the country,' he says, frowning.

'Why?' I ask, but he's already up and rifling through the sideboard drawers for our passports. 'What's wrong? Has something happened at work?' I ask, immediately fearing the worst.

'No, work's fine,' he replies. 'We just have to go somewhere that isn't Denmark. Soon.'

'What?' Life with Lego Man is, sadly, never dull. 'Are they transferring you? I thought you liked it here! You wanted to stay another year last month! And now you want to leave?' *I'm only halfway through my project,* I think. *I know that last month was a setback but I can't possibly leave now. How will I know why Danes are the happiest nation on the planet? I haven't had my first white Christmas yet. I haven't even sampled all the seasonal pastries this country has to offer...*

'Do you mean going back to the UK?'

'If you want to,' he says, 'but I was thinking somewhere sunnier. Maybe the Med.'

'You want to live in the Mediterranean?' This is new.

'Not *live*,' he says, looking at me as though I'm deranged. 'Go on holiday! There's literally no one in the office the whole of this month and Lars says that if we don't book something soon, there won't be any flights left out of here.'

Lego Man's colleague, Lars, has become our font of all knowledge on Danish customs. We'd be lost, or at least desperately under-informed, without him.

'Oh!' I exhale heavily.

'I knew lots of people were off in July but I didn't realise the whole country shuts down,' Lego Man explains. 'Most of my office takes all four weeks off.'

Like the Italians, the Danes like to take their holiday en masse, only they chose July as the month to hit 'pause' on normal life and decamp to foreign climes. I wonder if this need to travel has been entrenched in the Danish psyche since the Vikings set off into international waters in the 8th century. *Perhaps wanderlust plays a part in the country's impressive happiness record*, I think. The British philosopher A.C. Grayling described travel as 'expanding the mind and spirit' and scientists from the University of Pittsburgh recently discovered that regular holidays cut the risk of dying from heart disease by 30 per cent. There's also evidence that taking a break reduces blood pressure and stress levels, according to research from the UK's Nuffield Health charity. Which is bound to make you more upbeat. Lego Man has convinced himself (or Lars has convinced him, it's unclear which) that long holidays are another reason the Danes are so content and he's determined to get away on a summer break, Danish-style.

'I've been doing some research into what's still available and France and Greece are already out,' he tells me with a nod at a couple of *Lonely Planet* guides that have been hurled across the room once he'd discovered there was no flight availability from Billund airport. 'So is Gran Canaria,' he clicks to close the offending window on his screen, 'as well as Tenerife, Spain and Portugal.' Danes, Lars has informed him, love sampling the exuberance of the Southern European lifestyle as tourists on their holidays before returning to their own, more ordered lives in Denmark. 'Oh, but hang about…' Lego Man scans the lone remaining window before sitting back in his chair and taking a celebratory swig of gin: 'Bingo!'

'You've found somewhere?' I peer over his shoulder as he nods.

'How do you feel about Sicily?'

It turns out we both feel very good indeed about Sicily. So we book, pack our bags and head off two days later. The roads are virtually empty on the way to the airport, the rest of the country having shipped out a week ago, and when we drop the dog off at the '*dyrepension*' or 'animal hotel' (a jazzed-up kennel), we learn that the owners too are away. 'A month in Namibia,' the teenage daughter tells us, 'but don't worry, me and my boyfriend have this place covered…' This doesn't fill us with confidence, but the dog bounds off merrily to play with the other animals and doesn't seem to mind being left in the care of the substitute teacher equivalent, so we leave while the going's good.

Four hours later, we're sitting in Castellammare harbour, watching Italians fight, kiss, talk, laugh, pose, promenade and ride up and down on scooters. Car horns beep, tatty cats roam the streets, and generously proportioned old women with crinkly eyes make their way slowly up the steps of the small town to their homes or sit on stools in the shade. We eat pecorino cheese, salami and tomatoes that taste as though they're made from pure sunshine. Delicious cooking smells waft out from every home and I can feel my senses fill up as I take it all in. There is noise and colour and passion in abundance. It is the antithesis of pared-down, ordered Denmark and we revel in its difference.

I'd forgotten how much I missed *bustle* and *mess* and *chaos*. The security and stability and 'knowing what you're in for' in Denmark is great – really great – most of the time. But it does take some of the excitement out of life. You wouldn't get an obscenely glamorous Danish policewoman pulling over a motorcyclist to give him a snog then waving him on. You wouldn't catch her colleague issuing a parking ticket to a banged-up Fiat 500 whose driver has simply stopped, mid-street, before reapplying her lipstick in its wing mirrors and sashaying off in stilettoes, channelling Beyoncé. But in Sicily, this is a typical Tuesday.

Our first week away is a joy. We walk in the mountains, lounge about on sandy beaches and swim in a never-ending expanse of turquoise sea. But by week two we're flagging. In London, we never had the luxury of being able to take two weeks off. Even when we got married, we could only manage a week and a half for the big day itself *and* a quick honeymoon (it's a champagne problem, I know, but there you have it). We've never, throughout the course of our relationship, spent two weeks away together without the dilution of family, or friends or *work* of some kind. And now that we have the opportunity to do so ... well ... it's a bit weird.

It feels like an admission of failure to say out loud that spending two weeks with your life partner in beautiful surroundings can be anything other than idyllic. *And yet*, Lego Man and I find it tough.

I look at families frolicking on the beach and can't help wondering whether things would be different if we had children. Whether this trip would mean more if there was a child with us, experiencing everything for the first time. Lego Man asks me what I'm thinking about, but I know that telling the truth will only make him sad. So instead I say it looks as though his nose is burning (aren't I a helpful holiday companion?). My husband reluctantly agrees to apply factor 30 and I try to shake off my melancholy. There isn't any point getting down about this now. For the moment, it's just us. But I wonder how life will be if it's just us, for ever. I wonder how we'll navigate this. Whether it will be enough for me. And what I'll do if it isn't.

Week two doesn't begin well. By the Monday, we're repeating conversations and commenting on other diners for something to talk about over dinner. I start thinking fondly about work and wondering when I can get back to it. I finish all the books I've brought with me and stare, wild-eyed, at the empty boxes in my iPhone calendar calculating how many days are left before we go home.

Having adjusted to the shorter Danish working week and spending more time together than ever before, it feels as though the endurance test has now been extended to 24 hours a day. We are together *all the time*. Our normal routines and structures can't save us from ourselves out here and I start to feel irritable in our poorly air-conditioned pressure cooker of a hotel room. Soon, the petty grievances we both keep a lid on in everyday life start pushing through, like angry green shoots.

'You've left the loo seat up again.' It begins one evening, as we're getting ready to go out. There's some huffing as Lego Man pushes past me to flick the seat down.

'Is that what you're wearing?' he asks next, looking me up and down.

'Yes. What's wrong with what I'm wearing?'

'You said those shoes killed you the other night.' This is true. But they are pretty. So pretty. And they go with my dress.

'They're fine,' I lie, doing a few, already painful, laps of the room like a show pony to demonstrate their comfort.

'*Fine*,' he repeats with a barely concealed eye roll. 'But will you at least take a jumper this time?'

A jumper will not go with this outfit. A jumper will make me look bulky and accentuate the slightly bloated food baby I've become conscious of during the course of our trip. I do not plan on taking a jumper.

'It's still warm out,' I counter.

'Yes but it gets cooler once the sun's set. And you always get cold. And I always end up having to give you *my* jumper. And then I'm cold.'

This is also true. *Damn it*.

I agree to take a wrap with me in case of a chill and then sit on the bed of our hotel room, ready to go, as Lego Man potters around some more. I glance purposefully at my watch, seeing the numbers on my digital Casio flick over ever closer to the time of our dinner reservation.

'Ready when you are,' I say, hoping to prompt a response along the lines of: '*Great! Me too! Let's go!*'

Only that doesn't happen. Lego Man likes to cut things fine, as though life is one long *Top Gear* challenge. Even before moving to Denmark, the promptness capital of Europe, I liked to be on time. Life, I feel, becomes unnecessarily stressful if you're rushing all the time, when a little planning can ensure that you arrive on time, unfazed and Zen-like (at least, this is the goal). Lego Man does not share this rationale.

Midway through our year of living Danishly, my own fear of being late has escalated. I now find myself constantly on edge whenever Lego Man and I have to go anywhere, fearing the drama that will ensue and the sabotaging of my attempts to get to our destination on time. It makes catching flights, social engagements, even meeting people for coffee, a potential tinderbox of bickering. And tonight is no exception.

'We should probably get going or we'll miss our reservation,' I try saying, in as neutral a voice as I can manage.

There is no response, so I presume he hasn't heard me from the bathroom. I repeat myself, slightly louder this time. 'I said, we'll miss our reservation—' I start, but he cuts me off.

'—For god's sake, this is *Italy*! *Nothing* happens on time here! JUST. RELAX.'

It is a truth universally acknowledged that being told to relax makes the action itself impossible. Instead, we both fume silently until he is eventually ready to go. I hobble out in my impractical footwear and he follows, forgets the key, goes back, and returns with a bulky jumper that he insists I take with me. Over dinner, more mundane matrimonial feuds float to the surface.

Me: 'Why do you always drop your laundry next to the laundry bin. Why can't you ever just put your dirty clothes in the laundry bin?'

Him: 'You never squeegee the shower.'

Me: 'You leave wet towels on the bed.'

Him: 'You eat all the fun bits from my cereal when I'm at work, then pretend the manufacturers aren't putting in as many chocolate chips as they used to.'

We are both right. We are both ridiculous. We argue for much of the next day before declaring an amnesty until the end of the week when we fly home and immediately make plans to get out of the house. Independently. Lego Man goes to pick up the dog from kennels while I pop next door for coffee. Conducting a post-mortem of the trip with Friendly Neighbour, I run her through the highlights of our domestic disputes.

She laughs before explaining, kindly, that this is entirely normal: 'Everyone fights over their summer holiday – it's because we spend so much time together.' I'm just feeling comforted when she adds, 'I split up with my husband after three weeks in Tuscany last year. It was too long with nowhere to hide.'

'Oh, I'm so sorry—' I start. I had no idea she'd been married.

'No, it's fine. We're friends now. Besides, everyone gets divorced in Denmark.'

'They do?'

'Oh yes. July's the most popular month for it. People either row on holiday and realise they don't love each other anymore or get caught out cheating with text messages or emails because they're away from their lovers for too long. My ex and I were just the rowing types. It's our divorce anniversary next week,' she adds, cheerfully.

I attempt a nervous smile, unable to quite comprehend how she can be so cool and calm about her impending divorce-iversary, and I'm relieved when she changes the subject to update me on her travel plans for the rest of this month ('Norway, then France, then New York,' she says matter of factly).

When I get home, I look online and discover that two-thirds of couples end up arguing on their summer breaks, according to a 2012 poll by Ebookers. *This means that two-thirds of our couple friends posting loved-up snaps of themselves sipping cocktails in swimming pools are kidding themselves*, I console myself. *Either that or they're drunk.*

I call a few Danish divorce lawyers to test out Friendly Neighbour's theory that these rows often spark divorce proceedings and finally get through to Copenhagen-based lawyer, Anja Cordes. I ask her whether Friendly Neighbour's on to something: 'I've heard that there are more requests for divorces in Denmark in July because couples are forced to spend a lot of time together. Can this be right?'

'Yes,' one of Denmark's leading divorce lawyers tells me, 'there are more calls for assistance in July and we're always very busy after vacation time.'

Denmark, it turns out, has the fourth highest divorce rate in Europe – and living Danishly can seriously harm the health of your marriage. The latest figures from Statistics Denmark show that 42.7 per cent of marriages end in divorce. There's also a rise in the number of immigrants getting divorced, even when this goes against cultural norms. A study by the Danish National Centre for Social Research found that the divorce rate of Turkish immigrants in Denmark has increased from 3 per cent to 12 per cent over the last twenty years. Cağdaş Sağlicak, chairman of the Alevi Association in Denmark, called this 'a shift in the new generation' as more Turkish descendants pursued higher education. The right-wing Dansk Folkparti and Denmark's most left-wing political party, the Red-Green Alliance, both claim that this as an example of immigrants' successful integration into Danish society – making a break with their home country's norms. Divorce in Denmark *is* normal. And although going through the emotional distress of a marriage breakdown probably isn't on anyone's bucket list, it's so common that any stigma that may still be attached to getting a divorce elsewhere just doesn't exist here.

'Why is this?' I ask Anja. 'Why is divorce so *normal* in Denmark?'

'I think that so many women are working and so many children are taken care of outside the home that it's very easy to get a divorce and good financial help from the state,' she says.

Because both sexes get paid a decent wage in Denmark, women don't need to depend on their husbands for money. Most mothers return to work after having a baby and the state pays three-quarters of the costs of childcare – so there's no financial obligation to stay together if it isn't working out.

Danes also marry later, with most men nudging 35 before they get hitched and the average bride being 32 years old (compared to 30 for men and 28 for women in the UK and 28 and 26 respectively in the US). As Friendly Neighbour put it: 'You have a lot of fun with your friends in your teens and twenties, then you settle down with one of them in your thirties. It can feel like the fun stops after that so you feel like you want a change.'

Getting a divorce in Denmark is also famously easy. 'If parties can agree on direct divorce,' says Anja, 'you can fill out an application on the web and between one and three weeks later, your application will be handled and the divorce order will be sent out.' What's more, it's cheap: 'A straightforward divorce costs 900 DKK [around £100 or $170].'

But how can all this divorce make for happy Danes? Isn't the breakdown of a marriage, along with bereavement and moving house, one of the three most stressful life events that can occur?

I ask Anja how Denmark can keep coming top of the world happiness index in spite of this and she tells me simply: 'It's because we have equality and freedom.' A depressingly high divorce rate does at least suggest that Danes have choices. They can take their own destiny in their hands and take action if their lives aren't panning out as they'd hoped. They are free, and freedom makes you happy, even if divorce doesn't.

I ask Anja whether she counts herself among the contented Danes of the surveys, despite dealing with warring soon-to-be divorcees all day long. 'I'm an eight out of ten,' she tells me. 'I have a good, fulfilling and satisfying life.'

All these divorces don't put Danes off tying the knot again, either. Denmark is the number one country in Europe with regard to marriages, according to Statistics Denmark. So the key to domestic bliss, Danish-style, seems to be that if you're not happy with who you're waking up with most mornings, make a change – if you want something (or someone) else, go for it. And as Friendly Neighbour puts it: 'Danes *really* like getting married, so we don't mind doing it more than once. Plus most people here are pretty liberal.'

I tell her that this is something I've noticed. My mother was outraged during her last visit when we passed a selection of maternity wedding dresses in the local bridal shop ('Well, really! Couldn't she have waited?' was her tutting response), and many Danes have children before they get hitched. Danes don't mind a bit of public nudity, either, from organised skinny-dipping sessions to naked CrossFit classes (really) and plentiful nudist beaches sprinkled along the coastline. The latter are so common that my in-laws got an eyeful on a recent trip when they strayed too far from a *Lonely Planet*-listed sunspot.

Porn is regularly screened on public TV channels and a recent YouGov survey exploring sexual behaviour in thirteen European countries found that Danes consumed more X-rated content than any other nation surveyed. Danes are so open-minded that they even left their *hygge* family homes on Boxing Day 2013 to watch the premiere of director Lars Von Triers' five-hour sex epic *Nymphomaniac*. Because nothing says 'Christmas' like a six-foot-high projection of a phallus.

Those who aren't indulging in blue movies may still

credit celluloid with giving their sex lives a boost thanks to 'Disney sex'. Every Friday, Danish children countrywide sit down to an hour of Disney cartoons at 7pm, and a lot of parents use this time to 'cultivate each other', as Helena C puts it, while the kids are entertained. Every parent I speak to tells me that 'Disney sex' is a fantastic invention (despite the dodgy name) – 'and importantly, it comes at a time of the evening when we still have a *fair* chance of staying awake...' adds Helena C.

Even the clergy are pretty right on when it comes to sex here, and I write a story for a UK newspaper about a Zealand priest conducting a carnal-themed mass to promote procreation. Despite all this, Denmark's birth rate is currently at a 30-year low. With just ten babies born per 1,000 residents, the government, clergy and commercial parties are doing all they can to get Danes *at it*. A Danish travel company is running a campaign to get more couples jetting off on minibreaks together and encouraging them to '*Do it for Denmark!*' The advertisement claims that Danes have 46 per cent more sex when they're away from home, resulting in 10 per cent of the population being conceived while on a break (though not, clearly, if they go away for too long. One week = sexy times. Two weeks = imminent divorce). To get more Danes getting it on, the company is offering an 'ovulation discount' to women who enter the date of their last period when booking so that they can calculate the most fertile time for a minibreak. Anyone who sends in a picture of a positive pregnancy test after their trip is put in a prize draw for a three-year supply of nappies. No, this is not made up. This is the way Danes roll. Oh, and in case this all sounds a bit hetero-biased, gay couples are also encouraged to get involved because, 'the fun is in the participation'.

Sex is everywhere in Denmark, and it starts young. Sex education has been compulsory since the 1970s and from the age of six, Danish children are taught how babies are made during a national curriculum 'Sex Week' every February. By the age of ten, they learn about boundaries, how to take care of themselves on the Internet and the HPV vaccine. Danish preteens cover homosexuality, bisexuality and heterosexuality, and as the first country in the world to recognise registered partnerships for same-sex couples and the first European country to allow legal changes of gender without sterilisation, Denmark has long placed an emphasis on inclusion.

By thirteen, they're onto masturbation, contraception, sexually transmitted diseases, abortion, and sexual abuse. Danish pop stars and actors take part in public health videos to be used in sex education lessons and discussions in class are, apparently, frank and wide-ranging. *Wow*, I think, a *whole generation who don't have to find out about sex from reading Judy Blume or the sticky pages in the library copy of* Lady Chatterley's Lover... For someone who went to an all-girls convent school, this seems amazingly progressive. I had a biology teacher who blushed beetroot at the mention of stamen, let alone periods.

'And the classes are all mixed, right?' I ask Helena C over *snegles*, as she explains her young daughters' incredibly enlightened views on sex.

'Of course. We don't separate the sexes. That causes repression.'

This may be true, but it was far easier to concentrate in double Geography when I wasn't having lustful palpitations about Marco Terrinoni from the adjacent boys' school.

The legal age of consent is fifteen in Denmark, and once Danes get going, they don't stop. A recent public health survey found that 90 per cent of Danes aged sixteen to 95 said that a good sex life was 'vital' to them – which means that men and women in their tenth decade are swinging from the Scandi-style chandeliers in Denmark. According to figures from AgeForum, there has been a doubling in the number of divorces and marriages among Danes over 60 in the last ten years with many meeting new lovers online. The dating site Seniordate.dk now has 68,000 members, and Seniorcontact.dk has 34,000 users.

Singles can sleep with whomever they like without being judged, and those in relationships aren't shackled to sex with the same person forever either. A YouGov survey showed that 32 per cent of Danes had been unfaithful (tying them with the Finns for the 'most cheaty nation in Europe' crown) and 51 per cent admitted to one-night stands. Most Danes get around the problem of wanting to sleep with someone new by doing so in secret or splitting up and moving on. But for a growing number of Denmark's sexually curious, there's another option – and it's literally right up my street, as it turns out.

Late afternoon, the dog starts barking at the front door. This can mean only one thing: his nemesis, the tweenage paperboy is approaching. The dog and I play the daily game of '*which of us will reach the newspaper first?*' and this afternoon I triumph, saving the local rag from its usual fate of being shredded and liberally distributed around the house.

Scanning the inky pages in the hope that this might be the day my Danish lessons pay off and miraculously turn the collections of consonants and mystery vowels into a legible language, I'm delighted to spot a few words I recognise. Aside from a threatened strike and a special deal on pizza, there's a headline featuring the words:

Tucan Swinger & Wellness Naughty Nightclub!

Since moving to Sticksville-on-Sea, fast food offers and threats of union walkouts have been the apotheosis of excitement in my area. The very idea that I've been living in the eye of a *swinging* storm all this time is nothing short of staggering. I find myself coming over all Home Counties and having to sit down with a cup of tea and a biscuit. Then, I Google it.

The Tucan Club, it turns out, is Denmark's premier swinging establishment. The club was set up by husband-and-wife team Mie Hansen and Torben Nielsen, to 'bring secret dreams and wishes to fruition' by 'pushing the boundaries of accepted sexuality', according to the blurb on its website.

Even after a slightly tense holiday, I have no desire to swap Lego Man for anyone else's other half. But I am curious (just doing my job, honest).

'What if swinging is one of the keys to Danish happiness?' I ask a sceptical-looking dog.

He looks at me as if to say '*Really?*', then slinks off, still sulking at having lost out on the chance to eat today's paper. Unperturbed, intrigued, and in the name of journalistic endeavour, I pick up the phone.

'We got into swinging thirteen years ago,' Mie tells me, in

the same tone one might use to describe getting into juicing. 'We decided to start our own club and it just grew by word of mouth. Now, we're the biggest in Scandinavia.'

Mie explains that most couples arrive, have a look around to see if there's anyone they like the look of, then issue 'invitations' for whatever takes their fancy. 'There's no pressure,' she says, 'and there's also a disco, a sauna and a Jacuzzi for couples who aren't ready to swing yet. Then, when they do feel ready to try it, we have lots of facilities to make things more fun.'

The word 'facilities' conjures up chlorine-doused leisure centres but Mie soon sets me straight and I realise, not for the first time, that my life to date has been Very Sheltered Indeed.

'We have go-go dance poles, love swings, gynaecological chairs—'

'—Sorry?'

'You know, the chairs you have in hospital. With stirrups.'

'Oh,' I reply faintly.

'And then we have rooms for those who prefer privacy – without glory holes.'

'Right. And ... er ... why *would* the rooms have glory holes?'

I ask this at the precise moment that Lego Man arrives home from work. His laptop case slips from his hands to the floor in shock and his eyebrows hover somewhere around his hairline. I try to mime the action for '*nothing to worry about: I'm just interviewing a swinger*' (not easy, even with my charades skills). Lego Man plonks himself down at the kitchen table to compose himself as Mie clarifies the whole hole business.

'You know, glory holes: the normal holes you have for guys to put their dick into.'

I don't know where to begin with this information but it feels like the wrong time to admit that my 'normal' doesn't tend to include plaster-formed vagina substitutes. *Good god, I am vanilla*, I think and resolve to broaden my horizons, while stopping short of anything involving stirrups. Lego Man, looking quite pale now, makes for the fridge to revive himself with a stiff drink.

'Basically, everyone just does what they're comfortable with,' Mie goes on. 'It's good to experiment as part of a couple because then you've got someone you trust with you and the other pair understand the dynamics of the relationship. My husband and I started this way and have never looked back!'

Swinging, apparently, became big in Denmark in the 1990s and the community now has its own dedicated swinging hub. So naturally I call them up as well. 'Danes are pretty open-minded,' says Jesper Christensen of Swingerguiden.dk. 'Swinging in Denmark is really popular – especially compared to the rest of Scandinavia.' About 90,000 Danes say they swing regularly, though many more admit to being 'curious' and the website gets 190,000 visitors a year. Swingerguiden.dk promotes meet-ups, activities and even courses for newbies keen to learn about swinging etiquette. Enthusiastic Danes set up International Swingers Week in 2008 with events and functions all over the country – and the annual occasion now thrives worldwide.

And it's not just swinging. Dogging, I recently learned, is another popular pursuit in Denmark. American Mom nearly fell off her Arne Jacobsen chair when I told her this and I was forced to explain what the practice entails and how we Brits were the proud originators of this noble tradition.

'Basically, repressed Englishmen would tell their wives they were going out to walk the dog and cruise for sex in parks, or just watch other people at it.'

'So you called it *dog-ging*?' She asked, incredulous, drawing out the consonants to make the word sound even more ridiculous.

'Well, not me personally,' I said, keen to clarify, 'but generally, yes.'

'And now you guys do it in *cars*? In *rest areas*?'

'Again, not me *per se*, but yes. Although we call them lay-bys. From what I gather there's not really much "resting" going on...'

'So what happened to the dogs?' She sounded genuinely concerned.

'Um, well...' *If the nuns could see me now*, I couldn't help thinking: *a dogging-apologist cultural ambassador*. 'I suppose,' I hazarded a guess, 'fewer people had dogs as pets, but they still wanted to have sex outside so they just used it as a codeword. Maybe?'

American Mom seemed contented by this although she proceeded to cut our coffee date short to go and pick up her kids from nursery. I resolved not to take it personally and convinced myself that she just needed time for this new gem about her adopted homeland to sink in. *We've been friends for four whole months*, I tell myself, *she's not going to let a little thing like dogging come between us!*

Danes started to embrace the practice that originated in the UK (they gave us pastries: we gave them dogging. You're welcome...) in the 1990s. A recent YouGov survey reported in *The Copenhagen Post* showed that 41 per cent of Danes had tried dogging – the highest figure for a population in Europe. Danish sex therapist Joan Ørting recently explained her country's fondness for a good dogging session to *Metroxpress* newspaper by saying: 'In the old days we did it all the time in the open, so it is more natural for us to lie in the grass rather than on a bed. That's something we are discovering now and which is making us return to our roots.' *Or cars, in lay-bys, off motorways*. Either way, the pastime is now so popular that there are online guidelines and lists of upcoming events.

Thinking about it this way, it all starts to make sense. Knowing that these practices are conducted in a typically Danish way helps me to understand that there's nothing spontaneous about dogging, or swinging, or any kind of sexual proclivity in Denmark. *Lectures? Diarised events? 'Best practice' guidelines?* Danes may be wonderfully liberal but their approach to swinging and dogging sounds a lot like their approach to any other extracurricular activity or hobby club. *Sure, there may be slightly more risqué outfits or sex with strangers involved*, I think, *but still – there are rules! It is 'organised fun'! Someone, somewhere, is probably taking minutes!* A significant proportion of my fellow Jutlanders may well be indulging in partner swapping or bypass blowjobs on a regular basis. But by viewing these as just another form of evening class, I can carry on going to friends' houses and leaving my car keys unattended, safe in the knowledge that it's my own husband I'll go home with. Unless of course I've signed up for an organised event, months in advance, or attended some kind of course. With a certificate at the end of it. Assured, I set off to reassure Lego Man. And explain about the glory holes.

The next morning, after dreams of gynaecological chairs and Swiss-cheese walls, I feel drained and sick as a dog. This has been happening a lot lately. I even struggled to sample all the culinary delights that Sicily had to offer (most unusual). Yet despite this, my food baby isn't shifting, I notice as I get out of the shower and study myself in the bathroom mirror. I've been getting dizzy a lot. And grumpy. And sleepy. And probably a few other of the seven dwarves. I need to wee all the time, but can't seem to summon the energy. On the plus side, my chest is currently giving Pamela Anderson a run for her money and I have, frankly, fabulous hair. I locate my phone and turn to the hypochondriac's best friend, Dr Google, for a diagnosis, tapping 'irritable', 'bloated', 'big boobs,' and 'nausea' into a search. Before I have the chance to process this list of symptoms and apply any kind of basic logic, a slew of articles appear with titles like:

Congratulations, you're pregnant!
First trimester symptoms

and:

Positive test? What next…

'Oh. My. God.'

'What?' Lego Man is ironing in just his boxer shorts and socks next door while simultaneously eating a bowl of cereal and trying not to slop chocolate chip-infused milk onto a clean white shirt.

'Um … nothing, I'll be out in a sec.'

Back in the bathroom, I start opening and closing

drawers, furiously pulling out handfuls of slim, rectangular boxes. We've been trying for years. I have seen numerous specialists who have prescribed me a myriad of hormones to be ingested and then injected daily for the past 24 months. I've spent a small fortune trying every alternative therapy in existence, taken hundreds of tests and pretty much kept my local chemists afloat. Fortunately I'm still well stocked.

I tear open a dozen foil-wrapped packs and wee on as many as my bladder will allow. Three minutes later I emerge, brandishing two fistfuls of pink and white plastic sticks like a reproductively victorious Edward Scissorhands.

'I *think* we might have been a bit clever,' I say, as Lego Man sponges a brown milky splatter out of his shirt at the kitchen sink.

'Are they…?' he starts, setting down the dishcloth, 'are *you*…?'

'Yes!'

'And they're definitely…?'

'Uhuh.'

He comes closer to check off each double-lined window in turn. And then we both cry. And I make his white shirt even soggier. Lego Man and I have made a baby. With no swinging, dogging or stirrups involved.

Things I've learned this month:

1. Denmark shuts down in July
2. Holidays are good for you, but stay away too long and you're dicing with divorce

3. …which is fine in Denmark. Everyone's at it. And it may even make you happier
4. Danes do sex. A lot. And they're refreshingly un-British about it
5. It's possible to reach your mid-thirties without knowing what a glory hole is
6. Being pregnant can make you really cross (but you do get great hair)

8. August

The Kids are Alright

Having discovered, Jeremy Kyle-style, that I am already pretty far along in this pregnancy lark (the obvious signs having been absent, just to clarify – my biology teacher wasn't *that* bad), I am suddenly catapulted into the brave new world of parenting.

Lego Man and I are delighted; relieved that it's even been possible for us and grateful that it's happened. But we're also terrified. Conversations around the homestead start to go something like this:

Me: 'We're having a baby. I'm growing an actual living creature. Inside me. Like in the film *Alien*. And we're in a country where we still can't speak the language. And I'm going to have to push out a watermelon in approximately five months. I'm Going To Have To Push Out A Watermelon. Or have something alarming done to me with knives. *KNIVES*!'

Lego Man: 'I'll never be an astronaut now. Or James Bond...'

Me, momentarily distracted from my woes: 'Were either of those on the cards?'

Lego Man: 'Well, no. But it was nice to know the options were there.'

I want to be supportive, really I do. But I can't help suspecting that it isn't just impending fatherhood that has deprived NASA and MI6 of my husband's services.

I notice small, pink, squirming things wherever I go, and start seeing the prams routinely left outside cafés and restaurants in Denmark in a whole new light.

'Danes just *leave* their babies in the street? *Unsupervised*?' Lego Man asks incredulously, having only just clocked-on to this phenomenon. 'Can you imagine this happening back home? Or anywhere, in fact?'

I recount a tale that American Mom told me about a Danish mother who left her baby outside a restaurant in New York while she ate and was promptly arrested for child neglect and abandonment.

'God. Right. Good to know,' is his response. The idea of taking such a risk with your baby seems bizarre, but this isn't how Danes view it.

'We trust each other,' says Helena C, who, although happy for me, is mildly miffed that her every-other-Saturday-night wine wing-woman will be out of action for a while. 'It's like we plan for a positive outcome – we think, "let's leave babies outside to sleep in their prams and get fresh air, which is good for their lungs" – rather than planning for the worst and thinking, "if I turn my back for a second, my baby might get stolen". Plus people don't steal babies in Denmark.' *Ah, the famous Danish 'trust-in-the-system' again*, I think. *Nothing bad ever happens in Denmark...*

But because Helena C et al believe that their compatriots are, on the whole, 'good people' who are 'like them' and 'to be trusted', they feel safe and behave as though they live in a world without danger. This makes them happy and more inclined to act in a community-minded way. And so their trust is rewarded. And so on – until it becomes a self-fulfilling prophecy.

'There's nowhere else I'd rather be as a mother,' she tells me, 'and nowhere else I'd want my family to be raised.' This is a grand claim. But in the land of Lego and Hans Christian Andersen, children really do seem to be at the centre of everything.

'It's all geared towards the family here,' says American Mom when she's finished high-fiving me, and I ask about her experiences of raising children in Denmark. 'It's the best country in the world to have kids,' she tells me. 'Everything's been thought about here and it means that kids have a really fun time!' To prove her point, she ropes me into doing the nursery run the following week to pick up her two young children and see for myself. 'You can get some practice in,' she tells me. 'You also have to sign up for daycare practically as soon as you give birth anyway, so it'll give you a chance to look around and see if you want to send your little one there,' she points at my now swollen belly and I tug down my top self-consciously, to distract from The Bump. Already in love with my child-to-be, the idea of handing him or her over to anyone else feels strange. But Danes spend the majority of their early years being raised by someone else.

Every baby born in Denmark is guaranteed a place in daycare from when they're six months old to when they start school, aged six. *Vuggestue*, or nursery, takes children up to the age of three to be looked after by *pædagoger*, or social educators, who will have completed a minimum three-year education programme. There's also the option to send under-threes to a *dagpleje* – a child-minder or 'daycare mum', who may not be qualified but can look after up to five children in their own home. Packs of toddlers and their child-minders are a familiar fixture at parks and play areas nearby and they'll either bundle into four-seater prams to be pushed home or hop on a wooden trailer to be pulled by bike. Danish mothers often become so fond of their children's *dagpleje* that I hear of some women timing the conception of future babies to fit in with the availability of favoured child-minders.

From the age of three until they're six years old, kids go to a kindergarten or *børnehaven* (translated as 'children's garden', like the German) where trained staff prepare them for 'big school'.

Danes pay between 2,200 and 3,500 DKK (around £235–374 or $400–635) per month for under-twos and receive 45 hours of care a week in return. Prices vary slightly depending on which *kommune* you live in and whether lunch is included. There's also the option to send them for 25 hours a week instead, which costs even less. From the age of three, the price drops further (to 1,730 DKK, around £185 or $315 for 45 hours a week where I live). This is because less one-on-one care is needed and, as American Mom tells me: 'they shouldn't need so many diapers or wipes by then, which saves a few kroner. At least, that's the hope, anyway...'

Having heard horror stories from friends back home who've had to remortgage their house or sell vital organs to pay for childcare, the Danish rates seem surprisingly affordable. But this, I learn, is because the state picks up 75 per cent of the cost. If your annual household income is below 470,400 DKK (approximately £54,000 or $92,000), you'll get a further deduction, and if you earn less than 151,501 DKK a year (around £17,000 or $29,000), it's completely free. There's also a discount for siblings, so if you have more than one child in daycare you pay full price for the most expensive option and half-price for the others. A bit like a Richard and Judy's Book Club deal at WHSmiths.

'I pick up my kids any time from 3–5-ish in the afternoons – they're fairly relaxed about it,' American Mom tells me as we walk to their combined *vuggestue* and *børnehaven* the following Monday. 'And since most people who have proper jobs—' here, she shoots me a pointed look, aware that I get teased for my freelancer status in Denmark, '—since most of us work 8am–4pm, it works pretty well.'

We round a corner and I *hear* the nursery before I can see it.

'*Raaaaaaaaaaaaaaahhhhhhhhhhhhhhhhhh!*'

A roar of white noise is coming from the smart-looking cream-coloured house up ahead. A few men emerge, pushing prams or holding sticky hands.

'Do a lot of dads do the daycare run?'

'Of course, this is *Denmark*!'

It's 4pm. On a Monday. This would be unheard of outside of a few progressively trendy middle-class ghettos of North London.

We push open the metal gates to the nursery garden and a dozen mops of blonde hair flock to greet us, cheeks flushed, faces covered in a mixture of sunscreen, soil and sand, all grinning like mad. I look around at the *Teletubbies*-esque landscape in front of us, with swings, slides, sandpits and toys everywhere. Near-feral-looking children streak up and down grassy mounds, dodging smaller ones who sit in a circle under the shade of a tree with one of the few grown-ups I can see.

American Mom types a code into a wall-mounted monitor to sign her kids out before we set off in search of them.

'These are the kitchens, where a cook comes in and makes fresh organic food daily,' she tells me on our mini tour. 'Then there's also a whole room for the various kit we have to send them in with to cater for Denmark's crazy weather.' This, I learn, includes a rain suit, a 'warm suit' (usually a quilted jacket and trousers), a sun hat, rain boots, bike helmets, reflective vests, and a complete change of clothes, 'in case of bathroom-related emergencies,' she tells me. 'But that's just in summer: in winter, you need snowsuits, snow boots, hats, snoods and mittens too.' *More outdoors gear?* Lego Man is going to be ecstatic.

'And this,' American Mom pushes open a door to reveal a shady wooden appendage to the main building, 'is the "sleeping shed".'

I peer inside to see rows of pistachio 1930s-style perambulators, each with a mini ladder to help the more mobile (or heavy) toddlers clamber up.

'Wow. Retro...' I mutter.

'Yeah, and check this out,' she flips hinged wooden bars over the opening of one of the prams. 'These are the baby cages for the under-threes. So they don't escape when they're supposed to be sleeping.' The whole thing looks archaic.

'Don't the kids *mind* being behind bars?' I wonder.

American Mom shrugs: 'It works – they nap like a dream here.'

With neither child to be found inside, we head back out to the garden and eventually locate American Mom's little girl up a tree while her son is busy aiming a paper aeroplane at the roof of the bike shed. Shoes are the next challenge. After finding three in the sandpit and one under an apple tree, I presume we're good to go.

'Patience, grasshopper,' American Mom stops me and then addresses her kids: 'Empty!' Both children obligingly upend their shoes and turn out their pockets as trickles of sand fall into neat pyramids all around them. 'If we don't do it here, I find mounds everywhere at home. There's a good tablespoon most days,' she tells me.

Nursery in Denmark, I decide, is probably the most fun it is possible to have without artificial stimulants involved. It's like *Lord of the Flies* but with a happy ending. With the littlest one strapped into her buggy, we wheel our way to the metal gates that separate the playground paradise from the rest of the world. I ask the older child what he got up to today, expecting an answer along the lines of 'cutting and gluing' or 'face painting'. What I'm not expecting is 'tractor shopping'. I give the five-year-old a quizzical look then turn to his mother, presuming that this is a flight of fancy.

'He went *tractor shopping*?'

'Yes, I did,' the boy goes on, oblivious. 'A girl in my class loves tractors so the whole class walked to the shop to look around.'

'Is he pulling my leg?' I ask American Mom. *Could five-year-olds pull legs?*

'No, that's probably true. There's a girl in his class who does *really* like tractors and it's only two kilometres to the nearest dealership.'

I love how I now live in a place where such a thing exists. I can honestly say I've never given a moment's thought to where farm vehicles come from before now. I also love that I'm in a country where such an ad hoc child-inspired trip is even possible.

'So the whole class just went? And the parents didn't know?'

American Mom waves a hand dismissively: 'We signed some sort of disclaimer when the kids first started saying that teachers could take them out on excursions, so they go out and about quite a lot. It's not like the US – you don't need permission slips or insurance procedures or risk assessments for them to even leave the premises.' She tells me that there are daily expeditions where children are expected to dress themselves in outdoor gear to go out exploring.

'They came home the other day telling me they'd spent the morning looking at water in town – so everything from clouds to puddles, drains, fountains—'

'—the porny pony?'

'—the porny pony fountain, yes, and then the taps back at the nursery. It's kind of cool that they got these little kids to think about where their water comes from. They've also taken them to the grocery store to teach them "this is how you behave in a store". Things you'd expect to have to teach kids yourself – how to wash their hands, how to behave buying groceries, bike safety even – daycare does it for you.'

Many nurseries go above and beyond the call of duty. Several I've been told about in Jutland lead field trips to the home of any child whose birthday it is for an hour's 'cake and chaos'. A parent pops home in their lunch hour with baked goods of some kind, then the teacher arrives with the class and the kids go mad for 50 minutes before they all go back to school again. There's no social one-upmanship about whose parents have hired the hottest kids' entertainer or trumped their peers with the best party bag, and there's no infringing on 'family time' in the evenings or at weekends. It's just a ninja birthday squad: in and out. Staff at one kindergarten I hear of in Funen are so mindful of parents' needs that they offer them 'couple time' – caring for children outside of working hours to allow mums and dads to go out on a date night.

I wonder how organised the whole machine has to be in order to make this work, but American Mom tells me that there's not so much a structure to the day as a 'rhythm'.

'They arrive, do some gymnastics or dance, nap, have a snack, then go for an outing. The kids know what to expect next, but for the most part they're free to play.'

This sounds wonderful. I may have to rethink my plan

to come back as a golden eagle in the next life and opt for 'Danish toddler' instead. Danes seem to start life ridiculously well and just carry on from there. I start to wonder whether life as a Danish kid might perhaps set the blueprint for all future interactions – for a lifetime of contentment and well-being. *Have I, perhaps, stumbled on the secret to Danish happiness? Do they just build happy Danes this way, right from the start?*

'Of course there are quite a lot of fights, because teachers don't tend to intervene much,' American Mom interrupts my reverie, bursting my bliss bubble.

'Oh!'

'Yeah, there are bruises and sometimes scratches,' she goes on, 'but the kids are mostly OK in the end. And they always want to go back the next day.'

I hold a hand over my stomach protectively.

'Doesn't it scare you? Seeing your children get into fights?' I ask, mentally inspecting hers for bumps and feeling a ripple of relief when I note that their youthfully perfect skin is blemish-free – albeit covered in sand.

'It did a little, at the start – but kids have a lot of freedom in Denmark. And I think that's worth a lot in the long run.'

Numerous studies have shown that children growing up in the UK and US today are missing out on the full-throttled fun of being a kid because they're so micro-managed and swaddled in cotton wool; protected from dirt and dust and grazed knees, and stuck inside on iPads instead. But for kids living Danishly, there's more of a *Famous Five*-meets-*Swallows and Amazons* approach to childrearing. And the kids I've seen so far appear to be thriving on it.

Of course, the system has its critics.

'It's not freedom, it's laziness,' a Danish mother-of-three tells me. 'The staff at my son's nursery just sit there and drink coffee while the kids run wild.' Another expat says that stay-at-home mums are looked down on in Denmark: 'It's assumed that both parents go back to work here, and the fact that I haven't seems to reduce my status.'

I talk to as many Danes as I can about this and they all express the same sentiment: 'But why would you want to stay at home? Why wouldn't you want your children to have other kids to play with?' Most genuinely believe that sending under-threes to daycare is doing them a favour by allowing them to socialise early. No one can understand why a woman wouldn't want to go back to work, in a job that she probably *likes* and that pays her a decent wage. The job of stay-at-home mum has, in effect, been taken over by the state. Helena C even goes so far as to say that she thinks Danish children are better at socialising than the British kids because they learn how to get on with their peers sooner.

'But what about attachment theory?' I counter, coming over all Oprah. 'Don't Danish children grow up insecure or with abandonment issues or anything?' According to the late British psychologist John Bowlby, the difference between secure and insecure adults is determined by the kind of care you get between the ages of six months and three years. Not having your needs met in early life by your primary care-giver, usually a mother, is meant to make for needy and insecure adults who fear abandonment.

'Interesting,' says Helena C when I talk to her about this, 'but the whole of Denmark has been raised like this and we seem to be doing OK, don't we? Or do you think we're all insecure?' She's got a point.

I come across an article by Charlotte Højlund, parenting expert and mother of seven children. (Yes, *seven*. The woman has spawned her own netball team.) I figure if anyone can give me further insight into Danish childrearing and whether it makes for happier kids, it's her.

Charlotte is one of the most youthful-looking women I've ever clapped eyes on – and she has seven (*seven!*) children ranging from the ages of two to twenty. She also writes books on parenting and regularly appears on Danish TV as a commentator on childrearing. So I tell her to give it to me straight: does the Danish system work?

'I think so. I've read about attachment theory and understand that in some cultures mothers stay at home with their children until they're two or three years old, and maybe that would be better. But we can't go back. Most Danish mothers work now and it's just the way our society operates.'

Danes do indeed seem to be getting on perfectly well and, interestingly, all the studies saying '*working mothers spell the end of civilisation as we know it*' (I paraphrase) tend to come from America, with a few from Germany or Holland. None are from Scandinavia, where women routinely go back to work when their children are less than a year old. Charlotte tells me how children's development is taken very seriously in Denmark and how when they start at nursery, parents don't just dump them and leave for work as they do in some countries. Instead, it's a planned, gradual process where parents leave their offspring alone for ten minutes on the first day, then twenty minutes the next, and so on until they've worked up to a full day. The 'daycare-weaning' process can take up to three weeks. The local *kommune* will pay for extra members of staff if there's a child with special needs and a child psychologist is also on hand if children need extra help.

'There's also an intranet and parents get regular updates via email on what their children have been doing,' Charlotte tells me, confessing: 'in fact, I could do with a bit less of this – with seven kids, my inbox gets pretty clogged up!'

Because they aren't the primary carers for their children during the day, Charlotte thinks that Danish parents put in extra effort in the evenings and at weekends. 'A lot of parents feel guilt about being away from their children because of work and so they make sure they invest a lot of time in their kids whenever they can. This may be another reason our divorce rate is so high,' says Charlotte, a divorcee herself. 'Parents have to take that extra time from somewhere, and they don't want to take it away from their children or from their work – so relationships can suffer.'

I've just read an Open University study suggesting that couples without children were happier together than those who'd sprogged up. *Oh well, too late now,* I think, *that horse has bolted.* But interestingly, the research also found that women with children were happier than those without. *So my relationship might hit the rocks but I'll be happier than ever? Result!* I decide not to show the offending article to Lego Man but am consoled by the fact that mothers in Denmark must be some of the happiest in the world.

So is Charlotte happy?

'Of course!' she tells me. 'I'd say I'm a nine out of ten. Denmark is the best place in the world to have children.'

I'm pleased to hear this, of course, but I do start to suspect that everyone I speak to is a secret sleeper representative for the Danish tourist board. That, or I'm living in a Nordic version of *The Truman Show*.

Reassured and excited about the prospect of giving my unborn baby such a good start in life, I realise that this means I'm already thinking beyond my due date in January. By then, our year of living Danishly will have slipped into a sequel with us barely noticing. It would be easier to stay here, I rationalise, despite the language barriers, still not knowing quite how everything works and the daily opportunities for humiliation that even popping out for milk or trying to park here can afford.

Living Danishly is simpler than my previous existence back in London. It's not as exciting, granted. But all the rules, traditions, and rituals mean that a lot of worry and stress is taken away. And it turns out that I'm OK with this. You can just *be* in Denmark. Relocating either heavily pregnant or with a newborn might be more than my newfound levels of Zen are ready for.

Part of me wishes that I was having a baby with old friends and family around me, in a country where I could understand the doctor's information leaflets and knew where to buy decent clothes for my newly enlarged state. But I'm also aware that this may not have been possible in my former life. It seems likely that living Danishly is at least part of what has enabled this to happen – so I feel as though I owe the country a debt of gratitude. And if my wondrous university friends keep sending me care packages of pregnancy workout DVDs, magazines and Topshop maternity clothes, I'll be all set.

I'm beginning to think of Denmark as home. When we tell people our news over Skype or FaceTime (tech types really need to get cracking on inventing the 'virtual hug'), they keep asking, 'So you'll have the baby back in England, right?' to which I've started replying, a little defensively: 'We do *have* hospitals in Denmark, you know...'

The hardest thing about staying here would be making my mother a long-distance granny. She's wanted a grandchild for as long as I can remember, and all being well, I'm on course to deliver (literally) my side of the bargain in January. Only I'm doing it 900km away. OK, so it's not Australia, but she has a job, *a life*, a relationship in the UK. I can't expect her to upend everything and fly over to see us all the time. Having a baby over here means that she'll miss out on some of the firsts: the family outings, the bath times, the cuddles that grandparents who live around the corner take for granted. She'll have to make do with pictures and video calls instead. I tell myself that a year of this might not be so bad. But any longer might just break her heart.

There's still some time until we need to decide what to do, so exercising my right to be terribly British and repressed about the whole thing, I ignore the issue for now and eat my emotions instead. I distract myself with a packet of crisps – this being one of the few foodstuffs I can keep down at present. I'm just congratulating myself on my new life plan *not* to plan anything beyond the bountiful possibilities of baby daycare when I'm summoned to sample the Danish school system.

From the age of six, Danish children go to a state-funded *folkeskole* (public school) where they take classes with the same twenty-odd children for the next ten years. Being among the same classmates for the majority of their schooling is thought to help children feel secure and offer a safe, trusting environment to explore the key pillars of Danish education: equality and autonomy. As part of this, Jutland's schoolchildren are studying citizenship and I'm contacted by a colleague of Lego Man's and asked to give a talk at his daughter's school. There is an optimistic assumption that as a 'foreigner' and a writer, I might be able to a) string a sentence together and b) shed some light on how Denmark appears to the rest of the world, so, flattered, I accept.

I'm interested to discover that the Danish teens I meet all appear incredibly confident and relaxed – addressing their teachers by their first names and speaking out in class to debate and discuss at every opportunity. After a thorough grilling, I leave and seek the expertise of Karen Bjerg Petersen from the department of education research at Aarhus University to find out more about The Danish Way.

'We teach children to think and decide for themselves, not just pass exams,' she says first off. 'Education here is about developing the social and cognitive competencies of a child and experience-based learning. We encourage them to be critical towards the system.' She tells me that education and democracy have been tied together in Denmark since the Second World War: 'Children started to be encouraged to *think* and go against authority if they didn't agree with what they were being told – this became a priority after the German occupation of Denmark and was something Danes were very conscious of. We wanted citizens who were democratic and could have their own ideas, so self-development is a big part of learning in Denmark.'

'So Hitler drove the Danes to teach their schoolkids to question authority?'

'Pretty much.'

All this emphasis on a child's autonomy and self-expression can appear overly informal to an outsider. I tell her how strange I found it that children don't wear uniforms and address teachers by their first names here. When I was growing up, finding out a teacher's Christian name was the Holy Grail. It meant power. We would whisper it to each other before collapsing in fits of near-hysterical laughter, dazzled by our own daring, safe in the knowledge that Mrs Plews from Home Ec. wouldn't scare us half so much now that we knew her first name was '*Sue*'.

'Do Danish children have the same respect for – or fear of – their teachers?'

'There's still a lot of *respect*,' Karen tells me, 'but the idea is that even if you are a child, you're still equal to your teacher as a human being, even if they're older than you. A teacher may have a lot of knowledge, but children should also be respected as individuals.' This is an outlandish idea for a former convent schoolgirl to get her head around. 'So there's no hierarchy between pupils and teachers?'

'That's right. Jante's Law is very much present,' she says. 'Everyone is equal and no one is better than anyone else.'

The same goes for the pupils and their parents, and

Karen tells me how a CEO is likely to send his kids to the same school as a shop worker or secretary in Denmark. 'We don't like show-offs,' as she puts it. 'We're also a very wealthy society, so it's important that when we go out internationally, our children know not to go around saying, "*Do it our way! We know everything!*"'

Instead, Danish children are taught the tolerance that I learned about back in May. Throughout their school career, pupils take part in 'Friday *hygge* hour', where they take it in turns to bring in cake and the class talk about any pastoral issues together.

'My two children were told about bullying in their Friday *hygge* hour. The teacher explained it to them in a really calm way, making it clear that everyone had a right to feel respected and equal. Kids got told: "You might not like everyone you meet, but you need to respect their differences."'

There's obligatory physical education for one or two hours a week but most sport is done after school, when parents volunteer to run clubs in anything from table tennis to dance, theatre, football, and gymnastics. The Danish hobby club habit, it's clear, starts young. 'There are lots of possibilities for kids to do different things after school – it just depends on the parents' interests,' says Karen. I tell her about American Mom who's a marketing manager by day but now coaches volleyball in the evenings and another writer who moonlights as a gymnastics assistant.

'It's a really good system and it helps teach children that volunteering is part of doing your bit for society,' says Karen. It may also contribute to parents' happiness levels.

Researchers at Stony Brook and Arizona State University found that volunteering regulates stress and releases feel-good hormones like oxytocin and progesterone. And since more than 53 per cent of all Danes undertake some form of voluntary work, there are lots of happy hormones floating about.

After *folkeskole*, children can either leave or carry on for three more years at a *gymnasium*. This is the name of the follow-on school and not, as I originally hoped, a hothouse for late-flowering gymnasts (thus dashing my Beth Tweddle dreams). At *gymnasium*, Danish pupils study for an exam to get into higher education. They celebrate graduating from *gymnasium* with a hedonistic ritual of riding around in open trucks – or, round our way, tractor trailers – wearing sailor hats and having a drink at each classmate's house until they pass out, twenty beers in, often on the beach by our house. Any Jutland parents wondering where your children are, try Sticksville.

All of these mind-expanding educational experiences are free for Danish and EU citizens – and Danes over the age of eighteen are *paid* to study, between 906–5,839 DKK (£96–619 or $163–1,051) a month, depending on your age, the kind of education you're opting for, whether or not you're living at home and how high your parents' income is. 'We believe that education is every human's right and that you shouldn't take money for it,' says Karen.

From the ages of fourteen to eighteen, Danish teens can also opt to go to an *efterskole* (or 'after school'). This is a fee-paying boarding school that will often focus on sport, drama or the arts. Around 15 per cent of Danish children go to private schools, although in Denmark, a private school isn't terribly private. The government pays two-thirds of the fees and schools are expected to adhere to some key principles of the national curriculum. As you'd expect from a social welfare state, many Danes feel uneasy about the idea of paying to give their children an advantage. As one parent of a private school pupil I know puts it rather sheepishly: 'It's all a bit anti-Jante's Law.'

Jutland's tiny toy town of Billund has had its very own fee-paying institution since 2013, when Lego, the biggest employer in the area, funded its first school. The brainchild of Lego's billionaire owner Kjeld Kirk Kristiansen, the school was set up to cater for the toymaker's growing international workforce for whom Danish schooling proved a Scandi-step too far. With an emphasis on learning through play (Danish-style) combined with the International Baccalaureate, the plan was to give the children of internationals and globally focused Danes an education that was more 'transferrable' overseas. 'We just thought that The Danish Way, with all its focus on freedom and creativity, might be making things tough for kids once they get out into the real world,' admits Private School Dad. 'The Danes can be a little ... *soft* on kids.'

This is an interesting flip side to the overwhelmingly positive response I've had so far to Denmark's education system. For all the rigor and rules and *strictness* of my own school days, we were encouraged to work hard. Could the free-and-easy Danish approach really get the same results? Or are Danish kids leaving school happy (which is great) but ill-prepared for the big wide world?

A documentary screened in Denmark in 2013 pitted a class of Chinese children against Danes of a similar age and concluded that the Nordic nation was an academic flop. Danes were furious. Many claimed that the Chinese students had been selected from one of the best schools in the country and had been coached ahead of filming. These children, critics argued, couldn't possibly be compared to an average class in Denmark where the goal is to create well-rounded free thinkers. But could there still be a worry that young, carefree Danes aren't ready for the cut-throat international labour market? Despite the new emphasis on 'understanding citizenship', do they really have the skills and discipline to survive out there? I read about students at a school in Copenhagen who are so relaxed and laid-back that social workers have started making house calls to wake them up in the morning and coax them to their *folkeskole*. This, I decide, is insane.

As someone who's been raising children and observing the sea changes in parenting and education for the past twenty years, I go back to Charlotte, mum of seven (*seven*!), for her take on the current state of affairs.

'In Denmark,' she says, 'we have an education system where teachers are just as concerned about pupils' *social development* and happiness as the school's advancement up a league table – and I think that's something we can be proud of.' But, she agrees, some aspects of the school system may have gone astray.

'In the past, parents had the responsibility for a child's upbringing and school was responsible for their learning,' says Charlotte, 'but now the state seems to like to be in charge of both.' She cites a recent memo from her school that advised parents of pupils taking exams to '*keep them regularly refreshed with trays of tea and biscuits*'. 'I mean, I'm a parent, I have seven children [*seven!*]. I'm not running around waiting on them!' I agree wholeheartedly – if anything, they should be bringing *her* biscuits, I tell her. But because both parents work all day and then shower their offspring with love and affection during their downtime, Danish children can sometimes end up a little spoilt, Charlotte says.

'We have a lot of "curling parents" in Denmark, who do everything for their kids and won't say no to them. The expression is named after the sport – only it's the parents with the brooms who keep brushing in front of their kids, removing any obstacles to make their lives easier.'

Interestingly, research published in *Social Psychological and Personality Science* found that parents who prioritised their children's well-being over their own were happier and derived more meaning in life from their childrearing responsibilities. So perhaps curling parents are doing it to make themselves feel better? Maybe, agrees Charlotte, 'but it doesn't do our kids any favours in the long run, because life's not like that.'

'So do Danish kids, their parents, and their teachers, need to toughen up a bit?' I ask.

'I don't know if I'd say they need to toughen up,' she says. 'Kids should be allowed to be kids for as long as possible, and I think it's good that they're asked their opinion about things and encouraged to consider their views and beliefs, like: "What do I like? What do I want to do? How do I feel about this? How can I solve this problem?"' Despite everything, Charlotte says that she still has a lot of trust in The Danish Way.

Karen, from the University of Aarhus, agrees and says: 'We're never going to be China, but that's OK. The labour market is changing a lot – we don't have much industry left and we don't have oil, we're not Norway. But what we do have is great creativity among our young people, so this is our top priority.' This plan of action seems to be paying off. Denmark has just been ranked second in a global talent index, second only to the USA (according to a study by the leadership advisory firm Heidrick & Struggles International).

'So Danish talent is still very much in demand?' I ask Karen.

'Absolutely. Our young people may each learn at different levels, but they'll meet the standards in the end. And be happy at the same time.'

Karen talks me through the higher education options in Denmark. 'After gymnasium, Danes often work or travel for a bit to learn about the world and its problems before starting university. You're a better student this way as you're more mature, you know how to think for yourself, how to discuss, be interested, and be critical – you're not just regurgitating the opinions of your teachers or parents.' I think of my own first year at university at the age of eighteen and how difficult I found the transition from slavish retellings of my teachers' views towards original thought and can't help feeling she may be right. Going to university at all is a luxury today in most countries, following the abolition of grants and the introduction of tuition fees. But Danes get all of this for free *and* get paid for the privilege. And because students in Denmark don't have pressing financial worries, they're free to choose a course that they're really interested in, rather than something that will guarantee them a good income in future.

'This means that they're more likely to stick at their course, work hard, and enjoy the job they get in a related field as a result,' says Karen. It's just as Lego Man told me back in February – people here don't complain about their work much because for the most part, they're doing something they enjoy in an area that they're interested in.

'After graduating from your bachelors, you might do a masters or another degree after this,' Karen goes on. 'You probably won't finish studies before the end of your twenties or early thirties – but you'll have a wealth of life experience when you enter the workplace.'

This sounds idyllic, although ludicrously generous. I wonder whether you get a free car as well on graduation. And perhaps a pot of gold... But, Karen tells me, there's trouble in tertiary educational paradise: 'There are some who want to change the way it works at the moment and the length of time people can be paid to study for. Some politicians are saying they want to make kids finish studying at 24!' She sounds outraged by such a suggestion.

As a still-in-debt thirty-something who had to waitress to pay her university tuition fees, then work two jobs to do a postgrad and *still* only finished paying off her student loan last year, I find myself green with envy at the idea of Danish students getting all of this and more *for free, forever*, or so it seems.

'But is being paid to study for so long really sustainable?' I ask.

Denmark spends more proportionally on education than any other country in the OECD club of 34 advanced nations. Venstre, the largest opposition party, suggested introducing fees in 2013 but was accused by the ruling Social Democrats of 'gambling with the welfare and equality ... we have built up over generations' – and the proposal was spiked.

'We see education as an investment in our future,' Karen explains. 'It's important to us and I think it makes our kids happier.' She's backed up by OECD studies showing that education levels can influence subjective well-being, and that Danes with tertiary education have been found to be happier than those without. Danes pay one of the highest tax rates in the world – at around 56 per cent for the top earners – but the money is put to good use, in Karen's mind at least, educating the Danes of tomorrow.

I ask Karen what she thinks of the whole happy Danes phenomenon and she tells me she's very happy: 'I have my family, my kids are doing well, I'm satisfied with my career and I have really good work. I'd say I'm an eight or nine out of ten.'

'So why not a ten?' I ask, pushing it.

'Well, you know, Jante's Law – it wouldn't seem very modest, or very *Danish*, to say a ten...'

Growing up in Denmark, I decide, is a very cushy deal indeed. From the age of six months onwards, there's a rhythm to your day, your week and the seasons – celebrating every Danish tradition. As children get older, schools offer the same safe, secure framework within which to play and explore. It must be comforting, being in the same class with the same people for a decade. No matter how unstable life may be at home, with Denmark's sky-high divorce rate, education can offer a sanctuary.

This is something I know a little about. My schooldays were by no means perfect but the regularity and structure and *sameness* of them was reassuring somehow. It was a constant, when home life wasn't always as stable as the picture-perfect families of two parents and 2.4 children depicted in TV sitcoms. My mother and I did our best to muddle through together, often with unconventional results. Who else gets a lifetime ban from Eton Wine Bar at the age of eight for setting fire to the table? Or ends up at Notting Hill Carnival when her classmates are all at gymkhanas or tap class? I wouldn't swap these experiences for anything, now. But as a kid I longed to be 'normal'. I craved 'boring'. And school was a refuge. No matter how weird life was, I always knew that there'd be sanity come Monday morning. There'd be double history with lovely Mrs Monro, break time, bells, PE (aka hiding in the changing room during cross-country in winter or pleading 'periods' to get off swimming in summer), followed by lunchtime chatathons over sloppy tuna pasta bakes and fluorescent e-number-laden orange squash.

And that was in the UK, I think. *Imagine how much fun school must be in Denmark, with all their emphasis on creativity and play and arsing about – I mean, 'expressing yourself'*... I start daydreaming speculatively.

'Were we to continue living Danishly,' I tell Lego Man

when he comes home, 'our future offspring could look forward to a rounded education, for free, up until the age of eighteen, when he or she could actually be paid to study at one of the best universities in the world.'

I show him a newspaper article I've just read showing that Denmark is the fifth best country in the world at providing higher education, according to Universitas 21, the global network of research universities.

'Only fifth?' is his reply, before heading off for a run with the dog on the beach. I realise we may have already become spoilt by Denmark.

Things I've learned this month:

1. Danish kids are very lucky indeed
2. Being a toddler here is off-the-scale fun
3. It's possible to look seriously fabulous after seven (*seven!*) children
4. There's still a lot I have to learn about parenting

9. September

Butchers, Bakers & Culture Makers

A gentle breeze lifts my hair from my neck as I look out across the sea to Sweden and inhale the salty air. The sun is shining and the sky is blue, with just a few, perfect, *Simpsons*-style clouds scudding by. I trace my fingers over a Henry Moore sculpture, the bronze warmed by the sun, as a sailboat passes, appearing in the gaps between the free-flowing forms.

'Coffee's up,' Lego Man holds two cardboard cups aloft as he walks barefoot on the soft green grass to the shade of an oak tree. I tear myself away and join him, sitting cross-legged and savouring the one caffeinated beverage that I'm currently allowing myself a day. I can almost feel the adrenaline trickling through my veins and making my brain taut and alert once more.

'This is *really* good stuff.'

'Yeah, a woman in the café told me the coffee here's legendary. Even Patti Smith dug it when she visited.'

'"*Dug*"?'

'Yes.'

'Er, the Beat generation called, they want their term of reference back...'

He narrows his eyes at me and returns to reading the guidebook we've been desecrating for the past few days, ticking off sights. It's our wedding anniversary and we're in Denmark's pocket-sized capital of just 550,000 people to celebrate. Wonderful Copenhagen has just been voted the world's best city for the second year running by Lego Man's favourite magazine so we're in town for a long weekend to refuel on culture, decent cuisine and all that Jutland has been depriving us of. I've spent some time here for work over the past nine months but we've never just hung out together and savoured it – something I promise to rectify during our minibreak. I've even left my laptop at home. Now *that's* love.

We've already visited the National Museum, the grand Royal Theatre, the futuristic-looking opera house, and the Degas exhibition at Ny Carlsberg Glyptotek – the art museum founded in the 19th century by Denmark's biggest brewer. We've made the pilgrimage to The Little Mermaid statue, walked along the Langelinie promenade, eaten '*smushi*' – a combination of the famous Danish *smørrebrød* open sandwiches and sushi – in Strøget, strolled around the Botanical Garden and watched a lot of beautiful people on bikes ('You don't get that in Jutland,' nods Lego Man at a leggy blonde pedalling past in a dress and heels. I clock her equally striking, Viggo Mortensen-alike companion and murmur appreciatively: 'Mmmm').

Now, we're kicking back at the Louisiana Museum of Modern Art, just north of Copenhagen. After filling up on

Picassos, a Giacometti, Andy Warhols and our first taste of Danish painters Asger Jorn and Per Kirkeby, we take in the gardens and watch children attempt to scale a huge Alexander Calder sculpture. *God bless Danish health and safety…* Once we've finished our coffee, we walk around some more and come across a tree festooned with slips of paper. Each one has a handwritten message on it, *Alice in Wonderland* 'Eat Me'-style, with some sort of wish or hope for the future. These range from the profound ('*world peace*') to the fantastical ('*I wish my toy gorilla would come to life*'). Before we can nose around at more people's wishes, we're press-ganged into creating our own and handed white luggage tags and felt-tipped pens to get us going. 'You can have three wishes, two personal and one political,' a woman wearing a multitude of colourful scarves tells us. Yes, even wishes have rules in Denmark. We accept the challenge and Lego Man starts scribbling away furiously. I start writing too, but I'm surprised to find that when it comes to the personal wishes, I'm stumped. If someone had asked me what I wished for a year ago, I'd have said, without hesitation, '*to write more*' and '*to have a baby*'. Sickening though it sounds, both these things appear to be happening. I no longer have a diary filled with meetings about budgets or strategies or recruitment. I just write, every day. And miraculously, we're on course to start a family in January. *Am I,* I hesitate to even dare think it, *am I … happy? Just as I am? Danish-style?*

Lego Man is already tying his wishes to the higher branches of the tree so I jot down something about looking after the people I care about, then add as a postscript, '*…but a lottery win might also be nice.*' I start fiddling with the string to make loops and hang my tags on one of the lower bows when Lego Man comes over.

'So, what were your wishes?' he asks.

'The usual,' I reply. 'Lottery, gender equality, an end to all Nicolas Cage films. Yours?'

'Oh, you know, stuff about the planet.'

'Nice,' I nod, as we wander back inside.

Copenhagen is an invigorating place. I know we're probably making the most of it because we're here for such a short time before going back to Sticksville, but just having great art and sculpture and a sea view on your doorstep must be good for the soul.

I try to talk to Lego Man as we amble around, but he's made a beeline for the eye-wateringly expensive lighting section of the gallery gift shop, making him essentially deaf to the outside world for the next half hour. *I need a cultural guide,* I think, *someone to update me on 'the scene' here.* I need, essentially, Denmark's answer to Melvyn Bragg.

Fortunately, Denmark's answer to Melvyn Bragg lives and works nearby. Adrian Lloyd Hughes (his father is Welsh but he moved to Denmark aged three) is a broadcaster and host on DR, the country's public service broadcaster, and has been making television programmes on culture for the past 30 years. I track him down online and we arrange a time to talk before I get busted by Lego Man.

'Are you *working* on our anniversary trip?' he eyes me suspiciously.

'No,' I lie, feeling guilty now. I notice he has emerged from the throng of shoppers empty handed. This is unheard of but it may just give me some leverage... 'Wasn't there another design shop you wanted to go to in town?' *Bingo!* 'I could talk to this culture expert while you looked around a bit...' We stare at each other for several seconds, neither of us wanting to blink first.

'Oh go on then,' he tells me.

'Thank you!'

The following day, I catch up with Adrian. I tell him I've been to the Louisiana and loved it and he reels off a list of more galleries and museums I should take in during my stay.

'The best Danish museums have become like theme parks, with shops and cafeterias,' he tells me. The capital's cultural offerings got a facelift in 1996 when Copenhagen was made European Capital of Culture. 'It's like when you're about to host a dinner party – you get dressed up, get fresh flowers in, do some cleaning, and get your best self ready to present to the world. The same thing happened to Copenhagen.' This was then incorporated into the infrastructure to keep the city in good nick. So how's Denmark's arts scene faring today?

'Pretty well, actually,' says Adrian. 'The arts are well supported here and the boom in Danish TV and architecture (and food) can be seen as the result of three decades of financial support.'

Danish theatres are heavily subsidised, Adrian tells me, 'and if you buy a ticket, you can probably estimate that the actual cost is twice, or even three times, what you paid.' As a result, actors usually perform to a full house. Denmark has also been adept at fostering new writing talent. Christian Lollike attracted worldwide attention for *Manifesto in 2083*, his piece based on the Oslo killer Anders Behring Breivik, and Thor Bjørn Krebs, who wrote about Danish soldiers in the former Yugoslavia, is also celebrated throughout Europe. Many playwrights come up through Aarhus Theatre's writing school where they're paid to study (naturally) and have the opportunity to see their work performed at Denmark's second largest theatre. 'Private sponsorship is also growing in Denmark,' adds Adrian, 'but most of it goes to the ballet – probably because more companies want to be associated with this glossy, beautiful world than a controversial piece of theatre about a Norwegian mass murderer.'

Discounted ticket schemes make both classical and contemporary dance in Denmark accessible to all and Adrian says that it's more popular than ever with young audiences: 'Whenever I go and see something now, I'm stumbling through rows of high school students to get to my seat.'

Opera is heavily subsidised, too, but tickets still start at around 500 DKK (around £60 or $90), 'so if you want a babysitter and to park the car somewhere you're looking at 2,000 DKK (£240 or $360) for a night out,' says Adrian. The greatest success story to come out of the Danish Opera in recent years has been Kasper Holten, now director at London's Royal Opera House, who caused a stir with his retelling of Wagner's Ring Cycle. 'He staged it with a feminist twist, making the entire production a question of male superiority versus female superiority,' says Adrian. 'The "ring" became a DNA molecule and the protagonists were literally fighting over the future of humankind – it was a huge hit.'

The Danish film industry remains one of the most successful in Europe thanks to a proactive policy of grants and support from the government. Big names still working in

Denmark today include Susanne Bier, who directed the Oscar-nominated *After the Wedding*, Thomas Vinterberg, director of 2014's *Far from the Madding Crowd*, and, of course, Lars von Trier. 'Most Danes acknowledge his genius, even though we may find him incredibly irritating,' says Adrian. Von Trier was responsible for Dogme 95 – the filmmaking movement begun in 1995 with fellow Danes Thomas Vinterberg, Kristian Levring, and Søren Kragh-Jacobsen. Its goal was to 'purify' filmmaking by following rules of production that put an end to predictable plots, superficial action and technological trickery. The rules were later abandoned but Dogme helped legitimise low-budget digital filmmaking and cemented von Trier's reputation as a controversial figure to be reckoned with.

Of course, the biggest success story of recent years has been Danish TV. I ask Adrian how this came about and he tells me it was no accident: 'A decade ago, you couldn't find a Danish TV series that made it onto anyone's radar overseas. Then the Danish Broadcasting Corporation [like Denmark's BBC] took action with a policy of fostering home-grown talent, finding out what writers wanted to work on and helping them to develop their own projects – with huge success.' With an emphasis on social realism, tense storylines and a distinctive, stylised colour palette (i.e. 'gloomy'), Danish dramas *The Killing*, *Borgen* and *The Bridge* gripped audiences worldwide and inspired remakes in the US and the UK.

'They've been a real good news story for Danish culture and they reflect a lot about us and what's important in Denmark,' says Adrian. 'For instance, series three of *The Killing* showed a Dane compromising his own family for greed.' As the plot played out, writers made it very clear that this was A Bad Thing and the wealthy businessman suffered as a consequence. In another storyline, the Danish political system was portrayed as protecting a guilty man. 'This was controversial,' says Adrian, 'but it showed that the public service broadcaster felt free to criticise those in power.' Each of the three hit series had strong female protagonists who were ambitious, sexually active, complex and flawed – reversing traditional portrayals of women on screen. 'In both *Borgen* and *The Killing*, we saw women trying to balance home and family, conscience and ambition – something that's familiar all over the world,' says Adrian.

Yet despite the homegrown hits, Denmark has a dirty little TV secret. No, not the naked lady show Helena C told me all about, but the cosy British Sunday teatime classic, *Midsomer Murders*. The Viking, Friendly Neighbour and Helena C all admit to being fans of the craggy-faced DCI Barnaby, who solves a minimum of three murders an hour, and the British import is one of the biggest shows in Denmark.

'Somehow, *Midsomer Murders* is our best-rated TV import,' admits Adrian, reluctantly. 'It's been getting a 30–40 per cent audience share for the past thirteen years – as long as it's been around.' The show is so popular in Denmark that to celebrate the anniversary of the ITV crime drama, bosses teamed up with Danish producers and stars from *The Killing* and *Borgen* for a special episode. 'I think it's because people find it soothing or something,' says Adrian. I tell him that The Viking compared the experience of watching *Midsomer Murders* with eating soup: 'It's not the most exciting thing out there but it does make you feel all warm and *hygge*.'

But aside from DCI Barnaby and his assorted sidekicks, Adrian is keen to reiterate that Danish culture is in good shape. Government subsidies mean that creativity can flourish and cut-price ticket schemes mean that more Danes than ever can afford to attend art galleries, dance or opera performances, the theatre and the cinema. The Danish Broadcasting Corporation's strategy of developing new writers has cemented Denmark's reputation as a cultural force to be recognised and helped popularise the Nordic noir genre internationally.

'And all this makes people happier?' I ask.

'I'm sure of it,' is his response. He's backed up by a study from London School of Economics that explored the top five activities that made people content. After sex and exercise, these were revealed to be attending the theatre, a dance performance or a concert, performing and going to an exhibition or museum. It seems that culture really can make Danes (or at least Copenhageners, lucky enough to live close to civilisation) more content. Interestingly, men who enjoy art, ballet and other cultural pursuits feel even happier and healthier, according to a 2011 study published in the *Journal of Epidemiology*. So is Adrian happy?

'I'd say I'm a nine out of ten,' he responds. 'I love my work – I'd do it even if I wasn't being paid – I have a lovely flat, I bike everywhere, and my only problem in life right now is deciding between getting a Steinway grand piano and a Blüthner. I mean seriously, these are First World problems.' So is there anything that would make him happier? Other than choosing the perfect piano to fit in his flat?

'Having a view of the sea,' he says straight away. 'That would bring me up to a ten.'

I decide not to mention the fact that I live by the sea and just remind myself of the things I have to be thankful for.

Reuniting with Lego Man, high on retail therapy, he announces that he has procured us two new lamps. I wince, already imagining bank manager Allan with two 'l's' admonitions at such reckless spending. On the plus side, my husband says that he also has several recommendations for where to go for lunch.

'It was weird,' he says, 'everyone I spoke to presumed I was a tourist, then when I told them I lived in Jutland, they did this funny thing with their heads,' he demonstrates a now-familiar head-on-one-side-in-sympathy pose. 'After that, they'd say, "I'm sorry". Maybe they didn't understand my accent or something...' I haven't the heart to tell him that I suspect they understood perfectly and that this is the stock response when I tell people that a) I wasn't born Danish or b) that I now live in Jutland. Instead of ripping off this particular Band-Aid, I focus on planning out our remaining mealtimes. My appetite is now back with a vengeance and I plan on making the most of the choice and quality the capital has to offer. We find Japanese, Mexican, Lebanese, restaurants with *stars*, cafés that serve *vegetables*, and menus without pictures. For someone who has been *smörgås-bored* by Jutland's food offerings (aside from the pastries) for nine months now, this feels like heaven.

'We're not in Sticksville now...' I tell Lego Man as I inhale a truffle-dust-and-powdered-mushroom dish in one of the city's smarter canal-side restaurants.

'Not a curried pork ball in sight,' agrees Lego Man as he dabs off the remnants of a peppered loin of venison from around his mouth.

Copenhagen has been having a culinary renaissance in recent years and a total of fifteen Michelin stars were awarded to thirteen restaurants in the city in 2013 – more than any other Scandinavian city. Tellingly, no restaurants outside of Copenhagen gleaned a single star and Jutland is still, for the most part, a culinary wasteland. I want to find out more about why this is and whether Copenhagen's great foodie success story has had an impact on national pride – and happiness levels – but I need some help. Enter Bo Basten, chef at Meyers Madhus and the friend-of-a-shiny-*new*-friend back in Sticksville who I promised to look up and say '*hej*' to. Before joining Claus Meyer of Noma fame at his latest emporium, Bo worked in a double Michelin-starred restaurant in Copenhagen and as a chef for the Danish royal family. In short, the man knows his stuff. Plus he looks like a cross between a Scandi hipster and Jesus. So when Lego Man spots another design shop he wants to bankrupt us in, I take the time to talk food with Bo.

'So,' I ask him after the preliminaries (aka me trying very hard not to tell him he looks like Jesus), 'has Copenhagen always been pretty good for foodies?'

He laughs. 'Ha! The answer is no. I grew up in the 70s and 80s on canned food and frozen veg. The only flavour enhancers most people knew about were fat, salt and sugar. If Danish food had been a guitarist, it would only have known three chords.'

'A bit like Status Quo?'

'Sure. We ate *smørrebrød* and junk food.'

From what I've observed, a lot of Danes still eat this way. Even the smallest village here seems to have a pizzeria or a *pølser* van serving the Danish version of the hot dog – bright red wieners baked in their very own bready prophylactic. Every outlet also attempts to sell me the abomination that is salted liquorice, a substance so alarming that it makes my mouth feel as though someone's attacking it with poisoned sandpaper.

'And what's with the whipped cream from a can?' I demand. 'It's on everything! I mean, who eats whipped cream these days? Are we at a *Chippendales* show from the 1980s?' I'm on a roll now. 'Then there are all the burger joints!' I go on, recounting how I've read that McDonald's profits are up 10 per cent year on year in Denmark. Any remaining traditional eateries, I rant, just serve open sandwiches or meatballs.

'But in the last ten years things have changed a lot,' Bo protests, 'at least, in the capital.'

Lucky old Copenhageners, I think. Again.

Bo goes on: 'Danes used to look to French and Italian cuisine, but now they can do it their own way. These days, more and more farmers and producers are trying to make unique produce with a clear Nordic identity.'

It all started in 2004 when chefs Rene Redzepi and Claus Meyer turned a former warehouse in Christianshavn into a restaurant and named it after a combination of the Danish words '*nordisk*' (Nordic) and '*mad*' (food). Noma was born and the pair vowed to eschew the traditional olive oil-and-foie gras Mediterranean ingredients being used in top restaurants at the time in favour of homegrown Danish produce. The same year, Meyer brought together fellow chefs to develop a set of principles to help Nordic food move forward. Just as Dogme 95 put the emphasis on stripping things back to basics in film, the Nordic Cuisine Symposium, as they called themselves, vowed to focus on the raw materials of cooking by using local, often foraged, seasonal produce. After an eighteen-hour-long workshop, the chefs formulated the New Nordic Kitchen Manifesto. Its outline: to express 'purity, freshness, simplicity and ethics' by prioritising 'ingredients and produce whose characteristics are particularly excellent in our climates' and helping to 'promote Nordic products and producers'.

The manifesto was taken up by lots of chefs but it's Noma that's been key to New Nordic Cuisine, says Bo. 'A lot of people laughed at Noma to begin with. They'd be like, "How can you charge people for serving them live ants?" [another favourite was sea urchin toast] But it's really opened people's eyes.' Noma was awarded first one, then two stars in the *Michelin Guide*, and has been named the World's Best Restaurant four times since 2010. The restaurant's fame hasn't automatically meant fortune and Noma still barely breaks even, employing 68 staff for just 45 covers. Because it's Denmark, even the lowliest of waiting staff gets paid a decent wage and there's a 25 per cent value added tax (known as '*moms*' in Danish) on everything. Noma is a labour of love, but Rene Redzepi recently told the newspaper *Politiken* that he felt New Nordic Cuisine had 'done its duty' – having now filtered down to more wallet-friendly eateries and even affected the capital's grocery stores.

'Supermarkets in Copenhagen started stocking better selections because people were hearing about these different ingredients,' says Bo. 'Noma chefs also combined their experience at the restaurant with their own heritage so that when they left to work somewhere else, they spread and developed the New Nordic Cuisine ethos.'

I want to get a better understanding of what this is so I ask him how he'd begin to educate someone who, just for example's sake, only knew how to boil pasta until she was in her mid-twenties.

'For me,' says Bo, 'it's about the *easiest* way to the *most* pleasure. If you have a carrot that's full of flavour and fresh and juicy, eat it raw. Don't roast it or puree it. Eating in season is also key. Think about what's outside your window and what you can grow yourself, and get to know what local produce you can get at different times of year.'

I tell him that whenever I buy Danish fruit and vegetables, they go off more quickly than I'm used to.

'That's because we haven't stuffed them with chemicals – that's a good thing!' Bo chastises me. 'In Denmark, we prefer our fruit and veg fresh.'

That's me told. I ask Bo whether he's heard about the reports claiming that Danes are the happiest nation on earth and am surprised to learn that he hasn't. 'But that makes sense. I'd say I'm an eight out of ten. Eating makes me happy.' Any foodstuff in particular? I ask.

'I can't possibly narrow it down to one,' he replies in horror, 'it would be like picking a favourite child! I just love tasting food.'

So what would make him a ten?

'Well, I'd like a new car,' he says, before backtracking, 'but I have everything else I could want already. And really, I'm happier with healthy children and a great wife than I would be with a new car.' I tell him this is lovely. I only hope that Lego Man would say the same thing, though I suspect that his response might be slightly more along the lines of *'what kind of car are we talking?'*

We say goodbye and he leaves me with a parting rally call: 'Remember – next time you go shopping it's all about seasonality. Fresh is best!'

To keep Denmark's foodie scene 'fresh', the team behind Noma and the New Nordic Kitchen Manifesto set up the Nordic Food Lab in 2008, a not-for-profit ideas laboratory to research new techniques and share findings between food academics. Working out of a houseboat moored opposite Noma in Copenhagen's harbour, the lab team experiment with flavours and explore their edible surroundings – with an emphasis on foraging. I decide to make Ben Reade, head of culinary research and development on board the houseboat HQ, my next port of call.

Ben, fresh from a field trip to Uganda, tells me he's been investigating edible insects.

'I tried some great crickets out there and learned how the locals cook them,' he says. 'It's all about getting inspiration for what we can do at home and what insects we can raise specifically to eat – like crickets, which are easy to rear. People shouldn't rule out eating insects just because we don't in our culture at the moment. Some of them, especially wild ones, are really delicious.'

'Most of what we're using are ingredients we've always had in Scandinavia, where there are very specific, but diverse climatic conditions,' says Ben. 'Danish food is very seasonal. It's not just about root vegetables in autumn, meat dishes in winter, fish in spring, shrimps in summer etc. – we're talking *micro seasons* – week to weck.' Ben lists cabbage, kale, apples, potatoes, berries, rye and other root vegetables as being especially good in Denmark. 'We don't get them for long but when we do, they're fabulous. The first time you have something in a season – like asparagus tips or hare or elderflower – it's a really special moment and something that you absolutely look forward to.'

The seasonal, *traditional* Nordic diet has been proven to be as healthy as the renowned Mediterranean diet and researchers at Sweden's Lund University found that a diet rich in fish, berries, wholegrain rye bread and good oils (like the Danish-favoured rapeseed oil), can lower levels of harmful cholesterol and protect against diabetes. The fatty acids found in oily fish such as Denmark's ubiquitous herring have long been proven to help counter depression and new studies from Aarhus University also show that the traditional Nordic diet can help lower blood pressure – something that's bound to make Danes happier.

'I think the New Nordic movement really helped people remember all the great, healthy, fresh foods we already have here that are really well-suited to the northern climates,' says Ben. 'The lesson we can take from this should be about opening your eyes to your surroundings, to the nature around you. Noma has been about a change in perception and learning to be more curious about your food – and now more and more restaurants have caught on and are doing it brilliantly.'

Which is great for everyone living in Copenhagen. But the changes haven't quite hit Jutland yet. It seems to me that there are three distinct styles of Danish cuisine on offer: 'New Nordic' (interesting, experimental, award-winning Noma et al), 'Old Nordic' (*pølsers*, pizzas and whipped cream-o-rama) and 'Traditional Nordic' (healthy, seasonal, berry-heavy, and the one all the scientists get excited about). It's my guess that 'Old Nordic' cuisine is still eaten by 99 per cent of the country.

As I make my way back to our hotel to pack up the car for home, I arrange to speak to the woman dubbed 'The Danish Delia' for an insight into what *real* people are eating on a daily basis. Trine Hahnemann is a celebrity chef who's been fronting the Danish home-cooking movement for years. I tell her I'm interested in what the average Dane is eating in, say, Jutland, for instance.

'Jutland? Jutland where?' is her response, so I tell her where I live in Sticksville-on-Sea. 'I know the area,' she says, rather ominously. 'I'd say that exactly where you're living is probably the most deprived area, food-wise, in the whole country.'

Break it to me gently, Trine...

'On the plus side, you have some of the best organic growers and producers of chicken and eggs and beers nearby in Jutland. But you probably don't see any of the produce locally where you live. It all tends to be sold to the bigger cities, like Aarhus. The staple diet where you are is probably less "New Nordic" and more pork and potatoes.'

I tell her she's bang on. 'What is it with potatoes? It's like Danes are spud-obsessed!'

'That's really a Jutland thing,' she says. 'I don't know what Jutlanders think is going to happen if they don't have potatoes every day. Sometimes they double up with some rice or rye on the side as well for a double carb hit.'

Interesting. Carbs have been proven to raise levels of serotonin, the chemical in the brain that elevates mood, according to research from MIT. *Maybe Danes are essentially popping happy pills with every potato fix*, I think, as Trine goes on:

'And these carbs are served, of course, with pork.'

I was wondering how long it would be until we got on to pork. Since my month of animal magic back in April, I've been thinking about the pigs here. Every menu we've been presented with since arriving in Denmark has been pork-heavy and we've been served a porcine variant at each home-cooked Danish dinner we've been invited to. And yet in all this time, I haven't seen a single swine in any of the vast expanses of fields and agricultural land that I drive through every day in Jutland.

Denmark is home to 30 million pigs – that's more than five times as many pigs as there are people – but they're all reared in light- and temperature-controlled barns before being transported to the slaughterhouse to meet their meatball-y fate. Every weekday, 20,000 pigs are delivered to the Danish Crown slaughterhouse in Jutland alone. Watching the process by which pigs become pork has become something of a spectator sport, with every other Dane I speak to telling me how they've been on a tour of a slaughterhouse at some point. One of The Viking's female friends even went on an office outing ahead of the company Christmas party. Yes, this is what passes for fun in Jutland.

But pork is also political in Denmark, with ministers regularly debating how far Danes should go in accommodating the growing Muslim community. This is something Trine experienced first-hand when she ran the restaurant in the Danish parliament for seven years.

'The right-wing Dansk Folkeparti would only eat in the canteen if it was serving Danish food that day,' she says. 'If we had a tandoori on the menu or something international, there'd be a no-show at lunchtime from the whole Folkeparti. Each political party also had weekly meetings where they'd have supper sent up to them and the Dansk Folkeparti ordered the same thing every week.'

'Let me guess – a classic pork-and-potato combo?'

'Exactly,' she says, 'Danish meatballs with potato salad. Every week. At least they walked the talk, I suppose.'

I'm interested to hear that even the Danish parliament all sit down and eat together wherever possible. There isn't the same culture of grabbing food on the go and eating lunch at your desk or dinner in front of the TV as there is in other places.

'We have a real tradition of eating together,' Trine tells me. Danes also tend to eat at home most evenings and weekends, apparently – which could explain why the restaurant offerings outside of Copenhagen aren't exactly inspiring. 'Most Danes only dine out for a birthday or a special occasion as it's expensive to eat out,' says Trine. This is because everyone gets paid a living wage, including the pot washer, and as with Noma, every eatery charges a 25 per cent tax on top of the bill for food and labour. But most Danes don't feel deprived by dining out infrequently. 'We enjoy eating in,' says Trine, 'it's cosy at home and we like to cook for each other.'

I wonder whether this too contributes to Danish happiness and find a study in the *American Journal of Clinical Nutrition* confirming that home-cooked meals actually make people feel better than indulgent meals eaten at a restaurant. No wonder the Danes are content.

'Having family meals together is a very important part of life in Denmark,' says Trine, something she puts down to the days when most people made a living from farming. 'You'd be working hard all day and so mealtimes were the only breaks you had. They became a strong tradition. Because we haven't had many foreigners and we're still quite a homogenous society, these traditions have stuck.'

The welfare state is another reason Danes still have an evening meal together as a family, says Trine. 'We don't work as long hours as you do in the UK or the US and it's considered important to get home to your family. It's totally acceptable for a high-flying lawyer, male or female, to say to colleagues at 5pm: "I need to leave this meeting to go and pick my kids up and make them dinner." It's part of our culture.'

She thinks that the price of Danish real estate has also played a part in keeping the sit-down dinner intact in Denmark. 'Post-Second World War, housing became more affordable, so most Danes could have a separate room to eat in. In other countries, many young people can only afford one room or a tiny apartment where there's no dining room and nowhere to sit all together. Then, of course, you *have* to go out for dinner.'

I tell her about my experiences of dinners in Danish homes to date – notably that they seem to involve three courses, napkin origami, and last until midnight. 'And that's on a school night!'

Trine laughs and admits that there is a certain pride associated with inviting someone into your home to share food in Denmark. 'Danes love to spend a whole day planning a meal, cooking and entertaining, then once all the hard work is done we like to sit and talk for hours. We don't quite have the thing you have in the UK of knowing when it's time to call it a night.'

I confide in her that our last midweek dinner guests arrived at 6pm and didn't leave until 1am. 'It was exhausting!'

'I know. But hospitality is very important in Denmark, we take pride in it and we enjoy it,' says Trine.

Does it make her a happy Dane? I ask.

'I'd say I'm an eight out of ten. We're one of the best countries in the world for the welfare state, safety, benefits and free education,' she says, before adding: 'But people still like to moan. I'm like: "Why? You have everything!"'

This is an interesting observation. I wonder whether people can ever be truly happy or whether there's something in human nature, or at least the drizzly-skied Northern hemisphere, that means we rather enjoy a bit of a moan now and then. I had assumed that this was a British thing, having a grumble about the weather, and litter, and the youth of today. But perhaps it's more of a universal truth – something that brings us together, something we can bond over, reassuring each other that life's not so perfect this end either.

Maybe complaining is an extension of Jante's Law, I think, having a mini-Eureka moment. *If there's nothing to whine about, you're essentially showing off. And no one likes a show-off. At least, not in Denmark.*

Back in Jutland, on a comedown from my cultural and culinary adventure, I retreat to the sanctuary of the local bakery to console myself with the one Danish delicacy they still get right around Sticksville: pastries. Months in and I'm still fascinated by the names of the traditional *wienerbrød*. As well as the '*kanelsnegle*' or cinnamon snail, there's the '*spandauer*', known as 'baker's bad eye' after the yellow cream in the middle that makes it look like an infected iris (delicious...) and the '*frøsnapper*' or 'frog snapper', a sort of poppy seed pastry twist (no one has any idea who came up with the name).

In one of my favourite assignments ever, I'm asked to look into the Danish pastry scene by a UK newspaper and so pin down Anders Grabow of Denmark's Bakery & Pastry Masters Association to find out whether melt-in-the-mouth *wienerbrød* might hold the key to eternal happiness (I hope so...) and why the Danes are so famed for their pastries.

'Because,' he tells me, without hesitation, 'they are awesome! When you eat as much Danish pastry abroad as I do, you know why we are famed for it. It is really ingrained [no pun intended, I presume...] in the Danish tradition and something that every bakery has made each and every day for hundreds of years.' He tells me that you have to train for three years and seven months to be a baker in Denmark. 'We take pride in the skill and craftsmanship and we make the best pastries in the world. It's called a "Danish" for Christ's sake! No one makes them like we do.'

I tell him he's very much preaching to the converted on this one. So is baking big in popular culture here too? I ask, thinking of Lego Man's *morgenmad*-making colleagues.

'Absolutely,' says Anders. 'There are lots of pastry bloggers, posting and sharing recipes, and there's been a big rise in the amateur baking scene with TV shows like *Den Store Bagedyst* ['The Great Bake Off'], Mette Blomsterberg's *The Sweet Life* and *Kagekampen* ['Cake Battle' – this sounds like my kind of battle].'

'But can the average Dane whip up a pastry, just like that?'

Anders thinks about this. 'I'd say everyone knows how to make a few Danish staples,' he says. 'And because it's Denmark, men bake too. Every Danish man will have a basic cake in his repertoire.'

This is music to my ears. I can't wait to tell Lego Man that I expect nothing less than the perfect *kanelstang* (a delicious cinnamon and marzipan plait that I've recently discovered) from him by this time next month. I thank Anders for his time, but there's one more thing I need to know before I let him go.

'And, er, in your experience,' I start, feeling myself redden, 'how *many* pastries does the average Dane eat?'

Confession time: I've been chowing down on *at least* one a day since I moved here nine months ago, with only a small hiatus during a particularly bad bout of morning sickness. Before you judge me, go to a Danish bakery and try them out. All of them. It may take a while. Nine months in fact. During which time, I have been powerless in their custardy-and-cinnamony caress.

'I mean, for instance,' I go on, 'if I'd been eating one a day…' I try to sound as casual as possible, '…would this be considered *normal*?'

His instant, unguarded response tells me everything I need to know: 'A pastry *every day*? Wow!' Then, realising he's supposed to be promoting the consumption of Danish baked goods, he back-pedals slightly: 'But then, what is a typical Dane? I'd say the typical Dane does not eat one pastry a day – though I obviously wish they would!' he jokes. 'Most Danes have them as a weekend thing. You sit down with a huge breakfast of soft-boiled eggs, fresh bread and some pastries as a treat.'

Oh.

'Mind you, it is also custom to have pastries on Fridays in the office.'

'Yes?' I seize on this.

'Then I guess there are construction workers who eat one every day…' I contemplate a career change. 'And then there are the health nuts who wouldn't dream of eating pastry.' I decide I'm not so keen on this lot. 'But on average, a Dane eats a pastry once or twice a week.'

'So unequivocally not,' I want to clarify for the sake of my arteries, 'every day?' I'm still hoping he'll contradict me.

'No, not really,' he says. 'Because of our health.'

'Yes. Quite.'

Having said goodbye to Anders, I stare longingly at a display of assorted *snegles*, begin to salivate slightly, then leave with a loaf of rye bread instead, feeling worthy.

I get home to an empty house. Lego Man's car is in the drive but there's no sign of him or the overexcited mutt who normally likes to whip my legs with his tail while circling me for several minutes by way of a 'welcome home' greeting.

Savouring half an hour of peace, I settle down to type up my notes and contemplate doing something creative with rye bread for supper. To my surprise, I find that my laptop has already been powered up. On rousing the screen from its slumber, I see a slew of pages on foraging, including '*A Guide to the Wild*', '*What's in Season: September*' and the Nordic Food Lab's '*Guidelines to Sustainable Foraging*'.

Oh God...

I thought Lego Man had perked up when I told him about Ben and the Nordic Food Lab's boy scout-esque wilderness adventures. I might have guessed that he'd try to recreate the drama of eating ants/crickets/god-knows-what-else back on home turf.

Worrying about what on earth's in store for dinner tonight, I keep an eye out of the window in the hope that he and his faithful dog will return home soon, preferably unscathed. Another hour later, two figures appear on the horizon. One: tall, broad, wearing wellies and ruddy-cheeked from his endeavours. The other: small, yappy, woolly tail wagging. As they approach the house, Lego Man lifts a black plastic bag, the kind we normally use for picking up dog poo. He holds it aloft above his head like a trophy. The other hand, complete with dog lead, follows it up in slow motion. I can almost hear the Bill Conti *Rocky* soundtrack playing as he executes a double air punch, triumphant. I'm as pleased that the dog's bowels are working properly as the next pet owner, but really?

Lego Man has a wide grin on his face and passes by the wheelie bin before coming into the house with his bounty.

'You're not bringing *poo* into our kitchen are you?' I ask, horrified, eyeing the bag. 'I think even the Nordic Food Lab draw the line at that...' I start but he opens the plastic sack and shows me what's inside. 'Clams?' I ask, nose wrinkling slightly at the strong odour of sea that's just swept into our house.

'Yes! I found a mussel bank! On the beach.'

'What?'

'It was low tide and I saw this island a little out to sea. It looked like a load of pebbles but the dog went for it, so I followed him.'

'Right...'

'Only it wasn't pebbles – it was mussels!'

'Wow. And so you just,' I'm not sure of the right term here, '...*picked* them?'

'Yes! I wasn't sure if you needed a license or something—'

'—Well, this *is* Denmark—'

'—Exactly, but there was no one around so I filled my pockets.'

I look down and notice for the first time the bulging sides of Lego Man's trousers, complete with wet patches threatening to meet in the middle of his groin.

'But then I thought, "poo bags!"' he goes on, 'so I filled this, too.' He jangles the bag to illustrate. 'I reckon I've got enough for dinner here.'

This all sounds lovely but I'm slightly concerned that he

might end up with food poisoning. I delicately opt out of a foraged supper on account of our unborn child and the loaf of worthy rye bread I've got to work through as Lego Man sets about scrubbing and de-bearding several dozen barnacled black shells.

'Are you sure they're safe to eat?'

'Yeah, as long as they're tightly closed and then open when you cook them, apparently, they're usually fine.'

'"*Usually*"?'

Lego Man nods as he scrubs: 'I Googled it. There's a *very* small chance of diarrhoea, vomiting, paralysis or death—'

'Oh good.'

'—but that's only in extreme cases of *neurotoxicological poisoning*.'

'Great...'

Lego Man once dated a doctor and I sometimes suspect that his gung-ho attitude to illness is down to a secret belief that he's actually *done* the seven years of medical training himself.

'Anyway,' he nods at the mussels as he scrubs at them with the kitchen brush despite my pleas, 'you'd pay a lot of money for these in a shop.'

Half an hour later and we're sitting down together to eat. Me: an open sandwich of cheese and tomato on black rye bread. Hunter-gatherer: a steaming bowl of mussels cooked in what I have to admit is a delicious-smelling white wine and shallot sauce of his own creation and garnished with home-grown parsley. Ben, Bo and Trine would be proud.

'So, what's the verdict?' I enquire, as Lego Man slips in a shell-full of his first foraged seafood.

He pauses, closing his eyes rather dramatically and savouring the moment, before answering: 'Perfect!'

'Good.' I smile at the strangeness of it all: we'd never have imagined ourselves going so native in Scandi-land this time six months ago, let alone this time last year in London. 'Happy?' I ask. Lego Man eyes me suspiciously.

'Are you asking me because you really care or are you just using me as research material?'

'Both?'

'OK then. Well,' he looks around, at his design-festooned home, his sea view, his faithful, if scruffy, dog, and his bowl of home-foraged food, 'I'd say I'm a nine out of ten.' He reaches a white wine, shallot and mussel-smeared hand across the table and rests it on mine and we both feel a little warm and fuzzy inside.

Things I've learned this month:

1. Copenhageners get all the best food in Denmark
2. Ditto cultural offerings
3. ...and lighting shops
4. I am living in a culinary black hole, apart from the foraged seafood and pastries (which I shall henceforth only be sampling twice weekly. Sad face.)
5. It's A Good Thing that food goes off so quickly here, as this means it's fresh
6. Living Danishly is making Lego Man happy
7. ...and maybe, just maybe, I'm coming around to the place, too

10. October

In Sickness & in Health

After Lego Man's foray into foraging and having learned that the traditional, seasonal Nordic diet is one of the healthiest in the world, we're feeling pretty good about living Danishly as we plough towards winter. In fact, with morning sickness in retreat and a newfound energy, I'm feeling remarkably well in general. Although I'm not pounding the treadmill in a gym as I used to, I'm getting more fresh air and exercise than ever before – walking the dog or embarking on non-Lycra-necessitating bike outings. And because we're dining at home most nights (due to dire restaurant offerings in our part of Jutland – thanks for the reminder, Trine), we're eating more healthily too.

But then Lego Man has to go away for work, and I'm left behind with just the dog and deadlines for company. I've been advised not to travel until after my due date now, which means I won't see family or old friends for a long time, unless they come to me. I'll miss my cousin's wedding and several big birthdays. It also means that the decision about where to have the baby has been taken out of our hands. We're staying until the end of January, when we'll have to decide how we feel about a second year of living Danishly.

I've got a few months of 'research' left to go, and luckily, with a fortnight of maternity-related medical appointments ahead of me, I'm about to become a lot better acquainted with Denmark's healthcare system. It all starts with a visit to meet my midwife in The Big Town.

'Your lady cave looks *very* fine,' a large woman with flaxen hair scraped back into a ponytail tells me. She has big, fleshy hands that look as though they could deliver twelve sets of twins an hour if necessary.

'My "*lady cave*"?' I think back to GCSE biology but am pretty sure I've never heard this phrase before. She gives my abdomen a prod by way of explanation. 'Ah, my "*womb*"?'

'Sure...' she frowns as she carries on scanning. I'm lying on a wooden table with cool jelly smeared across my middle as the baby is checked for abnormalities. Between my still-limited Danish vocabulary (despite months of lessons) and the midwife's amusing memory lapses when it comes to English gynaecological terms, we're muddling through.

'And here is the, how do you say, "mother's cake"? Big thing. Feeds the foetus.'

'"*Placenta*"?'

She nods: 'That. It is looking *quite great*.'

Having never given much thought to what my internal organs look like, I'm relieved to hear that they're satisfactory, though I'm slightly alarmed that innards are now subjected to the same visual appraisals as the rest of the female form (*What if I have fat kidneys? Or a wrinkly brain? Oh, wait...*). I make a mental note to go home and Google what a 'normal' womb and placenta look like as the midwife sets down her tools and addresses me face on: 'Now, what about sex?' I wasn't expecting this.

'What *about* sex? Shouldn't we be having it? Should we be having *more* of it?'

'I mean, do you want to know the sex? Of the baby?'

Aha! 'Um, well, can you tell? I mean, if you can see either way, maybe tell me, but otherwise don't worry...' For someone who's paralysed by indecision over what to have for lunch most days, a choice on this scale is, frankly, terrifying.

The midwife pokes around a bit more: 'Hmm ... labia or scrotum ... scrotum or labia...' she muses, tilting the screen in my direction. All I can make out on the black and white fuzzy image is something that looks a lot like a blob of papier mâché mix. 'What do you think?' She asks. I have no idea. So she answers for both of us: 'I think ... *scrotum*.'

'You "think"?' *Is this roll-out-the-blue-bunting time? Should I be buying books on how to raise boys? Will I need some sort of coaching to work out how the heck the only daughter of a single mum who went to an all-girls school can possibly parent a miniature male?*

'I am ... 80 per cent sure there is a...' She proceeds to do some elaborate charades to indicate that she thinks it's a male foetus, including a particularly vivid mime for 'penis'.

Once I've re-robed and mentally adjusted for the fact that it's '80 per cent likely' our child is male, we sit down to discuss The Birth.

'So, pain,' she kicks off.

I look around for an escape route but remember that the only door in here was locked in case of interruptions. Instead, I stare helplessly at government information posters showing the various things that can go wrong during childbirth and the alarming row of metal implements glinting at me from the windowsill. *Just. Breathe*. I coach myself.

'OK,' I quiver. 'I'd like everything they've got, please.'

'Right then,' she sits, pen poised above my notes. 'I will write, "*oxygen as a last resort*".'

I wonder whether I've heard her right.

'"*Oxygen*"? What about an epidural?'

What I'm really hoping for is some new out-of-body-experience-causing (but entirely safe) general anaesthetic to be discovered in the next three months that will render any agony obsolete.

'The "princess stick"? Oh, we don't like to use that if we can help it.'

'Sorry, "*princess stick*"?'

'That's what we joke about epidurals!'

I'm not laughing. 'Real Danes', it turns out, don't need epidurals. 'Princessy types' may have a mini-epidural if absolutely necessary but are only given half measures, 'so you can feel enough pain to push,' she tells me. 'I will make a note in your file that you request this. Then when you arrive, they'll know you're an anxious mother-to-be.' Brilliant. I'm already a princessy, anxious, Viking *failure*. And there are still months to go. *Sheesh*.

'So I have to give birth with just *half* an epidural, gas and air?'

'Oh no, we don't do gas.'

'What?'

'We don't think it's very good. What we can offer you is a bee sting.'

This doesn't sound promising, but I'm desperate.

'*OK...?*'

'This is where we prick you with a needle in the back of the hand so that you're distracted from the big pain by a smaller, different pain...' she trails off at this point, possibly put off by my expression that I suspect conveys something along the lines of, '*If anyone does that to me, I will punch them in the face.*'

'...but perhaps we'll just stick to air and the mini princess stick, for now...'

I leave, traumatised, and seek out cake with Helena C for consolation. I explain about pain-reliefgate and she nods knowingly, telling me that she gave birth to both her girls with nothing but an iron will and profanity-laden threats to divorce her husband. I'm in shock.

'So are Danes quite anti-drugs?'

'That depends,' she tells me, 'on the drugs.'

Danes, I discover, have the highest levels of antidepressant use in Europe according to the OECD. It's thought that the increasing 'work stress' I learned all about back in February, as well as the use of medication in milder cases could explain the rising consumption levels.

'Of course, we're also fairly relaxed when it comes to non-prescription drugs, too,' Helena C tells me. Jutland teens, I learn, tend to 'dabble' a fair bit because 'it can be a bit boring growing up here.'

Danes demonstrated their liberalism in 2013 when the country's first state-funded drug consumption rooms opened in Copenhagen. The initiative hit the headlines worldwide but most Danes didn't get too het up about it and there are now rooms in each of Denmark's main cities and some smaller towns too. Locals haven't put up much opposition and police steer clear of the safe rooms, the theory being that giving users a safe place to take drugs will prevent deadly overdoses. The plan is thought to be working, although statistics to prove this are pending. The whole approach is in marked contrast to Sweden's strict zero-tolerance policy – something that's earned them one of the lowest illicit drug consumption rates in Europe but led to a high number of drug-related deaths, as addicts fear seeking help for overdoses.

'So I can't have a full epidural, but I *can* take smack?' I ask Helena C.

'It looks that way, yes,' she tells me.

Strangely, the Danes' liberal attitude to non-pregnancy related drugs doesn't extend to remedies for the common cold, as I found out when Lego Man was laid up with man flu the week before last. There are no Lemsip or Night Nurse equivalents and my attempts to procure paracetamol were rewarded with a single, dolly-sized packet sufficient to soothe the fever of a very small hamster. This, I learn, is because a teenage girl took too many some years back and so the state clamped down on the amount that could be sold in any one transaction without a prescription. When something similar happened in the UK, the limit was set at sixteen in the shops and 32 in pharmacies. But in Denmark, it's ten. *Ten!* Just enough to get you through a single day before you have to drag your delirious, fever-addled body back for more. There are, however, ways around this. During my last exchange at the local pharmacy, the woman behind the counter took pity on me and told me that she could only sell me ten without a prescription, unless it was 'an *emergency*'.

I was just about to accept the micro-dose and be on my way when she lowered her chin and looked up at me knowingly. '*Is* it an emergency?' She tilted her head and nodded slightly, coaxing me to agree.

'Er ... yes?'

'So you're *telling me* that this is an emergency?' She asked again, nodding slowly.

'Well, no,' I started to panic under the pressure, 'not really, it's just man flu—' The pharmacist shook her head furiously until I corrected myself: 'I mean, *yes*, yes it is. It's *definitely* an emergency.'

'Great!' She beamed, before handing over *two* mini packets. 'Feel better soon!'

In spite of the odd generous pharmacist, Viking spirit dictates that Danes stick to natural remedies wherever possible when it comes to minor ailments. 'We tend to make do with hot tea, *hygge*, and maybe some schnapps,' Helena C tells me.

Ah, booze. I suspected it wouldn't be long before this came up in a discussion about health in Denmark.

'Danes drink a lot. And I mean A Lot,' says Helena C. I tell her that this is something I'd gleaned during my first week here. There's a running joke that the reason Danes seem so happy when they fill in Eurobarometer surveys is that they're always drunk. Danes are among the highest drinkers in Europe, according to the World Health Organization (WHO), consuming 11–12 litres of pure alcohol per person per year. And Danish teenagers drink nearly twice as much as other Europeans their age (so say WHO reports). I can feel an empathy hangover coming on just thinking about it. Studies from the Danish National Centre for Social Research show that young people in Denmark are learning how to drink from their parents' approach to alcohol, characterised as 'controlled loss of control'. In other words, Danes are very ordered and controlled – until they're *not*. Until it's a planned party, or a Friday night, or there's an event with schnapps involved. Then, they let their Viking tresses down and things get messy (and I'm British – I *know* messy). 'It's like we reserve the right to damage ourselves by drinking too much if we want to, and we don't always think about the impact,' Helena C tells me.

The same is true of sex here. Despite Denmark's prowess as a nation of sexually liberated Scandis, as I found out back in July, Danes aren't always careful. A recent YouGov survey placed Denmark in the top spot for STI's in Europe and a recent survey from the Danish health authority found that only 56 per cent of 18–25 year olds used a condom the last time they slept with a new partner.

Another health contradiction is smoking in Denmark. Once I'd got over the shock of seeing people smoking while cycling on their daily commute to work, I began to notice that every second Dane I encountered was partially obscured by a small grey cloud. Danes smoke with zeal and tobacco use in Denmark has been found to be a contributing factor to approximately 14,000 deaths a year, according to WHO. The World Cancer Research Fund awarded Denmark another 'first' in 2012 when it was discovered that women here have the highest rates of lung cancer in the world, and Denmark also tops the overall worldwide cancer charts for all types of cancer in both sexes.

'You see people smoking everywhere here, even outside hospitals,' comments American Mom when I get her take on this as a fellow 'outsider'. 'I went in for a check-up with my daughter and there was this guy pushing past us on the way out, wheeling his IV drip, barely able to walk. Then the first thing he did when he got into the fresh air was to light up a cigarette. You'd never see that in the US.' I confess to her that this is something you see a fair bit in UK.

'That's because your healthcare's free as well!' she rails. 'You take it for granted, you think the state will sort you out!'

This last part is true – most Danes, and probably Brits too, do think that a free national health service will take care of them if they really need it. But are Danes taking their *health* for granted?

I ask The Viking what he thinks when he joins Helena C and me later on for dinner.

'No! Not "*for granted*", he scoffs at first, before ordering a beer and a burger. 'OK, sure there's a lot of smoking and drinking—'

'—And unprotected sex,' I add, helpfully.

'—Yes, and that,' he concedes.

'—And drugs,' adds Helena C.

'Well, yes, we do them too…' The Viking wasn't expecting to have to field attacks from his countrywoman as well. But then Danes do love a good debate.

'—And you eat a lot of fatty food,' this last one slips out at the precise moment the waitress comes over and slides a juicy burger on to the table next to us. 'Sorry,' I murmur in their general direction.

'OK, so maybe we're not the *healthiest*,' admits The Viking, 'but we're individuals, we should have the choice.' He attempts to persuade me that, sure, Danes drink enthusiastically and smoke rebelliously, but that they're *enjoying* it, so everything's OK. 'There's no stigma, you can decide for yourself, see?'

'I think what it really boils down to is that we know we're covered whatever happens,' says Helena C. 'More so than in the UK, even, because we have extra social welfare to help us out if anything goes wrong – we're looked after. This may make us a little complacent, I think.'

Attempts are under way to encourage Danes to take more responsibility for their own health. Some *kommunes* now bill patients who miss doctor's appointments or cancel with less than 24 hours' notice – something that they hope will also drive down doctor's waiting times.

'It used to be pretty bad,' Helena C tells me. 'People would just book a time to see a doctor then feel OK again and not turn up. It meant you could never get a time at some clinics and it cost the government a lot of money. Now, you have to remember to go.'

Since 2003, Denmark has also had an e-health database. Whereas the UK's abandoned patient record plans cost British taxpayers £10 billion (or $17 billion) and counting, according to parliament's public spending watchdog, the Danish system cost £6.6 million ($11 million) to set up and its reach is growing year on year. My yellow Danish CPR – or ID – card has a number on it that I use to log in to a special site that contains all of my medical records. There, I can choose which doctor or nurse I'd like to see, ask any questions and get repeat prescriptions. The medical bods can then access all of my information and history on the Danish Health Data Network via my personal ID.

'Studies show that patients who are well-prepared and feel co-responsible and invested in their own healthcare feel happier and healthier,' says Morten Elbæk Petersen, director of the country's e-health database, Sunhed.dk, when I get in touch to find out more. Denmark's answer to Hugh Grant (*Four Weddings*-era) is all floppy hair, Scandi cheekbones and tweed, but with nineteen years at the top of Danish healthcare, Morten is a man in the know.

'The e-health system is a cheap way to make people feel comfortable and keep them out of hospitals,' he tells me, 'and we can then use the rest of the money in the government's budget on roads, education etc.'

The plan to make Danes more accountable for their own health shows signs of working – if slowly. Despite the ridiculously high numbers of smokers I see out and about, OECD figures show that the proportion of Danes lighting up has more than halved from 45 per cent in 1990 to 20 per cent in 2010. The government is also tackling the country's cancer problem by getting better at screening – with women aged 50–69 being offered mammograms every other year since 2007 and colon cancer checks every two years since 2014. Morten insists that Danish healthcare is in a good place: 'In Denmark, we spend 12 per cent of our GDP on healthcare that works well, is efficient and is for *everyone*. In the US, for example, they spend 18 per cent of their GDP on healthcare but there's no equality or sharing – so some people have nothing.' The UK spends just 9.6 per cent, according to WHO figures.

There's a lot of interest in the Danish system from the Obamacare lobby, and Morten regularly meets with supporters in the US, keen to find out more. But many Americans remain reluctant to share their personal information. 'A lot of people still hate the idea of the public sector seeing or owning their data,' says Morten. 'Some people think the whole thing sounds too much like communism, that it makes you "unfree". But actually, you're freer and safer if people are well looked after – if you know your neighbour can get the treatment he needs if he gets sick, he's not going to become desperate and rob you. Any time, anywhere access to personal clinical data empowers people – and for me there's no doubt that there must be connections between this and Denmark's high score on the happiness index.'

This is all sounding splendid. But could it work anywhere outside of the tiny land of 5.5 million people and 50 per cent taxes? Morten thinks so.

'Australia is rolling out a personally controlled electronic health system like ours in a few years to their population of 20 million. There are five different states with strong boundaries there so in that way it's like five Denmarks, all working together.'

Another area that Danes seem to excel in is research. A staggering number of new medical and pharmaceutical finds come out of Denmark and in the last week alone Danish scientists have made the headlines for new discoveries about asthma, vitamin B12 and preventing heart attacks, to name but three. 'We have good databases that go back in time and provide resources for research,' Morten tells me when I ask why this is, 'plus the university hospitals here *really are* dedicated to research. Because it's free to study, there's always new work being done and so new findings and discoveries. And the results get used. Cures and treatments can go into practice very quickly in Denmark. This feeds back into the public who can see things improving due to the advancements in medicine and so people are happier to cooperate in studies and pay their taxes to fund the system – and so it goes on.'

Although I'm still not sure that living Danishly long term is necessarily good for your health, I'm feeling reassured that things are heading in the right direction. I'm also beginning to get my head around the Danes' libertarian attitude to life. They cherish their freedom to indulge every whim and really enjoy themselves, safe in the knowledge that they'll be looked after if (or rather, *when*) anything goes wrong. It's a bit like the school system and even the job market here – the individual has freedom within safe boundaries. Danes have a choice about what to do with their bodies, their minds, and their careers, but they agree to work together towards a collective goal: maintaining and championing The Danish Way.

To round off my month of medical discoveries, I call Niels Tommerup from the Department of Cellular and Molecular Medicine at the University of Copenhagen. I explain about my project and ask if he thinks there could be something else, something more fundamental, something *in the genes* that helps Danes to be so content.

'As a geneticist, I'd say that everything is genetics, especially mood,' Niels tells me. 'Genetics affect your basic disposition, whether you're optimistic or pessimistic. There are people out there who are just *always happy*. Even if you throw a brick at them.' I'm hoping he hasn't put this to the test during the course of his studies. But then the Danes *are* a hardy bunch.

So what does he make of the worldwide happiness studies that keep putting Danes at the top. Could the good people of Denmark just be naturally happier than folk from other countries?

'Yes and no,' is Niels' diplomatic response. 'It's difficult to isolate genetics from cultural factors and the total genetic effect on well-being is estimated to be in the order of 50 per cent – i.e. the other half is contributed by the environment. But even if you say Danes are happy due to environmental and cultural factors, you can still ask: "Why did the Danes establish this culture? Is it something to do with the Danish disposition? Did the social democrat movement come about because we're all *related* genetically, so that we feel obliged to take care of each other, just as you'd look after a poor relation in your family?" It's a hen and egg situation.' Danes love a hen and egg analogy. The few times I've suggested 'chicken' as an alternative, it's scrambled their brains. 'There's also a study showing a correlation between the genetic distance within a country and its well-being, even when factors like GDP per capita are taken into account,' Niels continues. 'And Denmark is the country with the *least* genetic distance between the population, because we've had less migration historically.' In other words, the Danes are an insular bunch who haven't moved around or mated much with people from neighbouring nations and this has made them, weirdly, far happier than the rest of us. 'A homogenous population is more likely to be more content and trust each other because we're closely genetically related – like a family.'

This is a rather uncomfortable revelation – the idea that cultural isolation makes you more content. *How's a girl supposed to integrate and get in on the 'happy Dane' deal if she's not really wanted as an 'outsider'?* The answer seems too dark to contemplate. But Niels' point about Denmark being 'like a family' does make sense – and sounds a little more palatable. In all but the most dysfunctional *Dynasty*-meets-*Jerry Springer* style families, people *do* look out for each other. And if the whole of Denmark is essentially related, it's no wonder that living here can occasionally feel like an extended episode of *The Waltons* (if the Waltons wore cooler glasses and did their darning in designer chairs. Less Amish chic, more minimalist Zen).

A study from the University of Warwick into happy Danes also found that the greater a nation's genetic distance from Denmark, the lower the reported well-being of their inhabitants. *So Danes are so damned happy that the more closely related your country's population is to them, the jollier you'll be?* I marvel. *This is incredible!*

There's another humdinger, too. Niels tells me that studies have shown that there may be a specific 'happy gene'.

'It's called the 5-HTT, or the "serotonin-transporter gene", and it's a major target of many drugs aimed at mood regulation. The 5-HTT gene affects how your brain handles neurotransmitters and there have been huge population studies showing the relation between your mood and whether you have the long form of this 5-HTT gene. And if you look at the frequency of long-form 5-HTT worldwide, Denmark comes out on top. The Danish population as a whole has been shown to have higher levels of the gene – we score in the top percentages in the world along with Holland.'

Hang about, so an elongated 5-HTT gene will make you happier than the average Joe and most Danes have just *got it*? This is amazing. But where does it leave the rest of us? Those not fortunate enough to have been born with the white cross of the *Dannebrog* going through us like a stick of rock? Does this mean I've been trying to live Danishly, all in vain? Niels reminds me that the genetic effect only accounts for 50 per cent.

'So there's still a 50 per cent chance that I can get happy, Danish-style?'

'Yes.'

'OK...' I cling on to this and ask Niels if he thinks that he's 'genetically happy'. He tells me: 'I'm sure of it. I'm a very happy person. I'd say I'm an eight or nine out of ten. It's a privilege to be Danish, I feel lucky to have been born here. We are a good nation with great culture and wealth. If we lose to the Swedes in soccer or get depressed for five seconds, it's nothing.'

I'm pleased for him. Really, I am (can't you tell?). But I hang up the phone with a sigh, resigning myself to the fact that I've only got a 50 per cent chance of nailing this Danish happiness thing. I attempt to console myself by walking the dog, in the hope that the exercise will release feel-good endorphins. On the way home, I pick up 50 per cent of my new weekly *snegle* quota, in the hope that the stodge will release feel-good serotonin. Health and happiness Danish-style is, I decide, all about balance.

With Lego Man away for another week, I get roped in to attending October's major event solo. This is the highlight of the Jutland calendar: the closing of Legoland for winter. To understand quite the impact that this has on the local community, you just need to look around at all the harassed-looking parents of small children, now desperately wondering how on earth they're going to fill their weekends and entertain their little darlings during the long winter ahead. American Mom is already frantically trying to arrange playdates and stockpiling *Dora the Explorer* DVDs.

As a final hoorah before the region goes into a state of mourning for the much-treasured theme park, there's a closing party to mark the end of the season. I'm hoping for a *Dirty Dancing*-esque end-of-season bash, complete with singing, choreographed dance routines and Patrick Swayze. So it's a disappointment to find that the reality is rather less glamorous and involves far fewer rippling torsos.

Wearing wellies and Lego Man's parka, the only coat that now fits me, I stand holding a bottle of fizzy water in one hand and clutching a sparkler in the other. Rain threatens to put out the latter at any moment, as though even the sky is sad that Legoland is closing. I hasten to write my name in air with the cascade of spitting fire before it's extinguished by drizzle. Fortunately my name is fairly short. A Danish girl called 'Karen-Margrethe' standing next to me is, frankly, buggered.

The rides are all open for a final adrenaline rush, but

from the 'Polar Express' to the teacups, not one of them allows pregnant women on them. I'm stuck holding the coats and the hands of small children as the rest of the grown-ups get giddy and gently sozzled on Carlsberg. In Denmark, walking around a children's theme park with a Danish beer in hand is seen as patriotic, rather than provocation for an ASBO.

It's getting cold now. My cheeks are burning, my fingers are tingling and my hair follicles are standing to attention, *Hellraiser*-style. So I'm relieved when Private School Dad spots me, waves, and tells me we're on the move to watch the end-of-season fireworks.

'Come on, they're lighting the rockets,' he says, wobbling towards me with roller coaster sea legs. He downs his bottle of Carlsberg and puts it into his toddler's nappy bag to recycle later on. *Living the Danish dream*, I think. We follow the crowd, now shuffling towards the open space at the end of the theme park, to marvel at the display. Or at least try to. In the rain. When only half of them will light.

'*Oooooh!*' We make the sounds expected of us as I inhale the aroma of charcoal and sulphur.

'*Ahhhh!*' A fountain of gold spills from the inky black sky and specks of rain (or are they pieces of firework detritus?) fall into our eyes. A few children start crying, either from the noise or the optical assault, and are bundled up and edged out. Catherine Wheels whizz, signifying that the pyrotechnics are coming to an end, and there is clapping and whooping before all is dark and still once more. The season is over. Legoland, the sole attraction in my particular corner of Denmark, is done for another year. All around me, parents are packing up their shivering children, ready to ship out.

'Even the penguins leave for winter,' Private School Dad tells me, blowing on his hands to try to keep warm.

'Are you joking?' I ask hopefully.

'No, really – it gets *that* cold.'

I don't want a fight on my hands but I can't help pointing out that penguins are from the Antarctic. 'Surely it gets a bit nippier there than in *Denmark*?'

Private School Dad looks at me, tilting his head to one side quizzically. 'This is your first full winter here, isn't it?'

'Yes...?'

He shakes his head and gives a slightly menacing chuckle: 'Good luck!'

I wonder what's in store, and how on earth I'm going to get through it without wine.

Things I've learned this month:

1. Vikings are tougher than penguins when it comes to surviving the Danish winter
2. Healthcare in Denmark is high tech
3. ...but that doesn't mean Danes are terribly healthy
4. ...instead, they reserve the right to abuse their own bodies in any way they see fit, safe in the knowledge that the state will pick up the pieces
5. Midwifery in Denmark is Old School
6. My mother gave me a *distinct advantage* in life when it comes to sparkler spelling. Bad luck all you triple-plus-syllabled lot...

11. November

'Here comes the Snow/ Sleet/Soul-destroying Darkness...'

It's extraordinary how quickly it has happened. The air turned black, a cold wind shook what was left of autumn's leaves off the trees and huge, icy raindrops fell from the sky, unannounced.

Suddenly, the outside world has become menacing: brimming with *weather* that seems as though it's out to get you from the moment you open your front door.

The country has been dunked, mercilessly, into the new season and we're on course to experience our first full Nordic winter in its endurance-test entirety. It is bitter out there. The kind of brutal cold that makes your forehead freeze with the effects of nature's Botox and your eyes scrunch up to shield your irises from the chill. Driving home from the supermarket one afternoon, I wonder whether the thermometer on my car has broken as the needle droops despondently to the left and hovers around the minus twenty mark. I give the dial a tap (the universally accepted method of 'fixing' any mechanical item, along with 'hitting it' and 'turning it on and off again'), but it does not move. As I drive along the harbour, I see children who look as though they've been inflated in puffed-up padded onesies taking tentative steps off the pontoon and *onto the sea*. One boy is a good twenty yards out, standing and waving from the middle of the fjord. I blink, in case the cold's playing tricks on me or I really am witnessing the second coming of the Messiah in an Adidas snowsuit. Then I notice the cloudy, opaquely swirled surface of the sea. Could it be? Is it now so damn cold that the *sea* has frozen over?

We're not in NW6 any more, Toto, I think and find myself feeling nostalgic for the insulating smog of London in winter. As if to rub it in, the Danish public radio station starts playing Billy Idol's *Hot in the City*.

'Is this some sort of sick joke?" I wail to no one as I follow the snow plough, careful not to stray from its tracks. I couldn't leave the house this morning until the tractor had been round to clear the roads, my red mobility tomato being ill-equipped to tackle two-foot-high powdery drifts, despite the winter tyres. Fortunately, there was plenty to occupy me until then, since all residents in Denmark are legally obliged to shovel snow from the area in front of their house in case someone slips over. Friendly Neighbour was kind enough to inform us of this fact before she sped off to Copenhagen to sit out the worst of the weather and asked whether we'd mind doing hers as well. Danes must clear the entire property-width of their pavement and keep it snow-free from 7am until 10pm (on Sundays you're allowed a lie-in and can wait until 8am to start shovelling). This, apparently, is a non-negotiable civic duty and the newspapers run daily pictures of the Danish prime minister doing hers – the implication being that if she can run the country and still manage to shovel snow, the rest of us have no excuse. Face burning, nose dripping, and 'helped' by the dog, wearing a full white beard of snow as he attempted to *eat* his way through the drifts, I finally got our drive clear while Lego Man tackled Friendly Neighbour's. But no sooner was the snow cleared than a white blanket started to settle again.

By the time I get home, it's a winter wonderland once more.

It's also dark.

Again.

Once I've made it inside and thawed out sufficiently, I peer out into the thick black nothingness for five minutes and estimate that it is now 'evening'.

'OK dog, this means it's probably dinner time ... right?'

The dog nods and starts to dribble before prancing around, whinnying slightly and lashing his tail with glee as though he's pulled the wool over my eyes in some way. *Weirdo*.

I reason that I might as well start supper too and stare blankly into the fridge for inspiration before retrieving a raw chicken. I'm just holding its chilly pink carcass in my hands, frowning at the controls on the Danish oven, when Lego Man arrives home.

'What are you doing?' (It's not his fault: he didn't have a TV growing up. He hasn't watched enough US sitcoms to know that 'Honey, I'm home! How was your day?' is a more conventional matrimonial greeting.)

'"Hello" to you, too. I'm making dinner.'

'Now?'

'Yes.'

'You do know it's only 4pm?'

'Oh.' I did not know this. I should really start wearing a watch. The bird gets a reprieve and we decide to walk the dog instead. Not as easy as it sounds when your dog is black, the sky is black, and you live in an area untroubled by streetlamps or defined paths. Add in a skewed centre of gravity from being eight months pregnant, some precariously icy undergrowth and a total disconnect with feet you haven't seen for weeks, and dog walking gets ramped up from 'gentle activity' to 'extreme sport'. One wrong step could send me tumbling into woodland/mud/sand/dog mess left by previous walkers. Torches don't really cut it against the all-absorbing darkness so we spend most of the time swinging them about, pretending we're Mulder and Scully in *The X-Files* or holding them underneath our chins and doing ghost impressions.

Our neighbours are nowhere to be seen (we establish this before any juvenile flashlight shenanigans) and the legion of retirees who spent the summer pruning rose bushes and swigging from bottles of beer in socks and sandals have now retreated to their homes following a flurry of activity where they all raked autumn leaves into trailers and drove them around, for days, or so it seemed. Now, we don't pass a single soul, and conclude that we are living in a ghost town once again. It's a little eerie.

The dog's confused, too. He has a wee and it freezes instantly. We get home and he trots obediently to his bed, assuming it's time to sleep. This is unheard of. I try to coax him back out and he takes a few steps before slumping down in the hallway with an audible '*harrumph*'.

'Do you think the dog's OK?' I ask.

'Yes, why?'

'He's just been acting strangely lately.' I think for a moment. 'Do you think maybe the dog's suffering from seasonal affective disorder?' I ask.

'*Do* dogs suffer from seasonal affective disorder?'

Neither of us has a clue, so I turn to Google and find '*Do dogs get SAD?*' brings up 1,020,000 results.

Stanley Coren, dog psychology expert from the University of British Columbia, is first up, saying that 40 per cent of dog owners see a downturn in their pet's moods during winter due to melatonin and serotonin levels. 'Melatonin, secreted when it's dark, makes you lethargic and serotonin affects appetite and mood,' I tell Lego Man. 'It says you need *sunlight* to make serotonin ... or Prozac.'

'We're not giving the dog Prozac.'

I shrug as if to say: '*OK then, it's your dog's welfare you're messing with...*'

'It's not as though the rest of Denmark isn't high on happy pills to get through winter,' I mutter, then read on. 'Apparently, dogs sleep longer and want to eat more in winter. So he might be comfort eating. To cheer himself up...'

'Good grief...'

'He brought home half a pizza yesterday. And he's started gorging on acorns.'

'Do dogs eat acorns? Isn't that Piglet from *Winnie the Pooh*?'

I'm not sure about this so I click on another link.

'Dogs with SAD can also suffer from depression and social withdrawal.'

'"*Social withdrawal*"? He's a dog! Does this mean he hasn't been attempting to sniff as many bottoms as usual?'

I have a think. 'He did give that Alsatian a wide berth yesterday...'

'Oh, *well then*, he's practically a canine recluse.'

Choosing to ignore Lego Man's mockery, I read on: 'It's all related to light levels, which are particularly crap in Scandinavia in winter.'

'Does it say that?'

'I paraphrase. This site says that in Florida, where it's sunny all the time, only about 2 per cent of animals get SAD.' I'm just imagining all these giddy Florida dogs, tails wagging, wearing muumuus and '*I Heart Orlando*' visors, having the time of their lives, when our dog comes and sits at my feet. He stares up at me from beneath long, cow-like lashes and I picture a thought bubble rising from his woolly head: *'Don't s'pose a trip to Disneyland is on the cards?'*

'Fortunately, there's also some advice to "help dogs battle the winter blues".'

'Oh good, I can't wait to hear it.'

I sense a tone of sarcasm but plough on: 'We should leave lights on for him when we're out. And the radio.'

'But he doesn't speak Danish.'

We think about this before logging on to internet radio and selecting him an English language station. We wonder whether he's more of a Radio 2 or a Radio 4 sort of chap. I'm erring towards Radio 2 when Lego Man raises a crucial objection: 'But what about Ken Bruce? *Pop Master* might be enough to push him over the edge...'

'Good point.'

We decide to stick with Radio 4 ('*everyone* loves Jane Garvey...') and resolve to leave it on whenever he's in on his own. We're just rewarding ourselves for having solved the problem with a cup of tea and a biscuit, followed by a Danish that's been lurking in the fridge and some crisps that were left open, when I look again at the SAD symptoms listed on my laptop. '*Increased appetite, craving for comfort foods...*'

'Do you think,' I start tentatively, '*we* might have it too?' Lego Man isn't listening: instead he has his head wedged in the fridge, inspecting the designated cheese compartment. 'Seasonal affective disorder, I mean?' He emerges with a matchbox-sized slab of cheddar distorting his left cheek.

'Whaa?'

'We went to bed at 8pm last night. And we turned down a drinks invitation in to stay in and watch *Orange is the New Black*.'

'It's "must-watch" TV...' he protests through his mouthful. 'That's why they *call* it that. We're *powerless* in its grasp...'

'That's as may be, but we definitely tick a few boxes.' The more I read, the more convinced I am that we have all the symptoms: lethargy, social withdrawal, tiredness, addiction to cheese and TV box sets (the last two were more implied that specified by the scientific journals).

It turns out that Scandinavians hold the gold standard for SAD. The Finns have it worst (well, they *would*) but Danes don't get much respite during winter. A recent study from the Danish Ministry of Climate and Energy showed that there were only 44 hours of sunlight in Denmark in November. That's just over ten hours a week – less than an hour and a half a day. Of sunlight! I'm practically living in Mordor. It's no wonder I'm mainlining carbs and on a permanent builders' tea drip.

I text Helena C to ask her whether or not this is normal and she sends a smiley face in reply. Danes, as I've mentioned, are fond of an emoticon.

'*No, but really?*' I write back.

'*Of course! It's totally normal. Everyone gets it. You just accept that you're going to feel like crap when it gets really dark. We call it "vinterdepression"!*'

Excellent: it's been escalated from an affective disorder to depression.

She texts again, with the subtle Danish humour I've come to know and love:

'*Loads of people kill themselves this time of year too. Try not to kill yourself!*'

The next day I come across statistics that show she's half right. Daylight hours or changes in the day's length are the most significant explanation for seasonal variations in suicidal behaviour. But it turns out that suicides and suicide attempts peak at two points during the year: November, when the days begin to shorten, and April, when the days get longer again.

'Why is this?' I ask Bo Andersen Ejdesgaard from Denmark's Centre for Suicide Research.

'People with severe winter depression lack the initiative to act while they are suffering from the depression,' he says.

'You need some energy to attempt to take your own life. It's only when people are feeling rejuvenated by the return of the sunlight in the spring that people have this.'

'So in winter, Danes are too depressed to even kill themselves?'

'Something like that. Spring is also the month of "broken promises". In the winter people look forward to the spring, associated with hope, activity and the rebirth of a new year. If spring doesn't live up to the promises it can cause suicidal behavior. But it's not all bad in Denmark – we have the same level of suicides as other Scandinavian countries apart from Finland – it's higher there of course.'

'*Of course*...' Excellent news. 'So, er, how do you recommend making it through winter?'

'If you feel like you're experiencing a life crisis, then obviously contact a professional psychologist or psychiatrist.' Right. Thanks for that. 'We advise getting some sun – either artificially or by going away somewhere hot,' says Bo. I tell him that I've seen a suspicious number of Danes sporting out-of-season tans without much talk of Caribbean breaks. 'Oh yes, tanning beds are very popular in Denmark.' This much I've gleaned. Away from Sticksville, even the smallest town has a bakery, a florist, and a tanning shop. Danes may get the winter blues but by God they are always well-fed, floral and nut-coloured. A recent article in *The Copenhagen Post* showed that young Danes are the most prolific sunbed users in the world.

'The third option is to get a lamp that can simulate sunlight,' adds Bo, and here I think he may be on to something. Flying somewhere hot is out until the sumo wrestler inside my stomach decides to put in an appearance and sunbeds have always been a no-no thanks to my mottled blue-white British complexion. But the fancy lamp idea could work. I go on a SAD-prevention, professionally-sanctioned shopping trip and buy an agonisingly expensive lamp that also doubles up as an alarm clock. Yes, it's ugly. Yes, it probably cost the same as a minibreak to Gran Canaria. Yes, Lego Man is going to despise it. But this lamp is going to change our lives. Or at least our winter.

The makers describe the ugly lamp as being like a 'light bath' that I can take at any time of the day. They promise that it will make me feel fresh and energised. By using it in place of my normal alarm clock, I will start every morning with more pep than usual. It will also improve my day-to-day well-being. It will make my '*wake-up experience*' more enjoyable. It will even boost my brainpower, give me slimmer thighs and make me pancakes for breakfast (OK so I made the last two up, but basically, if the manufacturers are to be believed, it's the bee's knees). Lego Man is sceptical.

'It cost *how* much?'

I refrain from pointing out how much *he's* spent on Danish designer lighting over the past eleven months and instead focus on our new ugly lamp's plus points.

'It's been developed by "*leading light therapy experts*",' I read out from the manual.

'It looks hideous.'

'It's "*inspired by nature's sunrise*"...'

'And it doesn't even play music?'

'It "*emits natural sounds to accompany your wake-up experience*".'

'What, like dolphins and whale song?'

'I don't know,' I frown at the small print. 'I haven't got to that bit yet...'

Still grumbling, he helps me set it up and we go to bed confident (at least, one of us is) that we'll have a good night's sleep followed by a gentle sunrise coaxing us into morning and building to a soul-lifting brightness that will fortify us for the day ahead.

Five hours later and I'm blinded by an enormous orb of iris-exploding luminosity, six inches from my head.

'Arghhh!'

It's not even time for the alarm to go off yet. *WHY IS THE LIGHT SO BLOODY BRIGHT?*

Lego Man snores on, oblivious.

I'VE NEVER SEEN A SUNRISE LIKE THIS! IT'S PREPOSTEROUS!

Squinting, I reach out a hand to find a button to turn the damn thing off but the streamlined ergonomic design means that it's impossible to distinguish one faint bump from another. Pressing anything I can find, I accidentally turn on the 'nature sounds'.

'What's going on...? Can I hear birds?' Lego Man, now conscious, is croaking and shielding his eyes from the glare. A panic rises in his voice: 'Are there birds in our bedroom? There are *birds ... everywhere*!'

I feel for more buttons to try to kill the crazy birds but fail to get purchase and accidentally knock the orb off its base. It tips over. Out of reach now, I attempt to hoist myself up onto my elbow to retrieve the lamp but as my fingertips make contact, it's propelled forward. I watch, wide-awake now, as the thing rolls, slowly, off the bedside table. There is a '*crack*!' as it hits the hard, wooden Scandi-issue floor. The light goes out, and the birdsong fades to a sad tweet before dying.

There is a thud next to me as Lego Man slumps back down in bed.

'Well, that went well. I feel more relaxed and refreshed already,' he says.

I say nothing.

'That must be the most expensive wake-up call we've ever had.'

I take several deep breaths before coming up with: 'Would you like me to make pancakes for breakfast?'

Tired, tetchy and thoroughly cheesed off, I spend the morning researching other recommended antidotes for the Danish winter. Many experts swear by vitamin D, known as the 'sunshine vitamin', and research reported in the *New England Journal of Medicine* (everyone's favourite bedtime read) linked a deficiency to depression. It's also supposed to help prevent skin problems, cancer, strokes, heart disease and autoimmune diseases like multiple sclerosis. Darshana Durup of the Department of Pharmacology and Pharmacotherapy at the University of Copenhagen has been looking into whether or not the Danes have been getting their Ds, and as she tells me when I get in touch, the prognosis isn't good. 'A report from 2010 estimated that up to 40 per cent of the Danish population are Vitamin D deficient in winter,' says Darshana. 'The Ministry of Food, Agriculture and Fisheries recommend that you get 10μg/day but the average Dane is getting approximately 3μg/day. The best source is the sun, but in Denmark there isn't enough of that from October to March.' Yes, the winters in Denmark are so grim that they're officially bad for your health. *This is getting ridiculous*.

I find out that Danes suffering from *vinterdepression* are advised to up their intake of Vitamin D-rich foods as a substitute for sunshine but many also start popping it in pill form come autumn. As I'm pregnant, it's recommended I do the same, so I go on a mission to score myself some D. As it's not currently snowing (a novelty of late) I decide to go by bike, in case I'm lucky enough to catch the 'hour a day' of sun that the Ministry of Climate and Energy have been teasing me with.

I don't. Instead, wind-blasted, with fingers blue from cold, despite woollen mittens worn *over* gloves, I make it to my local shop only to find that they are all out of Vitamin D. There is a handy gap in the shelf between C and E and the assistant tells me that they won't be getting any more in before Christmas. After a bit more pedalling and puffing, I reach a chemist. But it has such a confusing 80s-deli-counter-style ticket number and queuing system that I spend twenty minutes waiting in line before a busty lady barges in front of me and I'm at the back again. I leave in protest and decide to chance the supermarket.

'*Nej*,' ('no') the woman I ask in supermarket number one tells me when I ask if they might possibly stock vitamin tablets. A man in the second supermarket I try looks at me as though I am clinically insane and shuffles off. This happens a lot. I think it's the pigeon Danish spoken with a funny accent that does it. But a woman in the third shop speaks English and, more importantly, kindly *deigns* to. It turns out that she is also training to be a nutritionist on the side. God bless Denmark's obsession with qualifications for even the most seemingly basic shop assistant's post and the nation's love of lifelong learning. She tells me that clever Danes bought up all stocks of Vitamin D back in September (they like to plan ahead) and the shops are unlikely to be getting any more in, but that she can suggest some D-heavy foods I might like to try. You don't get that in a Tesco Metro.

'Sardines, mackerel and eggs are all good,' she tells me. 'Good, but smelly!' she jokes. Splendid. We're in for a windy week in the Russell household. I fill my bicycle basket with the offending items and set off home, resolving to order Vitamin D tablets online from the UK. Yes, eleven months in Denmark has turned me into an international drug smuggler.

Pedalling my now-enormous bulk back with the smell of fresh mackerel filling my nostrils, it starts to rain. I push on, but after five more minutes the temperature drops still further, making me catch my breath at the cold. My fingers are frozen into a rigor mortis-like grip around the handlebars and the wind whips through the crotch of my trousers. And not in a good way. Then something abrasive starts to hit my face and I wonder whether it's frostbite until I hear a *ting ting ting!* – as though some ghostly force is ringing the bell on my bike. I look down. I can't feel my own fingers but I'm pretty sure it's not me doing that. *Ting ting ting!* It becomes more insistent and I realise that the percussion sounds are being made by the hailstones now hitting my bicycle bell. *Ting ting ting!* Hail plus pregnancy hormones are too much to bear in one afternoon and I start to cry. Fat, hot tears mix with the rain and hail that now appear to be falling simultaneously in a full-on chicken-licken-type scenario as I pedal as hard as I can and the baby boots me for all (80 per cent likely) he's worth.

I make it home – flinging the bike in the shed in disgust as though it has been personally responsible for making my trip so unpleasant, and pawing my way inside to safety. And biscuits. It takes a lot of Earl Grey and ginger nuts until I feel fully human again.

I vow to continue my crusade to understand how the Danes stay happy in winter from the comfort of my own home and post an SOS on Facebook: '*Danes, how do you get through winter and stay so bloody happy? I've tried daylight lamps, I'm trying vitamin D, I've even tried exercise and going outside (endorphins and all that) but it was HORRIBLE. Yours, disgruntled Brit-on-sea.*'

The responses are instant:

'*Well that's where you've been going wrong! The secret to getting through winter in Denmark is to stay inside!*' writes one.

'*Suck it up, you can't change the way the sun sets,*' posts another (don't I have nice friends?).

'*Two words: "hygge" and "candles",*' adds Helena C. She goes on to explain her 'theory' (and I use this in the loosest sense of the word) that by lighting enough candles, seasonal affective disorder can be avoided and a harmonious, *hygge* holiday season can ensue. This seems unlikely. But can 5.5 million people really be wrong? I remember that Danes use more candles per capita than any other nation in the world, and burn through 6kg of waxen wicks a year according to the European Candle Association. Their nearest counterparts, the Swedes, come in at a measly 4kg of candles per person with the Brits lagging behind at 0.6 of a kg (big old waxy lightweights...).

I resolve to give candle therapy a go. We eat rye bread by tea lights for breakfast, then I spend the day working on Christmassy features to the soothing light and scent of a Jo Malone candle I've been saving for a rainy day (or month. Or season). For supper, we light tapered wicks on candlesticks and sit at a proper table. I'm not sure if it's making me feel any better but candlelight's certainly more flattering. I catch sight of our reflections in the mirror above the bookcase and see that we're both bathed in a warm orange glow. The bags under my eyes are almost imperceptible in the semi-darkness and no one can see that my roots need doing. Lego Man's cheekbones are accentuated and he comes over all Viking warrior. *We look hot!* I think. Feeling smug we eat (mackerel, obviously), talk, laugh and even relax a little.

'This is nice!'

'Isn't it?'

'Candles, eh?'

'Who'd have thought? Maybe these crazy Danes have been on to something, all along!'

We laugh and the dog, not liking to be left out, begins to bark loudly in appreciation. Startled, I knock over a particularly spindly glass candelabra (who buys glass candelabras? I'll tell you who: Lego Man. He has some sort of Liberace alter ego that only comes out in home furnishing shops). This, in turn, spills wax over the pine wood floor of our rented house and sets fire to a napkin. The industrial-sized

Ikea fire hydrant comes into its own and within the space of two minutes we've gone from a romantic candlelit dinner for two to an Ibiza foam party.

This isn't working. I need an expert: a professional to tell me the truth about these Narnia-esque winters and how to handle them. My knight in weatherproof armour comes in the form of John Cappelen of the Danish Meteorological Society who I call up the next morning.

It's 8.45am and the peninsular is still draped in darkness. I watch a slow drizzle wriggle its way down our double-glazed windows as I explain my dilemma: 'I've tried light therapy, I've tried vitamin D, I've tried going outside and even getting *hygge*: my house is currently 70 per cent wax, 20 per cent wick and 10 per cent *snegles* but nothing is working. My neighbours have all been abducted by the White Witch, there's no one around, it's freezing cold and pitch black outside. What's a girl to do?' I tell him that I knew it was tough when I arrived in January but that the prospect of four more months of this stretching ahead of me may be more than any human being should be expected to bear.

Getting into my stride, I tell him I've read the stats: I know the winter will get even colder, that it rains almost every day in Denmark and the average wind speed is 7.6 metres per second, which explains why 30 per cent of electricity in Denmark is produced by wind power, why the country is one of the world's largest exporters of wind turbines and why I've been sporting the late 1990s windswept look for nearly a year now. 'So really, John, give it to me straight: what's there to love?'

He pauses before imparting his words of wisdom; the

key to understanding the nation's psyche; the Holy Grail for depressed expats countrywide: 'To be truly Danish—' says John in lowered tones.

'—Yes?' I'm tense with anticipation.

'—you must learn to *embrace* the winter weather.'

'That's *it*?'

'Yes.'

'*Really?* Is that even possible?'

'Of course. Weather is the number one thing we talk about in Denmark – Danes love talking about what's happening out there, and there's always something new. Norway and Sweden have much more stable weather so there's less to talk about,' he says pityingly of our Nordic neighbours, though seeming to omit the Finns. 'In *Denmark*, we are just below two big weather systems,' he goes on, 'so we get the wet, humid Western frontal system from the UK and the Eastern winds from Siberia bringing cold weather in winter and sunny days in summer. It's just so variable! You can never plan around the weather in Denmark.

'You have to just go with it. We Danes like to plan most things but the weather is totally out of our control. That's what makes it so exciting! But it's not dangerous weather like you get in some other places. Danes don't have to be afraid of their weather here – it's just entertainment. Just think about the storm we had a few weeks back; it was all people could talk about. It took up three-quarters of the TV news. Not wars, not politics overseas or celebrities – the weather!' He's on a roll now: 'What do you think about when you get up in the morning? You think about what the weather will be like! It influences what clothes you're going to put on that day as well as what you might need to pack and take with you for later on, because the weather changes so much throughout the course of the day in Denmark. There's always something new.'

'But the endless winter, John,' I say. 'How can you *like* the weather in winter here? The other day my car thermometer reported minus twenty. The *sea* had frozen. It's dark all the time here. And cold. And, just, *miserable*...'

His reply is vehement: 'No! Winter weather in Denmark is *special*. It brings people together. It forces us to be inside and brings families and friends closer. In southern Europe everyone's still going out and spending time in restaurants and cafés—' I think how appealing this sounds right about now, but John has different ideas, '—but in Denmark, we pull together at home and get *hygge*! In the olden days, you wouldn't have been able to survive winter here without gathering wood and food beforehand, so you had to help out neighbours, your family and friends to survive. Then when the cold weather came, you could hide away inside.'

'Like hibernation?'

'Sure. Of course, now it's not like it was in the times gone by. Now we have supermarkets and shops and offices to go to in winter. But there's still a cultural emphasis on being together. It can be really bad outside but then you can just come home and have a cup of tea and everything will feel better.'

If I'm understanding him correctly, Danes stay happy in winter because it's so awful outside that coming home inspires an overwhelming rush of relief and gratitude at having survived the elements.

'So no one goes out?'

'Well, you can, of course,' he concedes, 'you just have to dress right. We have a saying in Denmark that there is no truly bad weather, just bad clothes.'

'So we should all be wearing snowsuit onesies?'

'Sure!'

'And Danish weather really makes you happy?'

'Yes!' I demand his score out of ten and he thinks about it for a moment. 'I'd say I'm a nine.'

'Nine?'

'OK,' he concedes, 'a *ten*! Why shouldn't I be happy? I'm living in one of the best countries in the world! In what way can I complain?'

I relay John's gem to Lego Man – 'He says there is no such thing as bad weather, only the wrong clothes' – and watch his eyes light up.

'That means we can buy stuff! Winter weather clothes! With high tog counts! And wicking fabrics! And dynamic water-repellent outer layers! Like *Gore-Tex*...' he adds, with that dreamy, faraway look in his eyes that he gets when he can combine his twin passions of shopping and technical clothing.

Later, I find him online ordering a gilet and a snowsuit for the baby. Our future child still has nothing to sleep in, no pram, no pushchair, and no car seat to transport (80 per cent likely) him home from hospital. But at least he'll be clad in North Face. And probably be born wearing a rucksack.

My mother has been keeping a close eye on the Danish

weather from the UK and sends daily emails entitled things like: ***'WOW! MINUS 15!!!!!!!!!!!'*** She comes to visit for the weekend and when we meet her at the arrivals gate she's wearing salopettes, a ski jacket and a red beret.

'Good grief...' I mutter.

'It's a strong look,' admits Lego Man. I look at him accusingly: 'Have you been briefing her?'

'I ... might have mentioned the forecast,' he admits, 'and the thing you said about "no such thing as bad weather, only the wrong clothes" and all that for her first trip over in winter.' I roll my eyes.

'Darling!' My mother looks flushed. She must be boiling but appears not to mind: 'I was the only one dressed appropriately on the flight,' she announces gaily.

I explain that even though it's cold, we still tend to wear semi-normal clothes when we're inside.

'Well I don't know why, with your circulation. Look, your fingers are almost blue.' She's right. I hate that. 'Anyway, it's not a fashion show...' (this, along with '*Shoulders back, darling*', has been her mantra since 1986). Lego Man finds himself agreeing with her, infuriatingly, and the pair of them spend the next two days comparing fleecy mid-layers and woollen socks.

The weekend passes too quickly and before I know it, I'm driving her back to Billund airport. I wish she could stay longer, and start planning her next visit already. I may be an Actual Grown-Up about to have a child of my own, but sometimes you just really need your mum. It's strange to think that the next time I see her, I'll be presenting her with a grandchild. For now, I offer her a *snegle* instead in

Billund's biggest (aka 'only') winter attraction: the bakery. My mother agrees to strip off some of her outer Alpine layers but manages to karate chop her way through an ornamental display of dried plaited loaves in the process while trying to free limbs from ski attire. In its brittle, desiccated state, the bread virtually explodes, propelling crumbs everywhere. Once we've apologised profusely, offered to help sweep up, and bought several buns by way of compensation, I spend fifteen minutes helping my mother to re-robe again before going back outside. Getting dressed to face a winter's day in Denmark is exhausting.

After an emotional goodbye at the airport, I turn up the hot air blowers in my mobility tomato, crunch into first gear and set off for home. It's hard to drive with mittens on but I'm managing it, somehow, though the idea of four more months of winter spent dressed like a yeti is starting to make me feel a little claustrophobic. I have a sudden urge to come over all Joan Collins and escape to St Tropez to drink cocktails on a yacht. In lieu of this, I think *WWJD: What would Joan do? How would Joan cope with this expanse of frozen nothingness?* Since G&Ts, strange diets, and the option of marrying a much younger man are out (for now, anyway), I rifle in the glove box for my emergency lipstick and apply liberally. Then I resolve to read a glossy magazine on my iPad and put some perfume on when I get home, until cosmopolitan balance has been restored.

Driving back, the sun is setting (at 3.30pm) and the sky is turning an orangey-purple colour. I reach the crest of a hill before turning off into Sticksville and see the remnants of the sun creating orange slices across a cool, navy blue sea.

I catch my breath at its beauty and for a moment, I forget how bleak it has been and will be again.

I wonder whether maybe this is a bit like childbirth – of course the experience *smarts* a bit, but then you're left with something wonderful and you forget the pain. Here's hoping.

Things I've learned this month:

1. Danes are adept at looking on the bright side, even in the bleak midwinter
2. You can get by with a little help from your friends, family, candles and cake
3. Dogs get SAD too
4. You should never wear salopettes on a plane
5. When things get really rough, stay home
6. ...or think *WWJD*. Joan Collins: an inspiration for *all* seasons

12. December

Trusting the Taxman (or Woman)

The twelfth month in Denmark is a time for taking stock, taking time out, and *taxes*. Doing life admin in your own country is arduous enough, but attempting to do it in a foreign land, in a language with which you're *still* not familiar, is nigh on impossible. After eleven months of Google Translating every document that came my way, I've become a little slack of late. Which is why I'm caught off guard when the romper-suited postwoman rings the doorbell first thing on Monday morning and hands me an official-looking envelope. It's a shouty red letter from the '*skat*' office and they want to know when I'm going to be sending some kroner their way. '*Skat*' means 'tax' in Danish – as well as 'beloved' or 'honey', incidentally.

'So, technically, when I pay tax, I'm giving my honey to the skatman...' I tell Lego Man, who fails to see the funny side and suggests I get on the case before we're sent any more angry missives from the state.

I nod and try to look sensible but can't get the 90s classic by Scatman John out of my head ('*Ski-bi dibby dib yo da dub dub, yo dab dub dub...*'). As well as racing to finish commissions and meet deadlines before junior arrives, I'm now being forced to address the depressing issue of how little of my income I actually get to keep in Denmark. As though being a freelancer wasn't tough anyway, negotiating the tax system of a famously levy-heavy country proves predictably horrific. After much ringing around and some tears (I blame the hormones), I find someone who speaks English and can explain what's required. I need help, fast, as well as advice on what to do next to a) not get deported and b) not be socially stigmatised for failing to treat Denmark's hallowed taxation system with the respect it so clearly deserves.

Kim Splidsboel is a real-life *skatman*. He somehow found himself having been volunteered by the state to take a 45-page PowerPoint presentation on a tour of the country to educate new arrivals. Unfortunately for Kim, I missed this gem of a night out when it came to The Big City, so now he's having to go through it one-to-one. Poor Kim.

He starts at the very beginning, explaining that the income year here runs from 1 January to the 31 December. Which is handy, as someone who is simultaneously trying to sort out her UK tax return for a financial year that runs from April to April. And all because Henry VIII wanted to get his end away (for a more comprehensive explanation of how a 16th-century monarch ruined my month, see http://www.taxadvisorypartnership.com/tax-compliance/why-does-the-uk-tax-year-start-on-6-april-each-year/).

'In Denmark we ask freelancers and the self-employed to pay their estimated taxes as they go, so that they don't skip town mid-year,' says Kim. 'You have a running income, you pay a running tax. That's the rule.'

'Ah...' This is news to me.

The kind but rather scatty lady at the local tax office I visited back in January assured me that I could pay what I owed at the end of the year. Admittedly her English wasn't great and my Danish was, at the time, non-existent. But I'm now suspecting that what she *actually* meant was that all accounts needed to be settled and any *extras* are paid annually. Not, as I had interpreted it, that I should just sit on my hands and whistle until Christmas came around.

'I, er, wasn't quite aware of the whole *monthly* system,' I confess.

Kim doesn't answer straight away and I feel a panic rising.

'I'm not going to be arrested or anything, am I?' I half joke. *Could I get a criminal record? Will I end up in prison?* My imagination goes into overdrive as I consider worst-case scenarios before reasoning that, actually, it might not be so bad. *I bet Denmark's prisons are some of the best in the world. Maybe it would be nice to have a rest there for a little while.* I'm currently facing the prospect of a houseful of relatives for Christmas. Lego Man's parents are arriving, expecting bed and full board for seven whole days and nights. *A bit of bird*, I consider, *might be a welcome break*. I wonder whether New Nordic Cuisine has reached the country's penal system or whether we're talking more meatballs and pickled herring. I'm just deciding it's probably the latter when the skatman interrupts.

'It's OK: you can still do your taxes now.'

'Oh! OK then.' It looks like I'm down for the Christmas catering after all.

'You just use your NEM ID to log on and check how much you should have been paying.'

'Right. And, er ... remind me how I do that again?'

There follows a lengthy and highly complicated explanation that takes up ten pages of my trusty spiral-bound reporters' notepad – in addition to Kim's 45-page PowerPoint presentation. NEM ID is the online login system used in Denmark for all government websites and banks. It combines the national ID number (from my yellow Central Population Registry or CPR card) with a surprisingly retro fold-out flap of bingo-esque number pairings that are used as authentication keys. Old school, but effective. Once I've got my head around this, Kim goes on to tell me what I'm likely to have to cough up.

'Income below 42,800 DKK [around £4,600 or $7,800 at time of scribbling, although the level is adjusted annually] is tax-free. Then you pay 37 per cent tax on earnings of up to 449,000 DKK [about £50,000 or $85,000 – a salary not uncommon in Denmark] with a top tax rate of 51.7 per cent, on anything you earn above this figure. Oh, and everyone automatically pays 8 per cent social security tax.'

Blimey, I think, *it's not as though living in Denmark has been exactly cheap as it is*. In addition to the sky-high income tax, the 25 per cent value added tax ('*moms*') is whacked onto virtually everything here. Homeowners also pay property taxes and members of the Danish national church (i.e. the majority of the country, as I discovered back in May) pay a separate levy. Oh, and of course cars, petrol and electricity are also heavily taxed to regulate consumption and try to make Danes even greener than they already are.

'And, tell me,' I ask Kim, curious now, 'do Danes *mind* paying so much tax? I mean, don't they meet Americans or people from other countries and think "*you lucky bastards*!"?' I've become a bit sweary in my third trimester. Apologies.

'Not at all,' Kim tells me. 'People pay their taxes with pleasure in Denmark because they know that we get the best social welfare in the world in return. We get free schools, universities, doctors, hospitals, automatic holiday pay that's very generous, and employers pay into a good pension system that really benefits Danes and those who settle here.'

'Most Danes will have needed the services of the Danish state at some point or another in their lives – they'll have had a family member who was sick or something – so they understand the infrastructure and know that their money is going to a good place.'

When he puts it like this, it sounds surprisingly sensible. Danes have a collective sense of responsibility – of *belonging*, even. They pay into the system because they believe it to be worthwhile. The insanely high taxation also has some happy side effects. It means that Denmark has the lowest income inequality among all the OECD countries, so the difference in take-home wages between, for instance, Lego's CEO and its lowliest cleaner, isn't as vast as it might be elsewhere. Studies show that people who live in neighbourhoods where most people earn about the same amount are happier, according to research from San Francisco State University and the University of California Berkeley. In Denmark, even people working in wildly different fields will probably have a similar amount left in the bank each month after tax.

I'm interested in the idea that income equality makes for better neighbours and want to put it to the test. But since I live in what is essentially a retirement village, where no one apart from Friendly Neighbour works, there isn't much of an opportunity in Sticksville. So I ask Helena C about hers. She tells me that the street she lives in is populated by shop assistants, supermarket workers, accountants, lawyers, marketers and a landscape gardener.

'Everyone has a nice home and a good quality of life,' she says, 'it doesn't matter so much what you do for work here.' Regardless of their various careers and the earning potential that this might afford them in other countries with lower taxes, professionals and non-professionals live harmoniously side by side in Denmark.

This also makes social mobility easier, according to studies from The Equality Trust on the impact of income equality. So you're more likely to be able to get on in life, get educated and get a good job, regardless of who your parents are and what they do in Denmark than anywhere else. It turns out that it's easier to live 'The American Dream' here than it's ever likely to be in the US.

I've known since 1986, when my mother first played me her *A Hard Day's Night* LP, that 'money can't buy me love' – but it turns out it's not much use in terms of happiness either. Research published in *Psychology Today* found that true happiness comes from having good relationships, meaningful jobs or hobbies, and a sense of being part of something bigger than yourself, like religion, or just *being*

Danish for folk round these parts. The Worldwatch Institute's 2011 State of Consumption report also found that wealth won't help you on your way to having a satisfying life and new research shows that there's even a cut-off point for the amount of income we need to be content. A combined study from the Universities of Warwick and Minnesota found that there was a basic threshold beyond which any extra money added nothing to levels of well-being. The figure is around 197,000 DKK a year (£22,000 or $36,000), after which we apparently get wealthier but less contented.

Earning less than this? No need to worry. Research published in *Psychological Science* journal found that people of lower economic status had more empathy than wealthier people and a study in *Psychology Today* showed that rich kids had a higher risk of succumbing to eating disorders, cheating and stealing. So yay for you, you're a better person than anyone on *The Sunday Times Rich List* and your kids are going to be all right.

Already taking home more than the happy-income threshold? Don't despair just yet. There are three solutions, according to experts responding to the report: work less, pay more tax or migrate to a poorer country. Clever Danes, already ahead of the game, have been doing two out of three of these for decades. If you can't work less or influence your country's fiscal policy and you don't fancy decamping to the developing world, I've come up with a fourth option: move to Denmark. But bring Lemsip. And a pullover.

'It's like the weather,' Kim tells me. 'You can't do anything about the tax situation here so you just have to get on with it. Besides, it's part of who we are.'

Having high taxes that fund a comprehensive welfare state does seem to be such a big part of Denmark's identity that I can't help thinking he may have a point. 'And are you happy, personally, giving away all your money?'

'Of course!' he sounds surprised that I'd even ask. 'I live in a beautiful country, I love Denmark. I'm a Dane in my heart, why wouldn't I be happy?' He scores himself a perfect ten out of ten for happiness. Having never interacted with anyone from Her Majesty's Revenue & Customs in the UK who sounded anything above a semi-suicidal two, I surmise that the Danish tax system may not be so bad after all.

I begin to tally up my receipts on a rudimentary Excel spreadsheet when I come across another hurdle and am forced to phone *skat* back. Further probing with a far less entertaining *skatwoman* reveals that because I'm a freelancer, a 'foreigner' and about to have a baby, my 'case' is even more complicated than usual. After a few more phone calls, I'm told that I'll need a chartered accountant to present my records to the local *kommune*.

I look up the Danish word for accountant. It is, according to my translation app, '*bogholder*', which cheers up my morning of taxes immeasurably. I add this to my mental tally of hilarious Danish words, then Google to find one locally.

The list of possible *bogholders* in my area includes a 'Jens Larsen', a 'Lars Jensen', a 'Lars Larsen' and a 'Jens Jensen' – as well as a 'Mette Jensen', a 'Mette Hansen' and a 'Mette Nielsen', just for variety. It turns out that one in every four Danes has the surname 'Jensen', 'Hansen' or 'Nielsen' according to Statistics Denmark. Also in the top ten of Danish surnames are 'Andersen' (as in Hans Christian) and 'Rasmussen', a name so common that three successive Danish prime ministers from 1993 to 2011 shared the surname. Poul Oluf Nyrup Rasmussen, Anders Fogh Rasmussen and Lars Løkke Rasmussen (no relation) had to be referred to by their first names by the press and fellow politicians to distinguish between them. The '*sen*' bit traditionally indicated that they were the 'son of' someone who had the name preceding this, so Lars Jensen would have been the son of someone called Jens, and Jens Jensen's dad would have been so crazy about his own name that he decided to use it twice. A bit like New York. (Confused? Welcome to Denmark!)

'Every other Dane I meet is called Mette or Lars, or Jens,' I grumble to Lego Man when he gets home to find me barefoot (did I mention the incredibly energy-efficient underfloor heating in Danish homes?), pregnant and plaintive: 'How on earth am I supposed to remember who's who?'

'It's easy,' he shrugs, 'just call everyone Mette if they're a girl and Lars, or possibly Jens, if they're a boy. Chances are you'll be right the majority of the time...'

Reader, I married a genius.

Turning back to my computer, I find out that the same names recur more frequently in Denmark than they might do elsewhere because there's a *rule* about Christian names here. *Another rule? Of course. Why didn't I think of that?* I inform Lego Man of my new discovery: 'Apparently, you can choose from a list of preapproved names but if you want something that's not on the list, you need special permission from the church and government officials.' Lego Man, now busy surveying the contents of the biscuit tin, doesn't respond. But after two years of marriage I don't let a small thing like this deter me. 'It says here that "creative spellings" are usually rejected—' I plough on.

'—Bad luck for any Danish will.i.am wannabes,' Lego Man chips in through a mouthful of chocolate chunk cookie, keen to prove that he's still down with the kids.

'—and that the list of names is reviewed each year. About a fifth of new suggestions get rejected, and recent no-nos include – oh my – "Anus", "Pluto" and "Monkey"!'

'Damn. Looks like I'll have to send back the personalised baby towels then…'

I start to laugh but then get winded by a baby's foot in my stomach and splutter tea out of my nose (surprisingly painful). I scan the list to make sure the names we've been tentatively considering for our (80 per cent likely) son are allowed and am relieved to find they're in the 'safe' column. Reassured, I continue my quest for a *bogholder* called Jens. Or Lars. Or Mette. With little to go on from the descriptions online, I realise that I'm just going to have to pick one at random to entrust with my financial future. I do an *eenie meenie miney moe* to decide and land on a 'Lars' who operates out of The Big Town. I get in touch, explain my predicament, and make an appointment to meet the next day.

Lars tells me that if I hand over my invoices and any work-related receipts, he can do the rest. All I have to do is pay up a not-insubstantial sum at the end. Grateful and relieved that it's being taken care of, I wonder whether this is how the Danes feel: they know that they're paying through the nose, but they suck it up for an easy life. The Viking once told me that he was happy to pay his taxes because the state organised everything for him, and he trusted them to do a decent job.

I'm starting to understand now, a mere twelve months in, how big a part trust plays in the Danish psyche. How it can make life simpler and hassle-free and reduce the capacity for worrying (something I've made a hobby out of since the age of two, according to my mother). It feels strange to let go of any semblance of control and just trust in the system. But having no other option, I'm doing it. And it turns out I'm *OK*.

'Do you think Danes are more trusting?' I call The Viking and ask him. 'Just *generally* I mean?'

'You know, I think we might be,' he tells me. 'We've got the whole welfare system and a tiny population – so we tend to think that most people, well, that they're *good* and honest.' He gives me an example to illustrate this. 'So I checked my bank account at the other day and found that it was totally empty—'

'—Empty?'

'Totally.'

'God…'

'—I know. So, I ring up Allan—'

'—Allan with two 'l's?'

'Yes…'

'—How funny! Our bank manager's Allan with two 'l's too!'

'Oh *everyone* banks with Allan.' It's at this point that I am reminded what a small place I live in. 'So I call up Allan, to be all, like, "where's my money?"'

'And what does Allan say?'

'Well, Allan's on holiday.' Allan takes a lot of holidays. Bank clerks, along with everyone else from lawyers to waiters, get paid well out here. Even after taxes, most Jutlanders can afford to treat themselves. 'So,' The Viking continues, 'I've got no cash and no Allan, I'm meant to be visiting my folks and I'm all out of gas. I phone my dad to explain what's happened. I'm like, "Dad, I have no money..." and he says: "oh, sure you do, I just moved it." And I'm like, "you *moved* my money?" And he's like, "yeah!"'

'What?' I'm lost. I'm also amused that The Viking regresses to teen-speak when addressing his parents.

'Dad said he just called Allan about his mortgage, and Allan mentioned this new account for long-standing customers, with extra interest and stuff. So my dad goes, "Oh, that sounds great. Why don't you move my son's money in there too?"'

'And Allan just *did* it? He didn't ask your permission or get you to sign something?'

'No.'

'And the bank didn't check with you?'

'The bank trusts Allan. Allan trusts that my dad is who he says he is. And my dad trusts that Allan is trying to help by offering me the best deal for my money. So he switches my account over.'

'He just forgets to tell you...'

'Right. But it all turned out for the best. That's how trust works here.'

Extraordinary. I call up the happiness economist Christian Bjørnskov who I spoke to at the start of my adventure to ask for his perspective. He confirms that this level of trust is key to keeping Danes so damned happy. As he told me before I started my quest, 'life is so much easier when you can trust people', and this is regardless of whether you're actually about to get your bank account wiped or have your house burgled.

'So if I feel safe and trust the people around me, I'm less likely to feel stressed or anxious. I have the *headspace* to be happy?'

'Exactly,' he tells me. 'And countries with a major welfare state tend to be high-trust countries, though the high levels of trust in Denmark aren't *necessarily caused* by the welfare state.'

Christian has studied data from as far back as 1930, before the welfare state was established in 1950, and tells me that there was a high level of trust in the very early 20th century as well. 'It's as though the trust allows the welfare state to exist – and not the other way around. Danes accept that they must pay high taxes because they trust that the government will use their money wisely and do the right thing. The system *works* and Danes are, on the whole, happy – *because* they have high levels of trust.'

'So where does the trust come from?' I ask.

'That's the million dollar question!'

Klaus Petersen, director of the centre for welfare research at the University of Southern Denmark, thinks he might have the answer – and it's Denmark's close affiliation with her Nordic neighbours.

'We're all Lutheran countries with a strong social democracy and from the 1930s onwards there has been extreme cooperation to create the "Nordic Social Policy",' he tells me when I call him up to find out more. 'Denmark may be small, but we are joined with others so we feel safe and trust each other.' International surveys consistently show that Scandinavian countries all share high levels of trust and that Denmark is one of the safest countries in the world. The Vision of Humanity's Global Peace Index ranked Denmark as the world's second safest country to live in after Iceland (and it's colder, darker, and even pricier there…). The number of Danes who say, 'I'm feeling safe' is higher than it was in the 1990s and Danes are the most likely in Europe to say, 'I feel safe out walking in the dark' (followed by the Norwegians) according to figures from Danish criminologist Rannvá Møller Thomsen.

So why is this? Klaus has a theory that the country's size helps its residents feel secure.

'Danes all know each other,' he tells me by way of explanation. I presume he doesn't mean literally but he assures me that the truth isn't too far off in a country of five and a half million. 'We've always been small and there hasn't been much migration historically so there's a common Danish identity. You can get a few million people to accept a universal system and feel a shared identity.'

This is all sounding great but I'm a little disheartened that there doesn't seem to be anything I can take away or that can be applied to anywhere outside of Denmark with its tiny population. But then I read about the work of Peter Thisted Dinesen from the department of political science at Copenhagen University, who researches into social trust. I call him up and badger the poor man in his lunch hour until he generously agrees to take time out to share his hypothesis

– that a culture of goodwill towards the state and education may be the reason that Danes are so trusting.

'We live in a society that's very fair with efficient institutions and no corruption, and where people are generally treated equally and fairly,' Peter tells me. 'Bribing of the police or politicians in Denmark is almost entirely absent, and most of us are well looked after, so this provides the basis for trust.'

According to the annual Rule of Law Index conducted by the Washington-based World Justice Project, Denmark has the world's most responsible government. Denmark is also perceived as the least corrupt country in the EU according to Berlin-based NGO, Transparency International.

Politicians, a notoriously untrusted sector of society in most other countries, enjoy a surprisingly good reputation in Denmark. What helps is that they've long been thought of as 'normal people' – so there's less of a pedestal for them to fall off. Even high-profile ministers working at a national level are famously down-to-earth and accessible, as I've found over the course of my research. The political TV drama *Borgen* helped emphasise this idea of ministers as real people, encountering the same problems as the rest of us, and the show has even been credited with combating voter apathy and boosting turnout at the polls, according to a Copenhagen Business School study.

'Trust has actually been on the rise in recent years,' Peter tells me. 'I wrote a paper together with Kim Mannemar Sønderskov from Aarhus University showing that trust levels between 1979 and 2009 rose by 68 per cent and that 79 per cent of the population said that they trusted "*most people*".'

So why the upsurge? Are they putting something in the water out here? I look suspiciously at the half-empty glass in my hand.

Peter has a better suggestion: 'If you look at immigrants from low-trust societies who are educated in Denmark, they tend to take on our levels of high trust,' he says. 'Interestingly there are no differences between children who are immigrants themselves or descendants, which I in part ascribe to encountering fair Danish institutions.' This means that it's living in the society of Denmark that makes you trusting. Not *just* 'tradition' or something Danes inherit from their parents.

This, I decide, is wonderful news. It means that living Danishly is helping me to become more trusting and this in turn can help me to be happier. Once you trust '*the system*' and can get your head around the fact that it's not trying to screw you over, it's easier to pay your taxes with grace – safe in the knowledge that the money is going to a good place. I don't begrudge paying taxes (so much, at least) if it means that I'm helping keep the Danish dream going, free from corruption.

This is an interesting shift in perspective for a girl raised in Thatcher's Britain. I've always been independent but I'm starting to realise that this was because I've had to be – because there wasn't much of a safety net. But it's different for Danes. And I'm learning to see the benefits of doing things Danishly. I'm even getting better at letting go – relinquishing control and striving for a better work-life balance. It's not always easy to forget my old ways. There was the day back in July when I found out that two of my contemporaries back in 'Media Land' had bagged themselves big, spanking new jobs. Jobs that, for years, I'd thought *I* wanted, and felt I should be aiming for. At the time, I felt unreasonably agitated, did some aggressive dishwasher loading, broke a plate, and then howled at the sky, '*Whhhhhhyyyyyy?*' But then I realised that I wasn't in that race right now. I was writing and being pregnant and seeing friends and walking a dog on a beach. I was having A Life. I could now *sleep* at night and didn't have to bribe myself with tissue-wrapped online purchases to get through the week. Before I got pregnant, I'd lost half a stone without even realising it or meaning to (and despite the *snegles*) because I hadn't been misery-eating or in thrall to an office treats table. I was at peace. And that felt like a pretty good trade-off.

Soon, we'll need to decide whether or not to stay in Denmark for another year. We haven't got long to make our minds up. Should our Made in Denmark baby spend (80 per cent likely) his first year here too? Or would our year of living Danishly be better off remaining just that – an imperfect, finite year of Nordic Narnia? I'm just about to go into list-writing mode to outline the pros and cons when Lego Man crashes through the door, making his usual percussive entrance. It's 4.30pm.

'Another busy day?' I ask, teasingly.

'It was actually,' he says, disrobing and dumping more bags than it can be possible for any man to need in the middle of the kitchen floor. Once he's said hello properly he starts upending clear cellophane packets all over the dining room table.

'What *are* you doing?'

He tells me he's making a Lego model of the Sydney Opera House. As though this is the most obvious thing in the world for a professional in his mid-thirties to be doing on a Tuesday afternoon.

'It was built by the Danish architect, Jørn Utzon, don't you know?' he informs me, rustling packets and raking through mostly-white bricks as he talks. Lego Man insists that this 'project' is 'one of the things there won't be time for when the baby comes along.'

'*Too bloody right*,' I mutter, then: 'Do you want to walk the dog or are you too busy playing with toys?'

'It's not "playing", it's "*building*"!'

This isn't the first time he's tried to convince me of the crucial difference, apparently acknowledged by AFOLs everywhere. 'Anyway, it's for grown-ups. See?' He points at the twelve-plus age-guidance banner on the box with pride. 'It's even called "*Lego Architecture*". *Kids* don't even *know* what architecture is.' I detect a distinct eye roll before he gets back to his 'build'.

I watch him, a blonde head of hair bent over, squinting behind his black-rimmed square glasses, sitting in his Arne Jacobsen chair, outlined by the gentle glow of a Poul Henningsen PH lamp. He's playing an album by the Danish pop group Alphabeats on his Danish Bang & Olufsen stereo, humming along out of tune and occasionally sipping from a Danish Bodum double-wall insulated beer glass that has appeared by his side. Yes that's right, we've acclimatised so much that a Carlsberg at 5pm in winter is a perfectly normal Tuesday treat. I've never seen Lego Man look more at home.

'Look who drank the Danish Kool Aid...' I mutter,

wondering whether I should pin him down and swab his cheek to test for the 5-HTT gene. *Maybe our child will be part-Viking and have the happy gene too*, I think. *Maybe that's why our (80 per cent likely) son never sleeps and is such a kicker: he's already marauding around inside me, all high on serotonin and the anticipation of* snegles.

Lego Man, I can tell, wants to stay. But I'm still not *totally* convinced. Maybe you can take the girl out of the British cynicism but you can't take the British cynicism out of the girl. Maybe...

Things I've learned this month:

1. Danes don't mind paying their ludicrously high taxes
2. ...because money can't buy you happiness anyway
3. What can make you happy is being more trusting and living Danishly (hurrah!)
4. Lego Man may be a secret Viking

God Jul!

There's something else I should probably mention. I haven't forgotten – it's not as though Scandis are so ice-cool that they keep it all on the down low. No, Christmas here is A Huge Deal. And it starts at 8.57pm on the first Friday of November.

Lego Man and I are just finishing off a quiet dinner in The Big Town when an almighty roar starts up from the street. We look out of the window, curious now, only to see a few youths hanging around the porny pony and cats with boobs fountain. This is standard and all is as it should be with the world. A few moments later, a second cry can be heard. It echoes along the street, gathering momentum as other shouts and shrieks join it until there's an unmistakable sense that Something Is Going To Happen. In a place where very little ever happens.

The sound of an engine can be heard and a truck rolls into view, complete with sound system and a countdown clock. The vehicle begins emitting a strange white substance. Great gouts of the stuff are expelled into the air, floating slowly downwards and smothering the street like a blanket.

'Ahhh ... snow!' Lego Man exclaims with glee. It's been at

least two days since we've had fresh snowfall and Lego Man is excited at the prospect of breaking out yet more recently acquired technical outdoor gear. But for once, it's not actually snowing. This white stuff is something else entirely.

'I think...' I start, before blinking and looking again, just to be sure, 'I think it's *foam*.' I didn't spend two weeks in the Costa de Sol as an impressionable teenager for nothing: I know professional-grade bubbles when I see them. Nonetheless, the place suddenly looks incredibly festive and after paying, we take to the streets to investigate.

The lorry comes to a standstill and the tailgate lowers to reveal a gang of girls in small blue outfits and men dressed in boiler suits congregating around a diminutive, dark-haired man. He's sporting a mega-watt smile and aviator sunglasses, despite the fact that it's been dark since 3.30pm.

'Is that ... *Tom Cruise*?' Lego Man squints at the tiny figure.

I feel very sober indeed and try to break it to him gently: 'I think it's *supposed* to be...' I'm pretty confident that the world's most famous Scientologist hasn't come to hang out in rural Jutland for the weekend.

The looka(little)like greets fans with a wave and they cheer and whoop while the other *Top Gun* extras hand out flammable-looking blue Santa hats and plastic aviators. Then the womenfolk step forward and we see that they are dressed as air stewardesses. Lego Man is appalled.

'There are no air hostesses in *Top Gun*! You don't have stewards on a fighter jet! That would be totally *impractical*! Not to mention unnecessary...' His outrage at the factual inaccuracies of the tableau seems to know no bounds, but I can't help feeling there are bigger fish to fry. Maverick and his lady friends are now lobbing glass bottles of beer into the crowd. The assembled throng is becoming larger, louder and less able to stay upright as the foam disintegrates, leaving the street slippery with soap. And yet the scantily clad flight attendants and Denmark's answer to Tom Cruise are *throwing glass missiles*.

I ask a semi-sober-looking woman standing next to me what's going on and she tells me that this is '*J-Dag*' or 'J-Day' when the festive beer, *julebryg*, is traditionally delivered to every town in Denmark by horse and cart. At least, that's what happens in Copenhagen. Here, we get an articulated lorry.

J-Day marks the unofficial start of Christmas in Denmark, when bars and restaurants serve festive beer from 9pm and promotional teams from the brewery dole out a few hundred freebies to get the party started.

'I should probably try it, since we're here,' says Lego Man, eyeing up the folk around him who are now glugging down their *julebryg*. I'm about to comment on how magnanimous he is, willing to overlook the besmirching of his favourite film for the sake of some free lager, but he's already disappeared into the crowd.

'Be careful!' I call out, dodging carbonated glass grenades.

He comes back victorious, clutching a bottle above his head like a football trophy.

'Well done.'

'Thanks,' he nods, accepting the praise before cracking the bottle open and taking a hearty swig.

'Well?'

'It's ... strong. Sort of liquorice-y.'

My nose wrinkles involuntarily, 'God, they put that stuff in everything round here!' A sing-song starts up in Danish, of what sounds like some sort of beer-based anthem to the tune of *Jingle Bells*, while more lager missiles are thrown out. 'Danes must have excellent hand-eye coordination,' I remark. 'I haven't heard a single bottle smash.'

'That, or they really love beer,' replies Lego Man taking another swig. 'And I'll be honest, it's pretty good. You wouldn't want any to go to waste.'

After Tom Cruise and his team have strewn their stash, the truck rolls out of town and everyone decamps to the nearest bar. We meet up with Helena C and The Viking and the merriment continues. Feeling horrifically sober, I try to imagine that I'm conducting some sort of important indigenous analysis, like a heavily pregnant Bruce Parry in *Tribe*. But it's hard to get the bottom of an anthropological phenomenon when everyone you try to talk to has drunk a lot (and I mean A Lot) and honks of liquorice. So I leave Lego Man to it with the usual suspects after an hour or so and head home.

The next morning, I call on the good people behind J-Day to tell me more.

'It all started from a TV ad that ran for the first time in 1980,' says Jens (another one!) Bekke from Carlsberg, the company that brews the Tuborg beers, including the *julebryg*. The advert was a rudimentary animation, depicting Santa and Rudolph forgoing their Christmas duties in pursuit of a Tuborg truck to the twinkly sound of 'Jingle Bells'. The subtext, I discover when I watch the ad on YouTube, seems to be that Santa and his helper are borderline alcoholics. Nevertheless, the commercial drove better than expected sales and so has been screened every winter since. 'It's probably the only advertisement in the world that hasn't changed in more than 30 years,' says Jens. Neither, apparently, has the beer. The strong 5.6 per cent ABV pilsner was invented by mixing three other beers together and is said to be a good accompaniment to smoked fish, herring, pork, duck ... and more *julebryg*. 'We keep the beer the same every year, as well as the packaging and the TV advert,' Jens tells me, 'because Danes love tradition!' I mention that I'd noticed this. 'Plus we'd get protests from all over the country if we changed people's Christmas beer!'

Julebryg is so popular that despite only being on the market for ten weeks a year, it's Denmark's fourth best-selling beer. In other words, Danes fill their boots.

'Screening the ad marks the start of the Christmas festivities for many people,' says Jens, 'and from 1990 onwards, we got the idea to travel around the country handing out *julebryg* to mark the start of its time on sale.' Now, 500 Carlsberg employees visit 500 locations each year for J-Day. At each stop, they sing a bastardisation of *Jingle Bells* with lyrics that translate along the lines of:

Julebryg julebryg, Tuborg Jul-e-bryg.
Enjoy it cold, and wish a friend Merry Christmas once again. Hey!
Julebryg julebryg, Tuborg Jul-e-bryg.
Waiting is never fun, J-day is a hit!

'We also like to have a theme every year for the trucks,' Jens goes on. 'We've had elves, then last year it was Christmas trees, so this year we went for *Top Gun*.'

I tell him that *Top Gun* doesn't seem terribly Christmassy. 'No. I'm not entirely sure why we did this. Some people in the creative team came up with it...' He changes tack by telling me that the Carlsberg teams distribute 20,000 bracelets and 45,000 synthetic Santa hats on J-Day as well. These are worn with pride for the remainder of the evening by the assembled hordes, including, one year, by unlikely J-Day reveller Salman Rushdie.

Having fled his home to go into hiding, and with a fatwa issued against him, *The Satanic Verses* author was spotted in a bar in Frederiksberg on J-Day of 1996 wearing a blue and white Tuborg Santa hat. He was papped with a smile on his face and a *julebryg* in front of him, making front-page news around the world the next day. 'We're not sure his security team were very pleased,' Jens confides in me, 'but it was great for us!'

I figure that if it's good enough for the Booker of Booker winners, it's probably good enough for Lego Man. I thank Jens for his insights before waking my husband from his liquorice-scented slumber.

'Good night?' I ask cheerily, opening the blind and letting in the gloom.

He makes a grunting noise that neither confirms nor denies that the rest of the evening was a festive success, though from the fact that he still can't open his eyes at 11am, I'm suspecting it was a large one. I selflessly offer to do a coffee run into town on the condition that he emerges from his pit at some point in the next few hours.

The roads are empty. The whole of Jutland, it seems, is nursing a collective hangover. Even the bakery staff look jaded, and they're used to getting by on a few hours' sleep a night. One of the girls in my choir is a baker and having made Danish pastries my *Mastermind* specialist subject over the past year, I'm now well versed in how my beloved *snegles* are brought into this world. The magical process starts, I've learned, when some poor souls turn up to get the ovens going at 2am.

Pastries and coffees in hand, I step outside to inhale the cold, thin air and dodge street-cleaning machines already at work to tidy up after last night's revelry. The normally spotless streets are strewn with snow-flecked beer bottles, blue Santa hats and muddy tinsel. I hear a crack underfoot and peer over my vast expanse of stomach to see a pair of cracked plastic aviators in a mush of slimy bubbles and soiled foam.

From this point onwards, Christmas is officially deemed to have begun and all shops and local radio stations are contractually obliged to play *Now That's What I Call Christmas* non-stop. Disclaimer: I am a huge fan of the festive season and regularly break out 'Fairytale of New York' before the start of December, but the Danes embrace Christmas on a whole other level. Lego Man and I take to playing Chris Rea roulette – it being a sure-fire bet that the gravel-voiced crooner's 'Driving Home for Christmas' will be playing on *at least* three Danish radio stations at any given minute of the day. One very special Friday, it's playing on five of the six stations in range as I drive to the supermarket. Now *that's* what I call Christmas…

For many, Tivoli Gardens is the essence of Christmas and millions flock to Denmark's capital at this time of year to marvel at the twinkly lights, eat traditionally shaped pretzels and pet the reindeer shipped in specially. But in rural Jutland, things are a little less fancy.

'So, Santa's coming to The Big Town tomorrow,' Helena C tells me casually in mid-November.

'Ooh, fun, where will he be?' I am aware that as a grown-up I have no business to be quite so keen on Father Christmas, but my year of living Danishly has taught me the importance of letting go and being myself. So now, I'm an out and proud AFOC (adult fan of Christmas).

'Well,' Helena C goes on, 'he used to come along the canal, handing out sweets from an old boat, but we had a few issues with kids surging towards open water and falling in. It wasn't great PR for the town. Plus the water is pretty cold at this time of year. So it was agreed that Santa should probably stick to dry land this year.' As I mentioned, health and safety: not so big in Denmark.

This year, Santa arrives by pony, smashes some '*slik*' (or sweets) around, then heads to the main square to turn on the lights. Danes insist on decorating their municipal trees to look a lot like gherkins. Not for them the artfully wound-around fairy lights adorning grand public trees throughout the rest of the world at Christmas. In Jutland, at least, someone goes up on a crane to the top of the tree with several strands of bulbs and drops them, vertically, creating a stripy, strangely phallic-looking centrepiece for every town in the region. I ask around as to why this is and find that the Ann Summers personal massager-style tree decoration is another case of '*tradition*'. Once the town's tree lights have been turned on, nets of fairy lights get cast over every object that remains stationary for more than a couple of hours in Denmark. Danish homes also get zhuzhed up with an assortment of spangly things and a bewildering array of foraged finds.

Friendly Neighbour is back from Copenhagen for the weekend and appears on our doorstep one Sunday morning with armfuls of what I can only assume is garden waste.

'For you!' she says, brightly.

'Er, thanks!' I try to reply equally brightly.

'Since I'm not going to be here for Christmas I brought you a few leftovers from the forest to decorate your home.'

'Wow...' I can see lichen, something that looks a lot like a toadstool, and some twigs. 'Thank you...'

'You don't do that, back in England? Decorate your house for Christmas with things from nature?'

'Um, *well*...' I don't know quite how to break it to her that I seem to have mistaken 'nature' for 'John Lewis' up until this moment in my life. 'I think people just tend to *buy* Christmas decorations back home,' I tell her.

'Well now you are in Denmark! You must use *nature*.' Friendly Neighbour won't be dissuaded so I invite her in for coffee and she gives me the skinny on decorating Danishly. 'It is quite all right to gather from the forests, but only for your own private use, no more than you can fit in one bag. Of course, you know that there are two kinds of forests?' I did not know this. 'Ones owned by the Nature Agency and private forests. In Nature Agency forests you can gather from the whole forest floor. In private forests you are only allowed to take what you can reach from the trail. If you find a nice branch or piece of bark, you are allowed to pick it up, unless it is from a fir or spruce tree as these are for forest owners only. Acorn, cones and beechnuts can be gathered when found on the ground only, but mushrooms and lichen you can gather as much as you like.'

'And, er, how *do* you decorate with mushrooms?' I eye up the slimy thing now winking at me from my kitchen table. Friendly Neighbour looks at me as if I'm simple. Again.

'In bouquets, of course!'

'Of course...'

As well as fungus, Friendly Neighbour has very kindly lent us one of her '*nisser*' – a statuette of an alarming goblin-like creature. Folklore has it that *nisser* were responsible for determining how fruitful a farmer's harvest would be in days gone by. If a family kept its *nisse* (singular) happy and well stocked with rice porridge (evil spirits had simple tastes in yesteryear's Scandinavia), then the goblin would make sure things went well. Like a sort of lower-stakes miniature Mafioso. The idea now is that they're spies for Santa, reporting back on any bad behaviour. But for the most part they just look creepy.

'It really does feel like he's watching you,' I remark to Lego Man once Friendly Neighbour's gone. The strange, mute, hunched figure appears to be staring into my very soul, no matter where I try to hide him.

'I know – some joker left one in the office loo the other day,' Lego Man tells me with a shudder. 'It was horrible. No one could relax enough to ... you know.'

Office high jinks reach a new zenith this month as Danes start winding down for the holidays and, more importantly, planning their *julefrokost*. This is the annual Christmas lunch that's been held in most workplaces since the 1940s. My cultural integration coach Pernille Chaggar has warned me that Christmas lunches in Denmark can be, 'six, eight, even *ten* hours long.'

'There's an art to controlling yourself so that you can eat to the very end and sample each new dish that comes to the table,' she explains. These, apparently, include pickled herring, pork, beer and schnapps. It sounds like an ant-acid advert waiting to happen. 'A lot of alcohol is usually consumed,' Pernille admits, 'and people traditionally let their hair down and suspend some of the everyday boundaries, both in relation to the social hierarchy and generally accepted social conventions.' This is something I'm now familiar with, having observed the 'controlled loss of control' approach to Danish drinking on numerous occasions since 'Christmas' kicked off.

As partners aren't usually invited to witness the debauchery of the office lunch in Denmark, I'd expected to experience *julefrokost* vicariously through Lego Man's reports and those of other friends. So I'm touched when an invitation arrives to go to one myself as a lowly freelancer – and consider it my Bruce Parry-esque duty to accept.

I push open the doors of the old town hall to reveal a vast, grand, banqueting room crammed with tables and around 200 revellers already in full swing. I'm pretty sure my party isn't this large and wander around aimlessly trying to find someone who looks like they might be in charge. Music blasts, lights dazzle, and Vikings maraud, helping themselves to wine and food from a table laid out like some kind of Bacchanalian feast. I feel a little like I'm in a Baz Luhrmann film and am grateful when a familiar face smiles at me. The woman who invited me scoops me up and takes me to a table populated by people I partially recognise. They all exclaim in horror about how huge I am now and one observes that I look like 'overstuffed ravioli'. Danes are nothing if not blunt. It's also fair to say that my *julefrokost* crew are already well lubricated and appear far more excited to see me than folk I've only met a few times have any right to be.

'You're heeeerrreeeeee! *Now* we can begin!'

As Pernille predicted, herring is first up – big bowls of the stuff in various 'flavours' from curry to cinnamon. It takes a brave seasoning to take on the heft of a pickled herring and the result is something of an oral assault, not for the delicate of stomach. The fish is eaten on rye bread and washed down with a shot of schnapps.

'To help the herring swim!' they tell me as they drink. The tiny glasses are refilled for another toast and soon, every other bite is accompanied by a '*skål!*' ('cheers') Next is a buffet of meat and fish, much of it of unidentifiable origin. I watch my fellow diners ladle a creamy sauce with cubes of something in it over sausages and pork, before discovering that the chunks are chicken.

'It's a *chicken* sauce on *pork*?'

'Yes,' the girl to the right of me nods, smiling. 'You like it?'

I can't deny that it's tasty, but even a committed carnivore can have too much of a good thing.

Dessert is *risalamande*, a form of rice pudding mixed with whipped cream and chopped almonds with a whole almond hidden somewhere in the dish. The lucky reveller who finds the whole almond wins a prize, but has to conceal their discovery as long as possible by secreting said nut in their cheek. This is so that the rest of the party is forced to gobble down the entire vat of the creamy, lumpy dessert smothered in cherry sauce before the big reveal. By serving number two I'm ready for a lie down, but the rest of my group is just getting started. At the table next to us, a spirited game of *pakkeleg* starts up – an aggressive form of pass the parcel where, as far as I can make out, everyone brings a small wrapped gift and then throws a dice for the chance to steal other people's presents before stockpiling as many as possible for themselves.

Wine flows, faces become flushed and lips, blackened with Beaujolais, move animatedly. A few hands seem to be resting in places that perhaps they shouldn't – notably the thighs and bottoms of colleagues they'll presumably have to face on Monday morning in the cold semi-light of day. By the time coffee is served, several couples are sucking each other's faces like teenagers, up against walls or still in the seats that they plonked themselves into, several hours before.

'So, what happens next?' I ask the girl next to me.

'You mean them?' she looks at face-sucking couple #1. 'I imagine they'll have sex. There are hotel rooms just upstairs,' she point directly above our heads.

'Oh, no,' I thank her for her candidness but explain, 'I meant more along the lines of how this group plan to spend the rest of the evening...'

'Oh, that. Well, there'll be dancing, probably. And then who knows?'

At this point, my heavily pregnant Bruce Parry pioneering spirit starts to desert me and I say goodbye to my table-neighbours before attempting to slip away quietly. This doesn't go so well. In my enlarged state, personal space is compromised and on my way out I have to edge past various couplings. Thinking that I am exempt from this orgiastic annual ritual on account of being a) happily married, b) sober and c) up the duff, I exchange a few pleasantries with a fifty-something man while I wait to pick up my coat (aka Lego Man's oversized parka). I'm just re-robing and preparing to leave when he propositions me.

'*What*?' is all I can splutter in response. Then, pointing at my stomach: 'Really?!'

He gives a '*can't blame a chap for trying*' shrug before adding: 'You know what they say – "pregnant, can't *get* pregnant"!'

I decline, fervently, and squeeze past more middle managers making out in stairwells before making a break for it and driving home.

The next day, we go for brunch with The Viking, Helena C and some other Danish friends and have a '*julefrokost* horror story amnesty' where everyone hands in their weapons of mass humiliation.

'There are a lot of hookups,' admits Helena C. 'It doesn't matter if you're married or not.'

Another girl tells us about a Christmas party fling she had some years back that made things decidedly awkward around the photocopier come January. And a third reveals how he and his team were forced to learn the dance from South Korean pop icon Psy's hit, 'Gangnam Style', and then perform it to senior management.

'It was weird,' he admits, still looking a little shaken. 'Then afterwards, we all watched some porn,' he adds as a throwaway remark before taking a swig from his bottle of *julebryg*.

'*Sorry?*'

'What?' He looks up. 'The bit about the dancing?'

'*No*!' the party cry in unison.

'The porn!' I say, far louder than was necessary and attracting the attention of the table next to us. 'Sorry,' I murmur.

'Oh,' he says, '*that*. Well…' he sets down his beer and starts, matter of factly: 'The dance teacher had left, the financial director had finished pretending to ride me like a pony, and we started watching this movie, projected onto a whiteboard in this hotel conference room at 4pm in the afternoon. Then this man appeared on screen who looked a lot like Jens in our team—'

Lego Man shoots me a look that says, '*see, I told you a lot of people were called Jens in Denmark*'. I give him a look in return that says, '*not now – we're about to hear a story about porn at an office Christmas party. This outranks Lars–Mette–Jens-gate*'. Marital telepathy is a wonderful thing.

'So anyway, we're all watching the guy who looks like Jens and thinking, "this is kind of weird",' The Viking's friend goes on, 'and then the guy in the film suddenly strips. He's totally naked, and then he starts getting it on with someone.

And the *real* Jens sitting next to us bursts out laughing, saying, "Don't you recognise me?" Turned out it didn't just look like Jens, it *was* Jens. He'd had a career in porn before retraining in accountancy. He found the whole thing really funny, but I haven't been able to look at him the same way since...'

There's a lull in conversation after this. Turns out it's pretty hard to top a communal-screening-of-a-colleague-having-penetrative-sex story.

By the time Lego Man's *julefrokost* comes around, he's a little afraid of what the night might entail. So I'm relieved when he makes it home, apparently unscathed.

'Well, how was it? Any porn? Promiscuity? Herring fights?'

'Nothing remotely porny,' he says, sounding a little short-changed. 'Turns out I work with a wholesome bunch. We started off with a *Top Gun* quiz—'

'—What? Why? What *is* it about this country and Tom Cruise?'

'—which naturally I aced,' he goes on.

A whole quiz on his specialist subject? Christmas really has come early for Lego Man.

'And then we sang a song about Volvos,' he adds, just casually, as he drops his bag on the bed and walks to the bathroom, slotting the head on our electric toothbrush.

'I'm sorry,' I set down the book I've been reading and follow him in there, 'I *thought* you just told me you and your high-powered colleagues spent the evening singing songs about Swedish family saloon cars...?'

'That's right,' he says. 'But not just any Volvo,' he has to raise his voice now to be heard over the whir of the toothbrush. 'The Volvo B18–210,' he tells me, through a mouthful of minty foam. 'There's even a song sheet, see?'

Dripping minty spittle all over our wooden floors, he walks back into the bedroom and fishes a stapled pamphlet of papers out of his work bag. I love that he has saved this for me. I love that he knows how happy this kind of thing makes me.

'Wow,' I exclaim, wide-eyed, as I flick through and see that other sing-songs for the night included Cat Stevens's 'Wild World' and the Ace of Base classic, 'All That She Wants'. 'And why,' I ask, 'were you singing songs about Volvos?'

'Apparently it's—'

'—"*Tradition*"?'

'Exactly. Everyone else knew the words already,' he nods at the lyric sheet. 'It was in Danish but Lars helped me out with the lyrics – they were things like "it's got teak interiors" and "a great undercarriage", and "we'll be together from now until eternity ... I love my Volvo".'

'How festive...' I shake my head in wonder. Every time I think I've got this country sussed, it throws me a curveball.

'Yeah,' Lego Man spits into the bathroom sink and sticks his head under the tap to rinse his mouth. 'It's all a bit of a blur after that ... in fact, I might need to go and have a lie down...'

After all this partying, it would be easy to lose sight of the true meaning of Christmas: the obligation to cook a meal no one chooses to eat at any other time of year and spend days cooped up inside with people you haven't seen for the last twelve months. The Danes have a saying: 'guests are like fish – after three days they start to smell', and yet somehow we've signed up to have house guests for *seven whole days* over Christmas. I'm very fond of my in-laws. They are lovely people. But a week-long visit while I'm nine months pregnant is a little more than I'd bargained for. *At least*, I tell myself, *there'll be plenty going on in The Big Town, what with Danes being so crazy about Christmas and all*.

'Oh grasshopper, how much you still have to learn!' American Mom shakes her head when I tell her my action plan. 'Sure, there's a whole bunch of parties in the *run up* to Christmas, but in the week itself, no one does anything. It's all about spending time with the family.'

This is a setback. Then a bright idea strikes me: *Perhaps we could combine our various families in some sort of expat jamboree!*

'So, er,' I ask, 'what are you and the kids doing for Christmas?'

American Mom gives me a '*well, duh*!' look: 'We're going back to the States, of course!'

'Oh. Right then. Well, enjoy.'

'We will! Good luck!'

American Mom wasn't exaggerating. During the Christmas week in Jutland, everything is closed. And I mean EVERYTHING. I look on the *kommune* website's calendar to see if there might be a few rogue activities or events still taking place but see only a row of blank squares. I scroll through the days. *Nothing, nothing*, and then, just as those wise men must have felt on noticing something twinkly up there on the horizon, I spot a *star* on the calendar.

'Look, dog: an event!' I click on the starred day, eager

with anticipation, only to find that the only fixture occurring over the next seven days in Jutland is my own choir's Christmas concert. Something I'm scheduled to be at anyway. Singing songs in a language I still don't understand and attempting to channel my inner gospel diva despite being both sober and, more crucially, British. 'Excellent, dog: we have *one* afternoon's entertainment.' The dog growls. 'And yes, I use "entertainment" in the loosest sense of the word.' This just leaves six days to fill. Our longest staying visitors to date were here for four days back in the summer, when Sticksville-on-Sea was 'open', and we still struggled to entertain them after day three.

'Don't Danes mind having nothing to do for a whole week and just hanging out with their family?' I ask Helena C between songs at our final choir rehearsal before Christmas. She admits to me in hushed tones that yes, her own relatives can get a bit much, but says that most Danes love it.

'They ran this survey in 1998 and it showed that spending time with the family over Christmas was important to 78 per cent of Danes,' she tells me, as though this proves it. I point out that there weren't smartphones, or iPads, or *Netflix* back in 1998. 'Hanging out with the family or watching *Friends* on terrestrial TV was about all there was *to* do back in those days...'

'This is true,' she concedes. 'Maybe that's why they haven't run a survey since. Oh well, good luck!'

Jeez, why does everyone keep wishing me luck?

'Thanks,' I tell her. 'It's beginning to sound like I might need it...'

The choir concert passes off without a hitch. I sing with

the Danish lyrics written out phonetically and Sellotaped to a soprano in front of me. At the end I'm congratulated on my Danish by the choir mistress ('not bad, *for a foreigner*') and my in-laws, unaware of the scribbled notes strapped to the back of my choral colleague.

'Thanks,' I nod, graciously. Helena C tries not to smirk and promises to keep my secret safe 'for now'.

Afterwards, we all share *æbleskiver*, a traditional spherical pancake of pure deliciousness served with jam and icing sugar. There is a lot of hugging and wishing each other '*God Jul*!' – happy Christmas – before we all go our separate ways. Me, waddling back to the car I now barely fit into (the driving seat being so far back to accommodate my bump that my feet only just reach the pedals) and heading home to stare into the abyss of six days of nothingness.

We've resolved to do Christmas as Danishly as possible and so I've taken counsel from all the Danes I know to compile a foolproof recipe plan for the big day. On the menu: duck with prunes, caramelised potatoes, boiled potatoes (because Danes can never have enough potatoes in any given mealtime) and red cabbage followed by *risalamande*. Helena C has offered to be on call at the end of the phone should any calamities arise, and so it begins. Danes celebrate with a traditional roast dinner on Christmas Eve, so my 24th December goes something like this:

7am: Wake up, try to let dog out quietly to avoid waking guests. Fail, so make them tea.

9am: Start peeling things. Stare at the duck currently taking up most of fridge. Try to dissuade dog from barking at duck by distracting with bone. Do something unspeakable with giblets. Feel a bit queasy.

11am: Make rice pudding to allow time for it to set and chill in fridge. Try to get over idea of a dessert that has same consistency as sick and forget about traumatic experiences with school lunches and the word 'coagulate'. Whip cream with handheld blender. Send cream up walls, down front, and over dog. Put dog outside to clean off in the snow. Melt more sugar for cherry sauce. Blanch almonds and chop up, then stir in to lumpy goo with more sugar and more cream.

1pm: Eat a light lunch of pickled herring on rye bread. House now smells of cream, melted sugar, fish and flatulence.

2pm: Finish off a feature for UK newspaper where Christmas Eve is still a legitimate working day. Check email and find one from a PR inviting me to a 'One-day Festive Resilience Workshop' and another entitled 'Coping Techniques for Christmas Stress'. Wonder how much they know…

4.30pm: Boil potatoes. Put duck in oven. Battle with six pans and a temperamental oven crammed with baking trays while perspiring in just a stretched T-shirt and shorts now, despite snow outside. Decide Danish homes may be too well insulated.

5pm: Go to mass at local church to experience 'traditional' Christmas service. Only it's long, all in Danish, and I have a duck in the oven. Realise haven't thought this one through. Keep eye on watch as elderly folk around me in furs begin nodding off and snoring gently. Small child in front row turns around, rolls eyes, and mimes hanging himself to express boredom. And he can understand what the priest's banging on about...

7pm: Waddle home. Attempt to extract bird's fat. Make brown sauce from cream, fat and cornflour. Wonder if have ever used as much cream, butter and sugar before. Decide have not. Melt yet more sugar in frying pan, add more butter, make face as drop in half of potatoes and roll them around until resemble miniature toffee apples.

8pm: Unscrew lid of supermarket-bought red cabbage (in Danish: '*rød kål*', which sounds amusingly like 'roadkill'), decant into rustic-looking dish and bury jar in bin. Mush up cabbage to pass off as homemade. Get all dishes on table, make Lego Man carve, collapse. Forget Christmas crackers, retrieve from behind sofa then wish hadn't bothered. These fail to go 'bang' but include such hilarious Danish jokes as: 'If you need to do something, do it right as the hassle is the same,' and, 'He who understands how to listen often sits and thinks about something else'. Oh, how we laugh!

9pm: 'Singing and dancing' commences. No one is hurt, but the dog gets drenched.

Let me explain. My Danish festive advisory committee assured me that to do things properly, we must also decorate our bushy Danish fir tree with the colours of the Danish flag – red and white – as well as the obligatory '*nature*', fairy lights and *real candles*.

'Then, after Christmas dinner,' said Helena C, 'you all dance round the tree, singing.'

'*Whoa* there,' I stop her. '*Real* candles? In a *dried-out* tree? In *wood-heavy*, Scandi homes?'

'Yes.'

'Do you do that when there are children about?'

'Especially then. The kids love it!'

'Excited children and naked flames? What could go wrong?'

'Yeah, I see what you mean,' says Helena C. 'I thought everyone did this until we had an Australian over for Christmas one year and he pointed out the fire hazard.'

'Quite.'

'But we make sure we're safe.'

'How?'

'Well,' she says, 'we always have a big bucket of water to throw over the tree in case anything happens.' Good grief.

'And you have fairy lights as well as candles? Don't you trip over the cord?'

She looks at me as though I'm a mal-coordinated imbecile. 'We just ... step over it...'

'OK, but how do you get round the tree?' I explain that we normally have ours in a corner. 'That way, you only have to decorate one side of it.'

Helena C gives me a judgey face: 'We tend to decorate *all the way* around and then we just pull the tree out into the middle of the room on a mat for the singing and dancing.'

'Right then.' *I can do this*, I think, *how hard can it be?* 'And what do you normally sing?' I ask.

'Well, there are a few Danish songs we all know that I can give you the words to,' she goes on, 'then my uncle always sings the first two lines of "Winter Wonderland".'

'Only the first two?'

'Yes. He doesn't know the rest.'

'Oh.'

'He *could* learn them. We tell him to every year. But so far, nothing.' She shakes her head as though he is a huge disappointment as singing uncles go. 'So anyway, you and your family should just sing whatever you like, then hold hands and dance around the tree. Easy!'

Only it doesn't quite turn out this way. Our vast, bushy fir looks lovely lit up by fairy lights and real candles. But there are only four of us and so reaching our arms out to hold hands around the tree proves a struggle. Flames flicker precariously close to the blinds, the sofa and Lego Man's acrylic Christmas jumper, and twice our guests trip over the cord of the fairy lights. It turns out that none of us are much cop at remembering any festive songs in their entirety and after trip-up number three, we collapse on the sofa, laughing hysterically in a release of cooped-up festive stress. At this uncharacteristic whooping, the dog makes a break for it from his sentry post at the front door to see what all the commotion is about. In slow motion he moves from the tree, to me, then to Lego Man, checking that all is well, before spotting the ominous black bucket on hand in case of fire. *This*, he assesses, *is new. This*, he suspects, *could be dangerous*. With an energetic leap, he pounces on the alien object, placing his front paws on its side to get a better look inside … and tips its contents all over himself, the wooden floor and the special 'tree mat' purchased for the occasion. My first Danish Christmas celebrations end with a mop in hand.

And then … calm descends. The shops are all closed as we were warned they would be, and the roads empty. Danes, it turns out, really do stay at home with their families. For a *week*. So we do the same. We read books, laze around, drink cups of tea and watch the snow fall outside from the warmth of the sofa. And then, when it finally settles, we go for a walk. And all is peaceful and white. It is, I have to admit, magical.

The enforced retreat means that we talk, properly, about everything from favourite films to foreign policy. I learn that my father-in-law can, if left to his own devices, get through a pot of honey *every two days* and once built his own wooden cage then sat in it for twelve hours in Newcastle's MetroCentre to protest against political prisoners for Amnesty International. I find out that my mother-in-law once created her own ice rink by flooding a car park during a particularly severe frost one year. I get to know my in-laws far better over these seven (*seven!*) days than I have during the years that Lego Man and I have been together. It's like bonding bootcamp. No wonder Danish families are so close – they don't have much choice come Christmas.

It's gone OK. Better than I had feared. But I'm happy to have the house back to ourselves at the end of the week. Since there's still nothing going on in the environs of Sticksville, we do some nesting. I wash everything in sight and Lego

Man demonstrates his full array of Viking-esque powers by assembling an Ikea cot single-handedly. We hang a print of the Danish alphabet, complete with the extra three letters and a few suspect squiggles, in our spare room. My desk gets shipped out into the hallway and all manner of baby paraphernalia is manoeuvered in.

On 31 December, the country finally wakes from its snowy slumber. Denmark's New Year's Eve rituals begin at 6pm with the monarch's speech – something that started in 1942 during the German occupation when the king called for national unity. We're celebrating the passing of the last year and welcoming the one to come at The Viking's house, and I've offered to help him cook. He fills me in on a few Danish customs while I poke uncertainly at a cauldron of green mush that he assures me is 'traditional stewed kale'. This, he tells me, is served with potatoes (natch) and cured saddle of pork for New Year's Eve – yes, Danes are firmly back in the pork saddle after a brief dabble with duck over Christmas.

We chat and occasionally stir things, or jiggle a roasting tin, with the Queen's speech in the background. I tell him that I'm surprised by how fond Danes seem to be of their monarch and The Viking reveals that he's a big fan, too.

'Margrethe gets these crazy high approval ratings despite the fact that most people here probably wouldn't describe themselves as monarchists,' he tells me. In fact, the Danish monarchy is the most popular in Europe and a poll published in the Danish newspaper *Politiken* revealed that 77 per cent of Danes are happy with their queen.

'We don't think royals *in general* are great,' The Viking clarifies, 'we just like our lot.' I ask him why he thinks this is and he says: 'It's such a small country that most people will have seen her in the flesh or even met her at some point. And she's just a nice, normal woman. She stinks, but she's lovely.'

'Sorry?'

'—Of cigarettes, I mean. She's a massive chain smoker – but we don't tend to mind. It just makes her seem flawed, like one of us.' And there you have it. Liz: next time you feel an *annus horribilis* looming, try lighting up.

In this year's speech, as far as I can make out, Margrethe tells everyone to keep being tolerant but to try and be a bit nicer to each other.

'Is that right?' I ask The Viking, unsure of my shoddy translating skills and not as fast on the Google Translate app as I used to be with my nine-month-pregnant fat fingers.

'You've pretty much got it,' The Viking tells me. '*Margrethe*,' I'm enjoying how he insists on referring to her by her Christian name as if she's an old family friend, '*Margrethe* generally tells us that we're doing OK, but that we could all try a bit harder.'

After this, pundits discuss any hidden meanings in what she's said for the following 50 minutes before concluding that her message is indeed: 'keep being nice'. It's all very civilised. What's less couth, I learn, are the other Danish New Year's Eve traditions.

'We used to blow up each other's mailboxes and smash crockery against friends' front doors at midnight to welcome in the new year,' The Viking tells me. Lego Man, having just invested in a new Scandi designer letterbox, looks horrified at this prospect. 'But not too many people do this any more,' The Viking assures him. 'Though it's a shame about the plate thing,' he adds, wistfully. 'You could tell how popular you were from how many broken plates you had on your doorstep the next day.' He sighs, nostalgically.

Now, he assures us, most celebrations tend to be restricted to 'jumping off the sofa at midnight, then going outside to look at the fireworks, then watching a black-and-white film of an old lady being brought food by her butler'. The sofa part symbolises leaping into the year ahead. The fireworks are just for fun. And the old lady?

'Yeah, no one knows why we do that part. But it's *tradition*.'

'Of course it is.'

Once the other guests arrive, we eat, and I come round to the idea of stewed kale. Then we count down (in Danish) to the second that The Viking's digital watch flicks to midnight, trying to ignore the cheers and celebrations of people in other apartments with premature timepieces.

'*Ti! Ni! Otte! Syv! Seks! Fem! Fire! Tre! To...*' we chant, before, '*Godt Nytår!*' ('Happy new year!' in Danish).

There is hugging and kissing and *skål*-ing all round, and then the furniture-jumping begins. As a walking blimp by this point, I am the designated photographer – exempt as the rest of our party all clamber aboard The Viking's sofa. On the count of three, everyone jumps.

'*Aaaaaarrrrrgggggghhhhhhhh!*'

They let out a blood-curdling roar as they leap and I

press the shutter, capturing for all time the end of our year of living Danishly. The Viking, arms raised in celebration, is letting out a war cry, mid-air. Other revellers look equally animated, limbs tangled, and Lego Man, I'm amused to note, is grinning with an expression of pure joy as he executes a sort of long jump into the calendar year ahead. He looks happy. And relaxed, and confident and handsome.

The moment has been frozen – the digital image encoded in a series of ones and zeroes, electronically recording the split second just before socked feet slid on smooth pine wood floors, resulting in splinters, bruised bottoms and a suspected sprained ankle that one girl probably won't feel until morning when she sobers up.

I study the image fondly as plasters, painkillers and yet more schnapps are sought out by our host to heal his guests' various ailments.

It won't be like this next year, I can't help thinking. There'll be three of us for starters, and who knows where we'll even be by then. But in the present moment, this feels right.

Once the jumping injuries have been attended to, we troop down the stairs from The Viking's red-brick apartment and convene in the street, along with all the other residents of The Big Town. A few revellers are dressed in funny hats and I learn that these are another Danish New Year's '*tradition*'. Looking around, I spot a leprechaun, a pizza hat and even a *pølser* cap. *Wow*, I marvel, *Danes love junk food so much they theme their millinery around it…* There are also lot of comedy plastic glasses on show. These range from the Dame Edna Everage to early-years Elton John and even physics teacher-esque visors.

'Are the funny glasses another Danish New Year's Eve tradition?' I ask The Viking.

'No – they're to protect your eyes from the fireworks.' *Oh*.

'Should we be wearing some too?' I ask, concerned, but The Viking makes a '*pffff*' noise as though I'm fussing over nothing. Having grown up with harrowing annual public safety campaigns warning of the dangers of returning to a lit rocket, it's with some alarm that I witness the DIY pyrotechnics on display in the main high street of The Big Town. I'm also a little perturbed to note that many teenagers and even younger kids seem to be letting off gunpowder propelled missiles, too.

'Is that legal?' I can't help asking.

The Viking tells me that although you have to be over eighteen years of age to buy what he describes as 'the major fireworks' ('like, beyond a certain amount of grams of gunpowder...'), Danish children are allowed to buy many 'lesser' fireworks themselves, and often start doing so at a young age. 'I was probably younger than ten the first time I got to shoot off rockets by myself,' The Viking tells me casually, as one whizzes past us at a right angle (in this case, a *wrong* angle). Roman candles start spitting to the left, spiders of white light spill out to our right, and a willow tree of green splays out across the sky, scattering debris as far as the bakery. A few more low-rent rockets do their worst and finally, a waterfall of gold starts to spurt from the not-quite-sky, getting stuck on some guttering above the toy shop and spraying its bounty liberally about twenty feet from our heads. Fire droplets spit upwards, then rage down, lighting up the night and silhouetting the manhood of the porny pony and the cats with boobs in their fountain.

Ahh, Denmark, how I've grown to love you, I think, while using Lego Man as a human shield.

Back inside, we eat dessert – a traditional marzipan ring cake – washed down with champagne, as our party raises a toast to the year ahead.

'*Skål!*'

When we leave, a couple of hours later, a sprinkling of powdery snow is starting to fall. We walk past candlelit homes and inhale the heady combination of gunpowder and *gløgg* (Danish mulled wine) that wafts from every window. I'm feeling incredibly festive now – more so, I think, than ever before.

On New Year's Day, my first without a hangover for, I calculate, twenty years ('*Dear Liver, I'm sorry. I promise to do better. Yours, for as long as you'll keep me going...*'), we tune in to watch the Prime Minister's New Year speech. I have to remind myself once again not to expect to see Birgitte Nyborg with her lovely bun and twitchy-nosed smile. Instead, Helle Thorning-Schmidt starts echoing the queen's sentiments and reminds us that January is an opportunity for a new start. I'm well aware of changes the next calendar year will be bringing to our house and the ju-jitsu junior in my stomach is showing off all his (80 per cent likely) moves tonight. We go to bed and Lego Man falls asleep straight away, but I can't seem to drop off. Sleeping on my back is out, as junior will crush my vital organs. Sleeping on my front is out because I now look like I'm shoplifting cushions. So I lie on my side, and then wonder what to do with my arms. I try everything from a sort of Michael Jackson *Thriller* pose to outstretched in front of me like a furry koala pencil topper I had when I was eight. But it's no use. So I get up and pad around the house for a bit.

The sky is wonderfully clear and the stars are out in a way I've never seen before. Great swirls of speckled light compete with brighter, bigger luminous spheres in a crowded, glittering sky. With no light pollution to dull the view, the sky looks bigger somehow, and higher up. As I stare, I think I see a shooting star, though this could just be the blurred vision that my midwife warned me about as another happy side effect of pregnancy (varicose veins, anyone?). I stop staring up at the night sky but find that I still can't see straight. There are two of everything, including the Christmas tree, which is jolly, and a pile of dirty dishes waiting to be tackled (less fun). I feel dizzy, then as though my whole body is heaving and stirring. There is a lurching feeling. Like everything inside me wants to escape. It hurts. A lot. But then it goes away again. *Weird*, I think, and head to the fridge to have a nose around. *If in doubt, snack*. But then it happens again. And again. I glance, casually, at the clock on the kitchen wall, watching the second hand stutter around for several minutes until I'm sure. *Shit*, I think. And then: *This is real.*

Slowly, gripping the walls for support, I make my way to the bedroom to fill Lego Man in on what's been going on and let him know that our Christmas wish is being granted – slightly sooner than expected.

Things I've learned this month:

1. Danes are big fans of liquorice, Chris Rea, *Top Gun* and schnapps
2. Even Salman Rushdie has experienced the benefits of living Danishly
3. You can counter the consumerism of Christmas with moss and mushrooms
4. Enforced family time can be A Good Thing
5. Singing is *always* An Excellent Thing in Denmark
6. Life is about to change immeasurably

Epilogue

Made in Denmark

After eighteen hours of psychedelic pain, much swearing, and several *snegles*, a slimy, squirming creature is placed on my chest for a heartbeat before being whisked away into special care. I drift in and out of consciousness for a while (minutes? hours? days?) until finally I'm in a wheelchair being pushed towards a tiny plastic incubator that looks a lot like an Ikea storage box.

'Your son,' a nurse tells me.

From my low vantage point, all I can see is a squashed-up face with tubes coming out of it and a giant woolly hat. A heat lamp is placed above him and he is naked apart from the hat and a nappy. I taste salt and find I'm crying.

'Is he OK?'

'He is going to be quite fine,' the nurse tells me as a doctor begins removing the tubes and checking him over. 'He can come down to your room tomorrow.' I'm doused by a wave of relief.

'So he's all right?'

'He is more than all right,' the doctor tells me, whipping off the woollen hat with a flourish to reveal a shock of bright red hair: 'he is a Viking!'

This is a surprise. Neither Lego Man nor I have any flame-haired family members and I quickly scan back to try and remember if I've ever teased gingers in the past (Katie Brooking from junior school, I can't quite remember, but if I did, I'm sorry). Somehow, our son has joined the 1 per cent of the world's population to have red hair. The rarity of this has apparently been drawing a steady crowd of visitors since he's been here, as most babies born in Denmark are blonde or bald. Lego Man, who has been shuttling between the postnatal and neonatal wards, checking we're both still breathing and developing a dependency on syrupy hospital coffee, is still in shock. Nurses, doctors, and passing midwives have all been calling in and congratulating him on his 'true Viking' son.

As soon as the rubbery creature is lowered into my arms, there is a winding *thump* of love for him in my chest and I never want to let him go. We're kept in hospital for a week before I'm patched up enough to go home and yet more visitors travel from far and wide (or at least the other end of the hospital) to see the fabled Viking child. They come bearing gifts of grapes, fleecy breast pads and knitwear, including a hat that the head midwife knitted during the birth. Yes, that's right: my active labour was so long that the woman in charge had time to craft clothing. She may well have sheared the sheep, too.

We struggle to know quite what to call the new arrival. Every male moniker we'd had on our 'possible names' list now seems insufficiently strong to cope with the might of the Titan mini god we've created. And so he is affectionately referred to as 'Little Red'.

'Not "Monkey" or "Anus"?' Lego Man checks.

'No,' I tell him firmly.

Once I'm discharged, we're offered the opportunity to stay an extra week at the adjacent 'Stork Hotel' as a family. This is for new parents who want to ease the transition from '*shit, we have a baby!*' to '*shit, we're taking a baby home!*' Here, nurses are on hand night and day for advice on how on earth to take care of the squalling pink thing that has somehow sprung from your loins.

'You wouldn't get *that* on the NHS,' Lego Man observes, leafing through the brochure of the well-appointed rooms at next door's hotel that could be ours for just 300 DKK (£32 or $55) a night. I agree that it's tempting but after a week away already and with a dog languishing at canine holiday camp (kennels), we decide to go home. We're both frightened, feeling a lot like we're not grown-up enough to be dealing with this, and wondering how on earth hospital staff have seen fit to allow us custody of an *actual human being*. (Me: 'I can't even keep our houseplants alive!' Lego Man: 'We have houseplants?')

But we're doing it. We go home.

Back in Sticksville, Friendly Neighbour has visited, having received the '*we're parents!*' panic group text from Lego Man the week before. She's left a wooden stork outside our house, as is the custom in Denmark, to let all and sundry know that there's a new baby in town and encourage the postwoman and the free sheet delivery boys to tread lightly for a while. She's also left a care parcel of muslins and a note that reads: '*Because I hear they puke a lot* ☺'

I'm touched. The Mr Beards, who haven't acknowledged my existence since winter drew in and they all went into hibernation, have left a knitted bib with a tractor on it in our mailbox. The girls from choir have dropped off a toy elephant and a card that they've all signed. American Mom stops by with two washing up bowls full of carefully packaged home-cooked meals to stock up our freezer. Helena C and The Viking bring cake and an achingly cool Danish designer kids' dining set. I well up. Or at least, more tears join the ones already brimming in my now permanently wet eyes. As well as having acquired a new child and some pretty extensive embroidery around my 'lady cave', I also appear to have developed emotional incontinence, though this could just be the sleep deprivation. My limbs pulse with tiredness but still I get up to stare at my son and tell him I love him ten times an hour before poking Lego Man and saying: 'Look what we made!'

Despite crawling with exhaustion, I feel vital. It's as though I'm raw (not like *that*. Though also, FYI, *exactly* like that), as though everything *matters* more now. The world seems saturated with meaning and my son is a blank slate – a little life who's never consumed junk food or watched Jeremy Kyle or been disillusioned by anything.

'Having a child is like having your heart outside your body,' American Mom tells me, and she's right. I want to protect him and make everything bright and shiny for him. Just having a small person around makes me resolve to do my best to make the world *better*. And in this respect, Denmark suddenly makes sense. With its world-renowned work-life balance, its focus on children and education and the great strides that have been made in terms of gender equality, Denmark is the smartest place for us to be right now.

After two weeks of paternity leave post-birth, Lego Man goes back to work before tying up loose ends to take *ten weeks* off to care for his baby. He has a big shiny job at one of the country's most profitable companies, but a dad taking time out, fully paid, to look after his child is recognised as something that's important and so is encouraged. Lego Man learns how to do bath time and bedtime, and also learns how you can feel like you're going insane by 2pm on a Tuesday when all you want is an hour's uninterrupted sleep, and maybe a shower. He understands how looking after a child 24 hours a day can be hugely rewarding but that it's also relentlessly tough. He knows that, some days, all you need is for someone to come home and say, 'You're doing a great job, here's a *snegle*'.

When the time comes, Little Red can start at a *vuggestue* or *dagplejer* with other under-threes where he'll get to play and create and learn, with 75 per cent of the cost picked up by the state. This means that Lego Man and I can both afford to continue with our careers far more easily than we could in countries where childcare is akin to bankruptcy.

US psychologist Abraham Maslow said that there was a five-tier hierarchy of human needs, each of which needed to be met before you could move on to worrying about other things, culminating in the hallowed goal of 'self-actualisation'. These needs started with the 'physiological' (the basics: food, water, sleep etc.), followed by 'safety' (security of body, health and employment). Both of these needed to be in place before you could move on to the third, 'belonging' (friendship and sexual intimacy), then the fourth, 'esteem' (confidence and respect) and finally to self-actualisation (morality, creativity and problem solving).

Danes have their physiological needs and their safety taken care of by the state, allowing them to move onwards and upwards more easily. They're in school with the same people for ten years, allowing deep friendships to develop, and they're well-informed and encouraged to get on with things in terms of sex. With a focus on creativity in schools and nurturing future job talent, many Danes are getting a leg-up right to the summit of the triangle. By contrast, some developed countries haven't even got past the second rung of 'safety' – with no healthcare or job security (hello, USA).

Thinking about it this way, it's no wonder Danes are so happy. They have an obscenely good quality of life. Yes, it's expensive here. But it's Denmark – it's worth it. I don't mind paying more for a coffee here because I know that it means the person serving me doesn't a) hate me or b) have a crappy life. Everyone is paid a decent wage, everyone is looked after, and everyone pays their taxes, just as I pay mine. And if we all have marginally less money to buy more *stuff* that we don't really need anyway as a result, well I'm starting to think it's a deal worth making.

'It's like Buddha teaches us,' pontificates American Mom one rainy Thursday.

'Buddha?' *God, I love Americans*, I think. *If it's not Oprah it's Buddha.*

'Sure. He teaches us that desires are *inexhaustible*. The satisfaction of one just creates new desires, like a cell multiplying.'

I dearly want to give her a good old cynical British eye roll in response, but in spite of myself, I find I agree. Living Danishly has given me a glimpse of a more meaningful way of being. An understanding of how life *should* be, or at least, how it could be. And I like it.

Of course, it's not perfect. Yes, the winters suck and I wish that Denmark's daylight hours were a little more evenly distributed throughout the year, so that we weren't living in Mordor in winter and the land of the midnight sun for three months in summer. But we are where we are, and despite my newfound Viking powers, I can't push Scandinavia nearer the equator (though I might have another try sometime soon). It's not Australia, or any of those other, slightly more climatically temperate countries that also jostle for the top spot in terms of quality of life and happiness on global surveys.

But I always feel as though these non-Nordic pretenders to the throne are cheating, somehow, by living in places with year-round sunshine. It takes strength of character to survive at the top as the world's happiest nation throughout six months of frozen darkness every year. And life can't always be a sunny, unicorns-using-rainbows-as-skipping-ropes-style utopia. But a steady, safe, nurturing environment that you can rely on today, tomorrow and in a year's time is a pretty special next best thing. There are still highs – the first summer strawberries, Little Red learning to smile, the day I can drink again (in no particular order...). And of course there are lows. But for all the Danes I've spoken to over the course of the year, the lows tend to be personal – unavoidable human truths. The rest? Well, that's taken care of in Denmark.

There are still problems. It's a homogenous country and there are sometimes gaps between the rhetoric of living Danishly and the reality. A small sector of society is intent on blaming immigrants for everything, from crime to missing meatballs. But there's nothing rotten in the state that isn't also afflicting other countries, with none of Denmark's advantages. Danes are facing the same issues as the rest of the world, but despite the Dansk Folkeparti's gains in the 2014 European Elections, Helle and her Social Democrat government are still in charge. And attempts are being made to help native Danes understand those from other cultures. In 2014, Copenhagen's low-rise skyline changed to reflect the continued attempts at accepting and welcoming the city's Islamic community with the addition of a 65-foot tower as part of Scandinavia's biggest mosque. This combines traditional Islamic features with some typically Scandinavian design touches in an effort to encourage integration. The place has changed even while we've been here, with The Big Town becoming more ethnically diverse and better provisions being made to help 'foreigners' like me feel at home. Danes want to be thought of as tolerant – it's important to them. And so The Danish Way is slowly adapting to incorporate new influences and arrivals.

A year on and I feel as though I understand more about what it is to live Danishly. Danes are a discerning lot. Not for them the overt friendliness of Southern Europeans or Americans, nor the rictus-grin-politeness of the Brits. Danes are blunt and direct and trusting and secure in a way I've never encountered before. It's very unlikely that someone will tell you to 'have a nice day' in Denmark. But if they do, you know that they really *mean* it. And if your neighbours ignore you in winter, you know not to take it personally: it's dark, it's cold, they just want to get inside and get *hygge*.

I've picked up some of the language too, so that I can now grasp a little more of what's going on around me and converse on about the same level as Friendly Neighbour's niece. Friendly Neighbour's niece is only two years old, but she *is* Danish, so this is progress. I can also order coffee, tea and almost any cake my heart desires in a bakery and be 90 per cent sure that I'll get what I ordered. I have friends here. Lovely, generous, strong, reliable, hospitable people. I'm regularly touched by their kindnesses, thoughtfulness and patience when I ask them endless questions about all things Danish.

Once Lego Man and I have emerged from the initial fug of newborn madness (who am I kidding, I'm still in it. Any strange typos are because I'm writing at the same time as jogging an eight-week-old over my shoulder while he vomits and defecates simultaneously, occasionally kicking out a few rogue characters on the laptop keyboard), we Go Out. It is my birthday and we make a reservation for lunch. This requires military-style planning and five trips to and from the car to make sure that all the equipment needed to survive remotely with a baby has been packed, checked and double-checked. Once this has been accomplished, I realise that I'm still wearing pyjamas so go back inside. I throw on an outfit that I hope says: '*I may well be covered in baby milk/bodily fluids, but I'm OK with that.*'

We drive to The Big Town, park the car, and then spend several minutes reminding each other how to assemble the pram. Fortunately, the day is mild and the sun is threatening to peek through the clouds, so for once, the elements aren't against us. Little Red doesn't wake when I lift him from the car seat and gently lower him into his bassinet, pulling a hat over that still-staggering head of licking flames and wriggling mittens onto tiny hands before tucking them under blankets. As we walk to the restaurant, I smile fondly at the porny pony fountain that I haven't seen for a couple of months now and then catch sight of myself in the toyshop window. I take in the girl with the scarf wound around her neck, the Wayfarers on to disguise under-eye bags and the messy topknot, to keep hair clear of little pulling fists. I'm amused to note that I look very Danish. But I also look relaxed. Like the kind of person I always hoped I'd be when I grew up.

I'd thought I was doing all the right things to get to this point in my former life – working hard to be successful and trying to please everyone. But I never seemed to succeed nearly enough to make all the effort worthwhile. I felt tired, hungry (often literally) and ephemeral, blown about by the currents of whatever was going on around me. But now I feel safe, secure and solid. In a good way, and quite apart from any post-pregnancy pounds I'm carrying. I'm content and, yes, happy. I'd say I was a nine out of ten (I'm still waiting to be crowned queen of Sylvania-land).

I loop my hand through Lego Man's arm as he pushes the pram up the small incline to the restaurant. He's busy telling me how he's already stockpiling Duplo – Lego's little sibling – for our son, assuring me that it's 'an investment'. I tell him that I can see my toes again in a stationary position.

This is about the level of our sparkling repartee at present (did I mention the whole lack of sleep thing?). I start thinking about what I'm going to order and can almost feel the bubbles of the prosecco I've promised myself exploding on my tongue.

'So next year,' Lego Man starts, and I realise I might have missed something after the bit about the Duplo.

'Next year? Yes, well...'

It's decision time and Lego Man is looking at me hopefully. He laid his cards on thc table months ago and I know that he'd like to stay. Now, it's down to me. I look around at The Big Town's new Latin Quarter that we're booked into for lunch and spot an Asian supermarket and an Italian deli I haven't seen before. *I could live in a country with snegles, dim sum and decent Parma Ham?* It's almost too good to be true. The sun is shining now and our son is napping. As a new parent, life doesn't get much better than this.

'I suppose Denmark's not so bad,' I say.

A slow smile starts to creep over Lego Man's stubbled cheeks (he's growing a beard for his paternity leave – everyone needs a project), but he still wants to hear me say it: 'So you've enjoyed your year of living Danishly?'

'It's been *o-kay*,' I concede.

'Just "OK"?' he asks. I shrug and his face falls slightly.

'But just to check, I think we should try making it two...'

He beams. Then he puts the brake on the pram like a responsible parent and gives me a bear hug. This is still slightly painful but I tell him I appreciate the sentiment.

We're staying. The Nordic dream may have its flaws but Denmark is still the best place for us, right now. And

I'm excited about what the next twelve months will have in store.

We arrive at the restaurant and we're shown to our table. It's by the window in a sheltered courtyard and Little Red is still sleeping. So we leave the pram outside.

Top ten tips for living Danishly

OK, so I can't drag everyone to Denmark and none of us have control over our chromosomal make-up (yet). But there are a few things Danes do differently that can be put into practice wherever you are.

1. Trust (more)

This is the number one reason the Danes are so damned happy – so try it. You'll feel better and save yourself unnecessary stress, and trusting the people around you can make them behave better, so it becomes a self-fulfilling prophecy.

2. Get *hygge*

Remember the simple pleasures in life – light a candle, make yourself a cup of coffee, eat some pastries. See? You're feeling better already.

3. Use your body

Cycle, run, jump, dance, have sex. Shake whatever you've got. Using your body not only releases get-happy endorphins, it'll also make you look hotter, Danish-style.

4. Address the aesthetics
Make your environment as beautiful as you can. Danes do, and it engenders a respect for design, art and their everyday surroundings. Remember the broken window syndrome, where places that look uncared for just get worse? The reverse also applies.

5. Streamline your options
If living in Sticksville has taught me one thing, it's that cutting down on choice can take some of the hassle out of modern life. Too many options for things to do, places to eat (ha!) or what to wear (hello London wardrobe) can feel like a burden rather than a benefit. Danes specialise in stress-free simplicity and freedom within boundaries.

6. Be proud
Find something that you, or folk from your home town, are really good at and Own It. Celebrate success, from football to tiddlywinks (or crab racing). Wave flags and sing at every available opportunity.

7. Value family
National holidays become bonding bootcamps in Denmark and family comes first in all aspects of Danish living. Reaching out to relatives and regular rituals can make you happier, so give both a go. Your family not much cop? Start your own with friends or by using tip #3 (the sex part).

8. Equal respect for equal work
Remember, there isn't 'women's work' and 'men's work',

there's just '*work*'. Caregivers are just as crucial as breadwinners and neither could survive without the other. Both types of labour are hard, brilliant and important, all at the same time.

9. Play

Danes love an activity for its own sake, and in the land of Lego, playing is considered a worthwhile occupation at any age. So get building. Create, bake, even draw your own Noel Edmonds caricature. Just do and make things as often as possible (the messier the better).

10. Share

Life's easier this way, honest, and you'll be happier too according to studies. Can't influence government policy to wangle a Danish-style welfare state? Take some of your cake round to a neighbour's, or invite someone over to share your *hygge* and let the warm, fuzzy feelings flow.

Acknowledgements

I am immensely grateful to all the experts who generously gave up their time to speak to some strange Brit. I continue to be humbled, amused, inspired and invigorated by all the things you taught me.

Thank you to my agent, Anna Power, for having the best superhero name in publishing and for endless encouragement and cake. And to my fabulous editor, Kate Hewson at Icon, for her expertise, enthusiasm and fun cat facts.

Big thanks to our Danish crew for their support and sanity – Team Vejle (Tara, Liberty, Henrik, Chesney, Fee, Kath, Hjarne, Christine, Fen, Jules, Ana, Matthew, Craig, the choir); Team Billund (Frauke, Stephen, Nichole, Jackie, Karina, Cindy) and Team Aarhus (Sophie, Mick, Emmerys Bakery…).

Team GB, you have been brilliant as ever with the 'you can do it!' texts and Cadbury parcels (especially Chrissy, Emily, Sarah, Joe, Caroline, Lucy, Sally, Kate and the Gail Plait Gang).

A huge 'thank you' to my family, in particular Rita, John and Andrew for their intrepid expeditions to Sticksville. And to my mother, for just being her.

None of this would have been possible without the serious-looking blond chap and his love of Lego bringing us to Denmark in the first place. Thank you for forcing me out of my comfort zone whenever necessary, and hurrah for Danish paternity leave, without which the contents of this book would have remained the deranged scribblings of a sleep-deprived new parent.